ABOUT THE AUTHORS

Major General (Ret.) Johan Jooste retired from the South African National Defence Force in 2006 after 35 years of active service. In 2012, after a stint in the corporate world, he was appointed Commanding Officer, Special Projects at SANParks, where he was responsible for anti-poaching strategy, planning and execution. He went on to establish a Wildlife Crime and Corruption Combatting Coordination Centre, with funding from the Peace Parks Foundation. He continues to serve in the fight against poaching as a Programme Manager for Law Enforcement and Security with the Peace Parks Foundation.

Tony Park is the bestselling author of 20 thriller novels set in Africa and several non-fiction biographies. A former journalist and press secretary, he also served 34 years in the Australian Army Reserve, including six months in Afghanistan. He and his wife, Nicola, divide their time between Australia and southern Africa. www.tonypark.net Social media: @tonyparkauthor

ALSO BY TONY PARK

Far Horizon

Zambezi

African Sky

Safari

Silent Predator

Ivory

The Delta

African Dawn

Dark Heart

The Prey

The Hunter

An Empty Coast

Red Earth

The Cull

Captive

Scent of Fear

Ghosts of the Past

Last Survivor

Blood Trail

The Pride

Part of the Pride, with Kevin Richardson

The Grey Man, with John Curtis

Bush Vet, with Dr Clay Wilson

War Dogs, with Shane Bryant

Courage Under Fire, with Daniel Keighran VC

No One Left Behind, with Keith Payne VC

Bwana, There's a Body in the Bath! with Peter Whitehead

RHINO WAR

MAJOR GENERAL (RET.) JOHAN JOOSTE

TONY PARK

INGWE PUBLISHING

Cover design by Leandra Wicks
Picture captions back cover (print edition):
Clockwise from top centre:
White rhinoceros
SANParks Chief Pilot Grant Knight with sedated orphan rhino
Major General (Ret.) Johan Jooste with SANParks, SAPS and SADF personnel and
captured poacher
Jooste conducts a briefing in the Mission Area Joint Operations Centre
Major General (Ret.) Johan Jooste in SANParks uniform.

For Arina, Queen of my heart

GLOSSARY

Big Five – lion, leopard, buffalo, rhino and elephant

'N Boer maak 'n plan – a farmer (boer) makes a plan – a common expression reflecting the can-do attitude of South Africans

Border War – South Africa's campaigns against the liberation movement in South West Africa (Namibia), and in support of anti-communist forces in Angola, lasting from 1966 to 1990.

Bakkie – light utility vehicle ('ute' in Australia); pick-up truck

Bliksem – Afrikaans expression of surprise or displeasure

Fiscus – the South African Treasury or 'public purse'

Groenkloof – location of SANParks headquarters, in Pretoria

HiP - Hluhluwe-iMfolozi Park, formerly the Hluhluwe and Umfolozi game reserves, large public game park in KwaZulu-Natal

Indaba – a meeting

JOC – Joint Operations Centre

Jong – young, a term of endearment for younger friend

Klapped – hit

KNP – Kruger National Park

Kudu – A large antelope with spiral horns

Kudu kop – Kudu head, the antelope's head insignia of SANParks

KZN – the South African province of KwaZulu-Natal

Lekker – good

Madala – African term of respect for an older person

Moer – to beat, or bash; 'get the moer in' – to feel rage, or fury

Muthi (umuthi) – traditional African medicine

NG Kerk – Dutch Reformed Church

NPA – National Prosecuting Authority

Oke – short for 'outjie', Afrikaans slang for a man

Oom – Afrikaans for uncle, also used as a term of respect for an older male.

Potjiekos – pot food, a slow cooked meal, usually oxtail

R1 - 7.62 millimetre assault rifle

Rondavel – a round dwelling, self-catering tourist accommodation unit in the Kruger Park

Recce – abbreviation of Reconnaissance Commando, South African special forces.

Sangoma – a traditional healer (plural: izangoma)

SADF – South African Defence Force (prior to 1994)

SANDF – South African National Defence Force (post 1994)

SANParks – South African National Parks

SAPS – South African Police Service

Sitrep - situation report

Skoonpa – father in law

Skukuza – the largest rest camp in the Kruger Park and home to the park's headquarters and nearby airport

Tekkie – running shoe

Tannie – Afrikaans for aunty, also used as a term of respect for an older woman.

Tjommie – friend or 'chum'

Vellies – short for veldskoen – suede bush shoes

Veldt – (also Bushveld), open grasslands or, generally, the South African bush

Vlei – an open plain or floodplain

Wors - short for boerewors, traditional South African 'farmers' sausage'

PROLOGUE

I t was a time for good cheer, prayer and war. My wife, Arina, sat smiling beside me in the South African National Parks Air Wing helicopter. Below us, the seemingly endless wilderness of the Kruger Park stretched away to the horizon. We had just left the Houtboschrand Ranger Post, in the centre of the reserve, smiling children waving as we lifted off. We had delivered Christmas gifts and much-needed amenities to the field rangers and their families.

At Mopani, the nearest of Kruger's rest camps below, local and foreign tourists would be relaxing, perhaps settling down to a lunch-time braai and a cold beer or a chilled glass of wine, or taking a siesta in their thatch-roofed rondavel after an early-morning game drive. Our daughters, Ilze and Liezl, were far away, in Johannesburg and Cape Town, but, now, in December 2015, after nearly three long years of living in the bush, Arina and I at last felt truly welcome in this new family we had joined.

The veld had shed its winter khakis and browns, and had turned a rich emerald with the advent of the summer. The seasonal rains brought new life, perfectly in sync with the timeless rhythm of this African landscape. From the open grasslands around Mopani, the pilot tracked south-east, towards the Lebombo Mountains, the 800-kilometre-long range of rocky hills that mark the border between South Africa and Mozambique.

Our next stop was the N'wanetsi Ranger Post in the centraleastern part of the park. At nearby Olifants Rest Camp and the N'wanetsi Picnic Site to the south, visitors could sit atop the mountains and watch game through binoculars. Elephants splashed through the Olifants River below; giraffe, easy to spot because of their tall, graceful silhouettes, browsed from trees bristling from the rocky landscape. An eagle-eyed, lucky onlooker might even see a rhino.

The stress of my job as Chief Ranger of the Kruger Park was seen and felt by Arina. We had been married for nearly 40 years and she had been with me when I had gone to war as a younger man, also helping to care for other men in uniform under my command, as well as their families. She had borne witness to the horrors of armed conflict, accompanying me during one terrible week when I made a sombre pilgrimage around South Africa to visit the grieving families of men who had been killed in action during the Border War.

She took my hand and squeezed it. Her smile lifted me. It was rare for us to be out together, taking in the natural beauty of the place where I lived and she was a regular visitor. 'You are so lucky to live in the Kruger,' so many had said to us. It was true; the park was a natural paradise, but those people never saw the dark side of the Kruger.

I was wearing a headset so that I could communicate with the chopper pilot. Through the earphones I heard a ranger come onto the radio net. 'We've just made contact; we have three poachers wounded, copy?'

I didn't need to give any orders; we were all too well versed by now. In the operations room, based at Skukuza Airport about 150 kilometres south of where we were, the police would be notified and officers would be sent from the town of Phalaborwa. A fixed-wing aircraft from our Air Wing, with Kruger's physician, Dr Gary Peiser, on board, had already been sent to Satara, the nearest airstrip to the contact. The aircraft would be used to evacuate the wounded poachers to the nearest hospital if necessary.

Our helicopter re-routed to Satara, where we picked up Dr Peiser and then flew to the location of the contact.

We came in low and the pilot flared the nose as we touched down on an open grassy vlei. Robbie Bryden, the section ranger for N'wanetsi, was already on the scene. I went to him, ducking under the still-churning blades of the chopper, and shook his hand.

'The guys picked up the spoor of the poachers, General,' Robbie said. I was no longer a major general in the South African National Defence Force (SANDF) – I had retired several years previously – but the form of address had stuck. 'They made visual contact and our guys were then shot at. A firefight ensued.'

Lean, deeply tanned, with a stubbled jaw, Robbie's face was grim. He was in full combat gear, his face streaked with sweat and dirt. He was hands on, as always, and the bush was in Robbie's blood. He had been born into a ranger family – his father, Bruce, had been chief ranger here in the Kruger Park and had penned the bestselling book *A Game Ranger Remembers*, before his untimely death. Robbie's wife, Judy, was also a qualified section ranger who had been heading up our tracking training before taking time off to take care of their children.

As we spoke, Arina was already organising for the cooler box to be offloaded from the helicopter. She handed out cold drinks to those on the ground. As she did so, Dr Peiser was assessing the wounded poachers. One, he said, could be transported by road in an ambulance, but the other needed to be flown to Satara and evacuated to hospital in the waiting aircraft.

It was like a scene from a war zone.

Fortunately, this time the rangers were not responding to the discovery of a rhino carcass; they had found the tracks of the poachers and had been able to stop them before they could slaughter yet another rhino. It was a small win, a tiny step in the right direction. A South African Police Service bakkie arrived on the scene while

Robbie and I were talking. Robbie nodded to a nearby bush, where the third poacher from the gang lay motionless on the ground.

Despite receiving first-aid treatment from our rangers, he had died awaiting medical evacuation.

The helicopter lifted off on its mercy flight with Dr Peiser and the wounded man on board, raising a cloud of dirt, grass and dust in its wake. A police officer began questioning Robbie about what had happened, and how it was that three men had been shot, one of whom had died of his wounds. The policeman's tone became overly assertive, asking the how, when, where and why – just as our rangers were trained to interrogate poaching suspects.

Arina looked towards Robbie and the police officer. 'Why is he treating Robbie like he's the one who's done something wrong, like he's a criminal?'

Any ranger who had shot a poacher and caused his death would automatically become the subject of a murder investigation, so our on-call legal counsel would be notified as a matter of course. The investigation would now hang over Robbie's head until the Attorney General dismissed it – no ranger had so far been taken to court on a murder charge – but the uncertainty was just one more example of the stress rangers have to deal with.

The area where the contact had taken place was bare; apart from a few sparse bushes, there was not a single tree, no shade within sight. For now, there was nothing more Arina or I could do, but wait for the chopper to return for us. The state pathologist had been called to collect the deceased poacher.

'You must never forget that this man has a family as well, Love,' Arina said.

I nodded. Arina was always quick to remind me of the human cost of the war we were fighting. Our rangers ran the risk, daily, of being killed or wounded by a poacher; they spent protracted periods in the field, often shunned by their own communities, who saw the poachers as 'Robin Hood' figures.

Poachers risked their lives in pursuit of a commodity: rhino horn, worth more than gold, diamonds or cocaine. The one lying just metres from us had paid the ultimate price. Across the border, in Mozambique, a family would soon be in mourning.

After three years of war, Arina and I were both exhausted. 'Life is to be lived,' we had told each other when we took on this fight, in what should have been our retirement years. But this was harsh living.

1

In another helicopter, in another life, in 1990, I was on my way to a very important event, a christening of sorts.

'Colonel, you must come,' Piet Bronkhorst, Park Warden of the Augrabies Falls National Park, had said excitedly on the phone, 'Blompot has had a baby.'

By then I was a colonel in the old South African Defence Force (SADF). As commander of 8 SAI, the 8th South African Infantry Battalion, I was also in charge of the 76 000-hectare Riemvasmaak training area on the banks of the Orange River. Here, in this wide-open expanse of rocky desert terrain, we could conduct exercises with a fully mechanised battalion, aerial bombing trials, and test firing of the South African-designed G6 Rhino self-propelled 155-millimetre howitzer.

Today, however, I was on my way to see a real-life rhino – my first. In 1988, during my time in command, the Defence Force signed an agreement with the then Department of Environmental Affairs to link our military training area with the adjoining national park. While we had competing aims, the very fact that the military had appropriated this huge area meant that it had become a sanctuary for wildlife, as well as a wide-open space in which to conduct manoeuvres. It made sense that our two departments should communicate and see what benefits could be shared.

We had landed and picked up Piet, and the pilot of the camouflaged Oryx helicopter now flew low over the reserve, following Piet's directions for us to rendezvous with his scouts on the ground who had found Blompot, a female rhino. This harsh, arid country was good habitat for black rhino, I had learned. Blompot – she was named 'flower pot' because of the particular shape of her spoor – was, like all her kind, mostly solitary, only coming into company with another rhino when she was ready to mate. When we spotted Blompot she was with another rhino, a tiny thing not much bigger than a pig. Its ears looked too big for its body – it would grow into them – and it scampered about, full of energy, almost hopping on its skinny little legs.

'The black rhino doesn't calve easily,' Piet explained to me over the chopper's internal radio as we circled. The single young stay with the mother for two to three years and Blompot would not come into oestrus again for that entire period, until her calf left her protection. Piet grinned and his eyes lit up. 'Look what has happened here in our park, Colonel!'

Not only had I just seen my first rhino, and her calf – now christened Blommetjie, or 'Little Flower' – I had also witnessed what could happen when two different authorities worked together for a common purpose, and borders were dropped for the sake of nature.

I WAS BORN IN POSTMASBURG, in the dry Northern Cape region of South Africa. The harshness of the semi-desert terrain was contrasted by the kindness of the solid, hard-working people who lived there.

I started my schooling in a small building in the mining outpost of Smith's Mine, along with a group of about 20 pupils, from grades one to seven. We only had two teachers and it was thanks to their sterling work that I could not only complete secondary school, but also ready myself for university.

When I was nine, my teacher, Mrs Dippenaar, said to my father: 'Johan is talented and gifted; I will do my best to give him extra stimulation.' This remark was not meant for my ears, but my father passed it on and it gave me an early lesson for life about the importance of appreciating and encouraging others and seeing what can be done with few resources but a positive attitude. With no library or organised sports at her disposal at the school, Mrs Dippenaar spent her own time and the art of tuition to provide that extra stimulation.

My father was a diamond miner and my mother cared for the home and my two sisters and me. We grew up in a working-class household where structure, ethics, values and religion were important. I achieved solid results in high school and was planning to enrol for a Bachelor of Commerce degree, with some law subjects, at the University of the Free State. However, I had enjoyed being in the army cadets at school and, with national service looming on the horizon, sought out information on the military academy.

When I decided to join the army, the postmaster and the school headmaster in the one-horse town of Barkly West, where we now lived, came to visit my parents.

'Please reconsider sending him to the military,' the postmaster said to my father. 'If you have money problems, we can help you. How can you do this?'

My father and mother, however, supported my decision and in 1971, at the age of 18, I left home to begin the coveted course at the military academy at Saldanha Bay on the West Coast, and become an army officer.

Around the same time, the Defence Force opened its first positions for women since the Second World War in a newly established Civil Defence College (CDC). The following year, in 1972, women were allowed to join the army; in 1973 a group of these female candidate officers was selected to do a leadership course at the military academy.

My classmates at the academy and I had seen photos of these women in the army newspaper. 'I want that one,' I had said to one of my fellow cadets and I pointed to an attractive girl in one of the pictures.

The young woman's name, I soon learned, was Arina. Having won the leadership trophy at the completion of her CDC training, she was one of those selected for the academy. It is there that we met. She finished her course, but flew back later that year to watch my passing-out parade, at which I received the trophy for best army student. We were birds of a feather, meant to nest together. Two years after we met, she and I were married.

Commissioned as an infantry officer in 1975, I served in 1 SAI as a lieutenant and then as a captain at the school of infantry in the late 1970s. Between 1981 and 1982 I had my first experiences of working in the Lowveld when, as a major with 7 SAI, based at Phalaborwa, the army negotiated with the owners of the Letaba Ranch to use their game conservancy as a training area.

On weekends, Arina and I would sometimes visit the Kruger Park, but the bush, for me, was also my workplace. I preferred to take my leave on the coast. It wasn't until my next posting, as a lieutenant colonel based at Jozini, in northern Natal, that I had my first real up-close encounters with wildlife. While there, operating in the uMkhuze, Kosi Bay and Sodwana reserves, I was co-opted as an honorary game ranger with the old Natal Parks Board.

Arina and I pulled night-time duties in 1983, assisting with measuring, recording and tagging endangered leatherback turtles as they made their pilgrimage ashore to lay their eggs on the beach in the Seven Lakes area. As we stood there under the moonlight, just the two of us, we watched this moving, ancient ritual, as a giant, prehistoric-looking female turtle hauled herself across the sand. She used her flippers to dig a deep hole, laid her eggs, then turned and silently returned to the sea.

I looked to Arina and we held hands; tears were rolling down her cheeks. I felt moved, humbled that we could be here, making a difference simply by watching over these amazing creatures. In the back of my mind I was already worrying about what would happen to the tiny hatchlings when they broke to the surface, and what dangers awaited them. For how long, I wondered, would this little piece of pristine beach remain the way it was then, unchanged for millennia?

Dog tired after our vigil, but still excited, Arina and I made a fire on the beach and talked about the miracle we had just witnessed. Finally, we went to sleep in a simple reed hut. It was heavenly.

AFTER COMPLETING the command and staff course, I was posted to the border and given command of a battalion group at Eenhana operational base, six kilometres from Angola, in eastern Ovamboland in the old South West Africa, now Namibia.

Arina and the girls stayed in Oshakati, 150 kilometres away via a white gravel road. I would sometimes visit them on the weekends. One Saturday evening, Arina shook me awake – the People's Liberation Army of Namibia (PLAN), the military wing of SWAPO, the South West Africa People's Organisation, were attacking Oshakati with rockets and mortars. Shrapnel had ricocheted against one of our windows, but by that time I was so used to the sound of mortar fire I had slept through most of the attack.

I was then offered command of the San Battalion, made up of 800 soldiers plus about 2 700 of their dependants. The San people, commonly known as Bushmen back then, were from across the nearby border in Angola. These men, who spoke a mixture of Portuguese and their own San languages, had been enlisted into the SADF to fight PLAN. Our base, Omega, was in the Western Caprivi area, subtropical bushland situated between Katima Mulilo to the east and Rundu to the west. From Omega, my soldiers deployed into various operational areas, including Angola, just 15 kilometres away, using their phenomenal tracking skills in pursuit of our foes.

At any one time I would have under my command six young South African national servicemen who had been trained in nature conservation. Their job was to monitor game in the area and to keep an eye on soil erosion and alien plant eradication. It was part of a hearts-and-minds campaign, to show we were protecting wildlife while a war was raging. While allegations have been made of SADF personnel being involved in poaching rhinos and elephants during the Border War, I can honestly say that I never came across evidence of those activities. Perhaps I was too naive, or too remote, but what might well be true was that our ally across the border in Angola, Jonas Savimbi, paid for his war with the proceeds from the trade in wildlife products.

It was terrible, what the war did to the people and wildlife of Angola and northern Namibia. Sometimes, when I went jogging, I noticed lion spoor in the bush, but I never saw an actual cat; the wildlife and the environment were under pressure. I had been told not to allow the San soldiers to cut down wood for cooking fires, or to hunt or set snares to catch antelope; it was a pity that they were not permitted to follow their traditional ways, but I was responsible for nature conservation in the area. They were excellent warriors and trackers and I learned much about them and about working with different cultures during my time in the Caprivi.

Because of the war, the San were exiles from their country and their traditional hunting grounds and had brought their families with them. Arina became involved in supporting the soldiers' wives and children, setting up a programme to teach the women needlework and on-base cooking skills.

These people were the nomads of Africa and had been pushed around and forced out of their lands by various other ethnic groups for centuries. I learned of their complex family structures and their concerns. When a San man told me his heart was sore, then I knew he was depressed or anxious.

Family was key to their emotional stability, so we developed a policy where one of the soldiers would always stay behind with the wives and children when the rest crossed the border on a mission. Each night the stay-behind warrior would radio through to the patrol, passing on news from the families and relaying messages back to the wives and children.

. . .

FOLLOWING my term in South West Africa I received an accelerated promotion and was given command of 8 SAI, based in Upington in the Northern Cape. As an infantry officer, with much of my time spent on operations, I had lived in the African bush for months on end, so it was little wonder that Arina and I liked our creature comforts when it came time for leave.

Change was in the air in South Africa. When Nelson Mandela and the African National Congress (ANC) were elected to parliament in 1994, I was commanding the newly established Army Gymnasium, a junior leader training establishment at Heidelberg in what was then still the Transvaal. I was fortunate to be the parade commander and share the podium with President Mandela when he was awarded the Freedom of the City of Heidelberg.

The following year, I played a part in the transformation of the old SADF into the new SANDF. My staff and I ran the first induction training for a number of newly promoted colonels and brigadiers who had been commanders in what was termed the 'previous non-statutory forces'. The men and women who attended that course had been senior fighters in uMkhonto we Sizwe (MK) – the 'Spear of the Nation', the military wing of the ANC – and the Azanian People's Liberation Army. These were people I had fought against.

On the Sunday before the course started, I visited the officers' mess for a meet-and-greet in the living quarters as the students settled in. As I walked from room to room, the atmosphere was icy. I stretched out my hand in greeting to one member and he refused to take it. Others would not make eye contact when I introduced myself.

We broke this ice the next evening when, as was customary, students and staff met for welcoming drinks in the mess. After much consideration, I decided to stick to the habit of everyone introducing themselves around the lounge.

When it was my turn, I shot straight from the hip, hiding nothing about my service and involvement in past operations. I urged them to do the same and right there we reached common ground. A few sentences shared as soldiers made the difference and brought about a degree of trust and respect, forming a basis we could build on.

During the course, the barriers started to come down, and I learned a great deal about my fellow South Africans. We had debates and made compromises. For instance, I had to explain to the new officers that in the mess the minimum dress standard for men was a sports jacket and tie.

'But for us, an African shirt,' the type often worn by the new president, 'is formal wear,' one of the officers said. And so we agreed on that, but sandals had always been banned in the mess and the new officers agreed to wear closed shoes.

While we could make allowances for some minor issues, I had to make perfectly clear our strategy for the transformation to the new national defence force. 'We don't negotiate,' I told the inductees, 'we do "joint planning". We are apolitical and we maintain high standards.'

Despite our cultural differences, I insisted that when it came to the matter of discipline in the new defence force, there was only one way to go about it: to set the example you want others to follow on a daily basis. I prided myself on being punctual; I polished my boots every day; I was respectful, and I expected nothing less than those basic standards from the future leaders of our defence force, that they be on time and keep their uniforms immaculate.

The new government had made the decision to stay with a conventional defence force, rather than a guerrilla army, and that was what we trained for. I was lucky that English had been chosen as the language for the army – it had previously been Afrikaans – because if the powers that be had opted for isiXhosa or isiZulu I would have been at a serious disadvantage. To my shame, I had never taken the time to learn one of the other official languages of our country. I was mindful that I should neither lecture nor talk down to these new officers; I tried to see the experience through their eyes, and then accompany them on their journey.

I had always believed that, as an officer, my leadership was ratified by what was in the hearts of the people I led. I was as an outsider, white-skinned, so I had to work hard, right from the outset, to build trust with the men and women who participated in that first course.

Many went on to become senior generals, including Rudzani Maph-wanya, who became Chief of the National Defence Force. I am proud to say that, some 17 years on, I count many of them as friends. Most importantly, I learned valuable lessons about respect for diversity and working with people from different backgrounds – even former enemies – for the greater good.

In the later stages of my military career, between 1998 and 2001, I served as the Director: Projects for the army. As an infantryman, I had not been required to embrace or understand cutting-edge technology, but in this new role I had to learn about the full spectrum of modern weapons and systems, including electronic warning systems, comput-erisation and radar.

I had a good deal of contact with the Council for Scientific and Industrial Research (CSIR), a very can-do organisation driven by that good old-fashioned attitude of 'n Boer maak 'n plan. My job involved travelling internationally to meet other military personnel and arms manufacturers. If all my wanderings convinced me of anything, it was that if you give South African engineers a million dollars and six months, they will come up with a plan; some other countries, which I will not name, would need several million dollars and many years to come up with the same result.

By 2006, I was a major general, with 35 years of service in the army. I was the Chief Director of Corporate Services. I had helped oversee the transformation of the military, but I realised it was time for me to leave. Also, at the age of 53, I was young enough to embark on a second career. I had been sounded out by various companies when I was still in uniform and now it was time for me to start considering some of those offers.

I took a job with a smaller defence contractor and, after a few years, moved to BAE Systems, employed in South Africa by the American branch of this UK-based firm, at the time the second largest armaments company in the world. My position was Director of International Business Development, mostly promoting South African-made armoured vehicles. Arina had endured me being away from home on manoeuvres and operations for weeks and even months on end, and now she was being left behind by a husband who needed to travel the world for business. I maintained two maxi-sized passports, travelling with one while the other was being submitted for a new visa to a new country. I was away as often as three times a month, travelling to every continent. I visited countries such as Brazil, the United States, Canada, Sweden, Ireland, Spain, Poland, the UAE, Singapore, Malaysia, India and Japan. These trips, however, furthered my understanding and appreciation of different cultures, and I learned that people in other parts of the world, even in other African countries, viewed our world from different vantage points.

After five years of jet-setting and concluding deals for BAE, I was becoming jaded in the corporate world. I had seen how the phenomenon of 'groupthink' – in which employees were rewarded for blind loyalty, rather than expressing different views or chal-lenging the accepted way of doing things – robbed senior manage-ment of the ability to self-correct when things went wrong.

I was turning 60 and Arina and I started to consider the next phase of our life. We talked about possibly finding work at a small game lodge. Arina would do the books and I would look after the guests; we would ease our way into retirement and still keep busy. It was a good plan.

IN LATE 2012, as I did whenever I was home, I went to the monthly gathering of the Infantry Association, a lunch – some formalities and drinks all round – at the Bronberg Restaurant in Pretoria.

Old soldiers know how to scout out a bargain and the owner, Flip Marks, offered us a very good deal. Flip was a former Special Forces operator who had moved to the private sector and made a success selling military vehicles before taking over the Bronberg. There were about 30 of us present and, as usual, the food was good and the wine and beer affordable. At the lunch was Marius Roos, who, in his early forties, was still serving as a colonel in the Army Reserve. Tall, fit and engaging, Marius was a master networker and highly respected by both the part-time and permanent-force members of the military.

'Marius,' I said to him as we walked out into the afternoon sunshine after lunch, 'apart from you, the young blood, I'm one of the youngest in that room. Do you realise how old we are?'

We lingered on the restaurant stoep and he asked how my work was going.

'Jong, I'm considering my options,' I said to him. 'Turning 60, I'll have to retire from BAE.'

'I take it you still want to work, General?' he said. 'Yes.'

'I might have something for you,' Marius said.

I thanked him and, giving little more thought to our conversation, went home and took advantage of a quiet night. The next morning the phone rang. It was Marius.

'I've spoken to Dr David Mabunda,' he said. Interesting, I thought. Dr Mabunda was the CEO of SANParks, South African National Parks. 'He's looking for someone to consolidate and para-militarise the ranger corps in the Kruger Park.'

Like virtually every other South African, I had heard that rhino poaching was escalating in the Kruger and other reserves. Marius, I had learned, had been doing some security consulting work for SANParks through his company, Pathfinder. Marius explained that the CEO was coming under intense political pressure to do something decisive to slow or even stop the mounting toll of dead rhinos. The fact that Marius had the ear of the CEO was further proof of his trustworthiness and people skills.

I asked Marius for some time to think about what he had offered, before I signalled my interest. When I ended the call, I told Arina. We discussed the possibility of an offer and I weighed the option up against another job I had also been tentatively offered at the Voortrekker Monument in Pretoria as general manager of operations and tourism at the Afrikaner Heritage Foundation.

'What do you think of Marius's offer?' Arina asked.

'My girl, this is a parastatal,' I said of SANParks, a government-funded organisation. 'What are the chances that they would want a "platinum status" like me?' I was referring to my hair colour by this time.

And so, although I did not fancy my chances, I called Marius back later that afternoon. 'I am definitely interested.'

The next day, Marius called me back and asked me to send him my CV. A few days later, he then asked if I would come and brief the CEO and the SANParks Exco, the executive council. I agreed, although I was surprised by the request. I had been expecting at least an interview – if I was lucky – not to brief senior management about an issue I knew next to nothing about.

I set to work concocting a presentation, based mostly on what I had seen and read in the South African news media about the issue of rhino poaching. On the appointed day, I arrived at the SANParks head-quarters, a collection of two-storey, pinkish-coloured office buildings in Groenkloof, Pretoria. Marius met me and showed me to a board-room. Six individuals sat around a table, including David Mabunda, who I recognised from the picture I had found on the internet, and had cut and pasted into the PowerPoint presentation on my laptop.

Dr Mabunda was taller than I had expected, good looking, articulate and quite formal in his manner. I greeted them all and started my digital briefing. From what I had learned, there were several agencies involved in combatting rhino poaching – the SANParks Ranger Corps, the police and military, as well as private security companies operating in private game reserves.

'I would start by establishing clear lines of command and control in a JOC,' I said.

'What is a JOC?' one of the Exco members asked.

I paused. 'A Joint Operations Centre,' I said. ''Joint', commonly used in the military, is a term used to describe an operation in which there are several different forces on the same side. How, I wondered, could they even begin to target a problem of armed incursions into a national park without a JOC?

I ran through some basic ideas I had about how I might tackle the issue, but stressed that I would need to do a proper appreciation, as a military commander would, of the 'enemy' – the poachers; the friendly forces – the various agencies involved in fighting poaching; and the terrain – the Kruger Park.

I had mixed emotions as I walked out onto the tree-lined street after that meeting. On the one hand, I was excited; I could already sense that this was a huge opportunity to achieve something worthwhile. On the other, I thought: Is this what you really want to do at the age of 60? I had already made the transition from army officer to businessman, but this would require me reinventing myself all over again.

SANParks – or, at least, its CEO – wanted to turn his rangers into a paramilitary unit, but my instinct told me that I could not go into this task being 'too military'. There would be those who would object, I was sure, not just to my platinum status, but to having an army general put in charge of what was basically crime fighting in a national park.

The more I thought about it, the more the doubts began to creep into my thinking. I was clueless, I realised, about rhino poaching except from what I had read online and seen in the media. I wondered whether an entire corps of rangers could actually be turned into a force capable of thwarting armed criminals. The other job, at the Heritage Foundation, I realised, would be a lot easier and I said as much to Arina when I got home.

'That's not you, anyhow you'd be bored,' Arina said of the other position, with her customary honesty.

I had some news for Arina, which I had gleaned from my meeting with Exco. I took a deep breath – this would not be easy. 'If I get the job, we will have to move to Skukuza ... They will give us a house in the staff village.'

I could see mixed emotions on her face. This would be our thirteenth move to a new home, although it had been some time since our army days when we had to change houses every couple of years. Also, Arina would have to leave her job as head of a non-profit organisation supporting schools for children with disabilities. On the plus side, we would be living in the bush, in the iconic Kruger Park, surrounded by wildlife.

'OK,' Arina said, sensing there was more to come.

I braced myself. 'And we can't take Jonty.'

Her eyes widened in shock. With our daughters gone, Jonty, our little Jack Russell, was like a third child to Arina. 'But I thought there would be fences around the houses, to keep the wild animals out?'

I shook my head. 'No pets allowed, not even for staff.' Arina burst into tears.

I tried not to think about the offers before me, or about Jonty, but a day later I received another call. This time it was from someone from the human resources department of SANParks.

'We have decided to take you on board, sir,' he said. 'It's a five year contract.'

That, at least, told me they were serious. If, as I had half-feared, I had been offered a 12-month contract then I knew the idea of bringing in someone to transform the ranger corps would have been nothing more than a public relations stunt. I would have been set up to fail, because there was no way this mission could be successfully completed in a year.

At the personal invitation of Dr Mabunda, Arina and I attended the Kudu Awards, the annual recognition of achievements by individual national parks, departments, rest camps and people in SANParks. I put on my camouflage – a dinner suit and bow tie – and Arina dressed up. We went to the awards undercover.

We sat at a table at the back of the auditorium at the Gallagher Estate, the large convention centre in Midrand, Johannesburg. Only David Mabunda and the members of the Exco knew about my appointment. We sat with the secretary of the SANParks Board of Directors. I ate and listened as about a hundred awards were made. I did not blow my cover; I was there to gather intelligence.

Amidst the good cheer, food and wine, people were talking about one thing above all else: rhino poaching. SANParks was doing well commercially – tourism was growing – but its reputation was suffering. The two points I picked up that stayed with me was that this was an urgent problem, far greater than I had realised, and that the people whose lives and incomes were dependent on wildlife were hurting.

It began to dawn on me that this was a mission of great importance, not only to those of us in the room, who were putting on a brave face, but to the entire country. As I later said to the CEO of SANParks, you do not have 50 million stakeholders to deal with, but rather 50 million shareholders. This fight, I realised, was going to be bigger and more important than anything I had done in my life.

On stage, making his keynote address at the Kudu Awards, David Mabunda made the controversial announcement that the ranger corps in Kruger was going to 'go military' in the fight against rhino poaching.

In my previous life, I had been in combat and sent men into battle and now I was about to do so again. With a growing sense of sombreness, as I picked up snippets from conversations here and there about what was happening in the Kruger Park, I realised that once again I was going to war.

2

I was told to report to Lanseria Airport, north-west of Johannesburg on the twelfth of the twelfth 2012. David Mabunda had specified that I be issued a SANParks ranger's uniform, as I was to be taking part in a media event to announce my appointment as Chief Ranger of the Kruger Park.

No uniform could be found for me. Was this indicative of some serious logistics problem, I wondered? I couldn't help feeling concerned and disappointed, not because I wanted to dress up, but rather whether this was an indication of things to come.

Instead, dressed in my jacket and tie and polished shoes, I looked like a whore at a christening; everyone else at the airport was in casual summer clothes. Also waiting for the chartered aircraft that would take us to Skukuza in the Kruger Park were senior executives and board members from SANParks, high-profile conservationists, and a large contingent of journalists.

'Is that him?' I heard one reporter whisper as I arrived at the private terminal.

I met up with David and then the contingent boarded the aircraft. Although word seemed to be filtering out to the journalists, the official announcement of my appointment would only be made at

Skukuza, where I would also be introduced to some of the people I would be leading. My job title was 'Commanding Officer, Special Projects'. That conjured up images of both the military and covert operations. From David, my mission had been made clear – consolidate the ranger corps and turn it into a paramilitary force. I was not being sent to Skukuza to advise on this transformation, but to command it.

The flight took us east, over the sprawling farms and grasslands of the Highveld, and beyond the escarpment to the Lowveld bush and the vast expanse of the Kruger, South Africa's largest national park, roughly the size of the country of Israel. As the pilot descended, we crossed the Sabi Sand Game Reserve, privately owned land on Kruger's western boundary, also home to the Big Five. There, private security forces were responsible for protecting their rhino. At the very edge of that reserve, and similar private landholdings in the north, were up to two million South Africans who live on or close to the border of the Greater Kruger Park, as it had become known.

When we touched down and disembarked, as an old military man, I pitched in and helped with the unloading of suitcases from the baggage hold. A man walked across the tarmac and introduced himself. I shook hands with Ken Maggs, the head of ECI, the Environmental Crime Investigation unit in Kruger. In that role, he had, over time, assumed the responsibility for anti-poaching operations in the park. He was cordial, but stared at me for a moment – he had just learned over the past week that he would no longer be keeping that role.

David whisked me away to a car. He'd had time to open his bag and take out a spare SANParks shirt, khaki, with the green Kudu kop logo over the left breast pocket. He gave me the shirt and told me to put it on when we reached the conference centre at Skukuza. David had also borrowed a cap from one of the rangers and he told me to wear that as well. This would pass for my uniform, at least for the media event.

There was much to be announced. On stage in the conference centre, with the media contingent watching on with cameras, voice recorders and notebooks, David announced my appointment and ran through a summary of my CV.

'SANParks is serious about eradicating the scourge of rhino poaching,' David told the media and assembled Kruger staff. 'We know that we will not be able to put a ranger behind every rhino. Thus, we need to develop innovative, modern ways of protecting the rhino in the wake of this well-organised onslaught.'

I watched from the front row, weighing up his remarks and any response I could detect from the audience. I had prepared my own statement for the event. Next on stage was Yusuf Abramjee, the media personality and anti-crime activist. As the head of Crime Line, Yusuf announced that a million-rand bounty would be paid for information leading to the arrest of a poaching syndicate kingpin.

'Crime knows no borders and even if the kingpins are outside South Africa's borders, we need to hunt them down,' Yusuf said. 'The number of rhino being killed is worrying and it's clearly a crisis. We need to stop the madness and get the poachers and their bosses behind bars. They are threatening our heritage.'

At that time, 618 rhinos had been killed in South Africa in 2012, about half of them in the Kruger Park. There were predictions that more would die before the end of the year. Poachers, like everyone else, I learned, need extra money at Christmas time, so there was traditionally a spike in activity in December. I was up next and it was clear that the tone of this press briefing was one of getting tough on rhino poaching.

From my initial interview with SANParks, I had been getting a feeling that many saw my appointment as some silver bullet. The mood was: Right, we have appointed a general, so now the problem will be solved. To my way of thinking, that was not so lekker, and I wanted to address it here and now.

'I am not a Messiah, but a proven leader and team player,' I told the assembled media, as I read from my prepared statement. I swept the faces of the Kruger staff in the audience. Some seemed interested, others looked up at me with blank faces. 'I will do my best to bring acceptable results. This fight against poaching is not about an individual, and success depends on the collective collaboration and commitment from the men and women tasked with the responsibility of conserving our heritage.'

There were lights shining in my face as I spoke and digital camera drives fired in bursts at the rate of automatic weapons. After giving my statement I faced a barrage of questions from the journalists, which I did my best to answer.

'The battle lines have been drawn and it is up to my team and me to forcefully push back the frontiers of poaching,' I said in response to one question.

A reporter asked whether the fight against poaching did, in fact, amount to a war?

'It is a fact that South Africa, a sovereign country, is under attack from armed foreign nationals,' I said. From what I had already learned, the main threat to our rhinos at that time was coming from across South Africa and Kruger's eastern border with Mozambique. I wanted to send a clear message to the government and people of that country. 'This should be seen as a declaration of war against South Africa by armed foreign criminals. We are going to take the war to these armed bandits and we aim to win it.'

A murmur rippled through the audience. While I tried to be optimistic and positive in my statement and the rest of my answers, it was those more cavalier remarks, about 'taking the fight to the enemy' that, predictably, received the most prominent coverage in the media. After the briefing, several journalists took me aside for one-on-one interviews. They saved their more thoughtful, probing questions for these private talks, out of earshot of their competitors.

'What will you do differently?' one reporter asked.

Those five words unsettled me. The truth was that I had no definitive answer to the question – yet. I still needed to learn more about what had been done, and to formulate my strategy for what I believed should still be done. I skirted the question. I knew this would not be the last time I would come under the scrutiny of the media – although I could not have imagined back then just how intense that overwatch would be. I realised then and there that I would have to manage external communication directly and professionally from now on.

Away from the glare of the cameras, I was taken to lunch with senior leaders from the ranger corps and Kruger's management.

Louis Olivier, whom I soon learned was a legendary 'elder' among the rangers, shook my hand and slapped me on the back.

'Welcome, we will support you!' He seemed genuine, and while everyone was polite during the lunch, I did not see anyone rejoicing. I couldn't blame them. I had been parachuted into this job.

David Mabunda's message to the leadership team and the other players in anti-poaching – most notably the police and the military – was: 'This is the man I have selected and I request that you support him.' I appreciated that David had made such a bold decision, but a strong case could also have been made that the decision to appoint an outsider to the position of chief ranger should have warranted extensive consultation and collaboration.

The military was no stranger to the Kruger National Park – the founding warden, Major James Stevenson-Hamilton, had served on the British side in the Anglo-Boer War. South African troops had been deployed in the park on the border with Mozambique throughout the latter's struggle against its former Portuguese colonial masters, as well as during the ensuing civil war. Also, a local reserve force unit, the Kruger Park Commando, had been part of the security force in the old South Africa for many years. I hoped that I would be able to work productively with my old comrades in the army.

However, I could read the faces of the men in uniform at the lunch. If I thought that I would find strong support and allies in the ranks of the military people who had been working in Kruger, then, for the most part, there was nothing in those looks that told me that would be the case. If a commanding officer was to be appointed to run anti-poaching then it would be no surprise that the both the police and the army would think that he or she should have come from within their own ranks.

Likewise, I could see how my appointment had caused an issue for the SANParks people in the room. Bringing in a new leader from outside poses real challenges for any organisation. I realised that the buck stopped with me, and hoped that view would bring out the best in me and allow me to encourage maximum effort from those reporting to me. For the staff in the Kruger, however, I could see how my arrival made them uneasy, and perhaps created a perception that none of them was up to the task.

AFTER THAT FIRST blaze of publicity, I went back to Pretoria. In the first week of December we had received sad news – Liezl's husband, Grant, had lost his father. I travelled to Cape Town for the service and a dinner at the False Bay Yacht Club in Simon's Town. After the service, Grant and I reminisced about how we and Ian, his father, had enjoyed some good fishing off Cape Point on Ian's boat.

Several people, including Grant, congratulated me on my new job. Even though he was in mourning, Grant, who is as passionate about nature as any human can be, wanted to know more about my role and wished me well. 'Skoonpa, be sure we'll visit often and I'm sure you will be able to show us some unique places.'

I smiled and thanked the people who wished me well. Yes, there would be a certain romanticism about living in the iconic Kruger Park, but I did not want to bring the conversation down by sharing with them what I had already learned about the situation in the bush and how daunting the task ahead was. I knew my tenure was not going to be a proverbial 'walk in the park'.

Arina and I retreated to Ballito, north of Durban, for a much-needed holiday on the coast. I'd been working hard at my old job and was about to take on a mammoth task.

Together with our youngest, Ilze, and her boyfriend, we stayed in a holiday flat on the beach. It was a lovely spot and we could spot dolphins in the sea from the pool deck. Although I didn't sequester myself away from my family, I did use the time to conduct a command appreciation of how I would carry out my mission.

That was the first problem, I thought, as I lay back on the sun lounger and closed my eyes, Arina and Ilze chatting in the shade nearby. I had no mission. In the military a mission revolves around a task verb, a word that sums up the purpose and the end-state of the operation: to seize, to deny, to capture. What was I, Johan Jooste, retired general, to do about poaching? Was I to eradicate poaching? That was probably not possible. Poaching, in one form or another, had existed as long as man tried to put lines on maps or fences around protected areas.

In planning, one has to consider the battle space, and the intelligence one has – or needs – in order to do the job. As I swam in the pool or the warm Indian Ocean, or braaied wors, my mind turned to an analysis of the enemy – the poachers and the middlemen, kingpins, exporters, buyers of rhino horn and consumers. At the time, these were mostly outside of South Africa, with the majority of poaching in the Kruger being carried out by people from Mozambique, who would retreat across the border, safe in the knowledge that rangers or other security forces could not pursue them once they crossed that line.

The market for rhino horn was in China and South East Asia, notably Vietnam. So, although a war was being fought on the ground in the thorny, inhospitable bushveld in South Africa, much of the problem lay beyond the park. This would be a task that would also require engagement with people outside of my 'battle space', across international borders.

Apart from the poachers, I had to consider our own 'friendly' forces. If I had some clear guidance, a verb, it was to para-militarise the ranger corps so they could better prevent poachers from getting through to kill a rhino, or to disrupt or neutralise the poaching gangs. That could very well mean shooting a poacher in self-defence – killing or wounding him, if he opened fire on our rangers. That brought into question another issue – rules of engagement.

I made notes as I went. There were already plenty of people on social media and elsewhere calling for South Africa to implement a 'shoot-to-kill' policy in national parks, as was in force in some other African countries. Such a measure seemed inconceivable in a liberal democracy, but the rangers would need the right skills and equipment to ensure that if they were ever in armed contact with a poacher they would come out of it alive and on top.

On our side, I also had the army and the police force. I would need to try to bring them along with me on my journey and I knew, already, that my appointment had ruffled their collective feathers.

I scoured the internet, magazines, newspapers and books for as much information as I could digest about the trade in rhino horn and the problem of poaching. In previous decades, rhino horn had been marketed in Yemen, in the Horn of Africa, for use as the carved handle on ceremonial daggers. In Asia it had been used for centuries in traditional Chinese medicine as a tonic, and in recent years had been touted as a cure for cancer. Rhino horn was a status symbol, something for a wealthy businessman in Hanoi or elsewhere to show off as proof of his success. It was used to provide relief from headaches and, if one drank alcohol from a cup carved from rhino horn, it would supposedly prevent a hangover.

The international trade in rhino horn was banned by CITES, the Convention for the International Trade in Endangered Species, in 1977 – but by then, rhinos had disappeared completely from much of their traditional home range. South Africa was in possession of about 70% of the world's remaining African rhinos and only a handful of other countries on the continent were considered as having significant 'range states' for rhinos. South Africa had avoided the epidemic of poaching, with only 13 rhinos illegally killed in 2007.

Despite the CITES ban, rhino horn had been making its way, legally, out of South Africa, thanks to a loophole that allowed trophy hunting to take place in a country that had plenty of rhinos. However, in 2009, South Africa banned the legalised hunting of rhinos. Clearly some of the horns taken from animals killed by trophy hunters – many of them from Asia – had been illegally fuelling the market for rhino horn in user countries. South Africa soon found itself under attack from rhino poachers seeking to fill the gap in the market.

The southern white rhino, which differs from the black rhino (a different species) not in colour, but in size, shape of the head and body, and behaviour, was near extinction in South Africa in the early twentieth century. Accounts of the remnant population, in KwaZulu-Natal (KZN), varied from 20 to 150, but whatever the true figure, rhinos were nearly wiped out by white big-game hunters and pastoralists.

An intensive and ultimately successful conservation effort led to the stabilisation and expansion of rhino numbers, with rhinos progressively relocated from KZN to the Kruger Park and other game reserves. Even other countries, where rhinos had become extinct, received translocated animals from South Africa. By 2007, there were about 17 000 to 18 000 white rhino and the number continued to rise during the early years of the poaching epidemic in South Africa.

Many of South Africa's rhinos were in private hands and I very soon learned of the fierce debate raging over calls to legalise the trade in rhino horn. The 'pro-trade' lobby believed farmed rhinos, whose horns could be humanely removed and would grow back, would bring prices down and save the wild rhinos. The antitrade argument was that legalisation would bring legitimacy to the claims bandied about around rhino horn, and lead to even more rhinos being killed in the wild. Clever marketers in user countries, such as Vietnam, were already trying to convince their customers that the horn of 'wild' rhino was more potent and desirable than farmed product from a humanely dehorned animal. This debate was pitting conservationists against each other.

At times, the problem seemed overwhelming, but, while still trying to enjoy my holiday, I continued my analysis, reading and making notes by the pool, then typing them up on the computer at night. One bit of philosophy that guided me during this period was a well-proven concept: 'What you cannot address in the first hundred days, you will probably never get around to, and what you cannot achieve in the first thousand days, you will probably never achieve.' I was thus thankful for the five-year contract – it might just give me enough time to make a difference. I kept coming back to the closest thing I had to a mission: 'to consolidate and para-militarise the ranger corps'. If only it were that simple, I thought, that the rangers alone could stop poaching. It wasn't.

My introspection also led me to analyse myself. I was an older white male, with an apartheid-era military background, and some limited conservation experience. I wondered whether I was perhaps too strict a disciplinarian for the rather informal environment.

I had witnessed on my fly-in visit to the Kruger Park, where not even a uniform could be found for the new chief ranger. Was that just politics at play, or gross inefficiency, and if so, what did it mean for the future?

On the other side of the balance sheet, I thought, as I gazed out over the sparkling sea, there was the fact that I was still fit and well conversant with contemporary and concurrent leadership thinking. The last 10 years of my military career had centred round all facets of transformation and I had a wealth of knowledge and experience about project management and technology as Director of Projects for the Army and in my business career. My service in the Western Caprivi with the San Battalion had unwittingly prepared me for working with people from different backgrounds to my own, in the context of training and border protection.

Back in Pretoria, I met with David Mabunda again in early January, at the Blue Crane Restaurant, a popular place with the SANParks crowd from Groenkloof, as head office was generally referred to. On the deck, overlooking the dam and the adjacent Austin Roberts Bird Sanctuary, I told the CEO about the analysis I had been conducting at Ballito.

I still felt somewhat inadequate. I wanted to tell David what I could achieve for him, but all I had at this stage was my appreciation of the problem and perhaps an outline of a concept of operations.

'I'm still a long way from being able to present a fully formed strategy,' I told him. 'I appreciate your trust in me and you will have the benefit of my best effort. I know the where and the when, and some of the what, but I have to invent the "how".'

He looked at me across the table. 'General, if you fail, then fail trying.'

3

'I am not going to give Jonty away,' Arina said on the phone to our daughter Ilze in Johannesburg. 'Will you please look after him and I'll come fetch him when I can?'

Two of the biggest obstacles to my starting the next phase of my life in the Kruger Park had been overcome. Ilze agreed that Jonty, the Jack Russell, would live with his friend Tekken, the dachshund, in Johannesburg, and that Arina would continue with her job, working remotely part of the time. Arina's plan was to spend three weeks at a time with me at our house in the Skukuza staff village, and then go back to Pretoria for a week or two. I wished all the problems facing me could be resolved so easily, with compromise and cooperation.

Kruger is hot in January. The grass and leaves are lush and green, the air heavy and humid. The shrill call of woodland kingfishers, bright blue and white, with red-and-black beaks, can be heard everywhere as dark clouds build, most days, and thunder rumbles like distant artillery. The thwap of helicopter blades overhead, I learned very soon, was a harbinger of death, a sign another rhino had been killed, that more poachers had entered our park.

I arrived at Skukuza on the seventh. The park's headquarter offices are located in a separate building, behind the large thatched structure that serves as the reception to the rest camp. I walked down the corridor, noting the number of empty desks and chairs – many people were still on leave. My office measured five metres by five, but I had been allocated no staff. Other senior staff, I saw, had connecting offices where their personal assistant sat. I was dressed in a grey office-dress SANParks shirt and a pair of my own chinos – still the closest I could get to a uniform. I was given no induction to the park, no duty sheet, and no handover briefing.

David Mabunda flew in and I met with him and Abe Sibaya, the Managing Executive of the park. My appointment had been so swift that no decision had been made about who I would report to. Abe and David deliberated at length and, in a compromise, it was decided that I would report to Abe, but with a dotted line to David. Intuitively, and given my experience in the military, I felt that a paramilitary force needed a unity of command and this arrangement might dilute that. The compromise got us past the immediate problem, but I was worried that it might cause problems in the future.

Arina joined me at Skukuza later in January and together we inspected the house we had been allocated. It had stood empty for some time, and needed a good deal of work. Arina and I decided that it would be best for her to go back to Pretoria. She knew I would be very busy, initially, finding my feet, so decided to return around Easter 2013.

I had my own work cut out for me, but it was slow going. During my first week, I called in anyone who was not on leave. For administrative purposes, Kruger was divided into four regions: Nxanatseni North, covering the area north of the Shingwedzi River; Nxanatseni South, from the Shingwedzi to the Olifants River; Marula North, from the Olifants to the Sabie River; and Marula South, from the Sabie to the Crocodile River. One of the regional rangers sat down opposite me.

'I hear there's another strike planned,' he said.

'What the fuck is this about a strike?' I asked, adding, 'Excuse my language.'

I couldn't believe my ears. Six months earlier, in 2012, he filled me in, there had been a total strike by rangers over a number of griev-ances. Staff had complained about their allowances, uniform supply problems – that I could understand – and a shopping list of other things they were unhappy about. Morale, it seemed, was rock bottom.

'Three rhinos killed yesterday,' the statistics clerk from ECI said, 'and we've found some more carcasses.'

We sat in a room at the Air Wing building at Skukuza Airport, which was also ECI's headquarters. Every morning there was a meet-ing, in which the numbers of dead rhinos and contacts with poachers were summarised. It was almost an administrative process, a routine reeling off of statistics. There was no planning, nor methodology to analyse what was going on.

Command and control were done by cell phone, with section rangers communicating with their people and each other, the Air Wing, and head office as required. There was no operations room, except for the conference room, in which we were now sitting.

'How do you plan operations?' I asked the leader group. 'How do you ensure in-time control?'

I looked at their faces. They were tired and I sensed that I was irri-tating them with my questions. They wanted me to help, rather than interrogate them, but I could see there was a long and challenging road ahead. Apart from telling them to switch gears, I had to be cognisant of the hard work they had already put in.

I learned that 150 new recruits had been taken into the ranger corps in 2012. This was a credit to the tenacity of the Minister of Envi-ronmental Affairs, Edna Molewa, who had obtained the funds for extra manpower from the fiscus, but no one in SANParks seemed to grasp that manpower alone was not enough. We had more people, but they could not be effectively deployed, because they lacked lead-ers, equipment, proper accommodation and logistic support.

As I had seen for myself, there were shortfalls and inefficiencies in the logistics chain. The new intake had represented a 40% increase in the corps, but what had not been taken into consideration was the need for more corporals and sergeants to be trained and promoted to lead these raw trainees.

One thing was clear: I needed to act decisively and swiftly and have the courage to take calculated risks. While I needed more information, there was no time for 'analysis paralysis'. This task would require renewal projects that might take months or years to bear fruit; I was already making a long list of things that required immediate attention. In my mind and notebook, and on my laptop at night, I was developing a CONOPS, a concept of operations, but I also needed to work on a long-term strategy.

Meanwhile, the death toll was mounting day by day. I needed help, but first I had to get out of Skukuza. If only, I thought to myself, as I sat in the stuffy, hot conference room, they had hired me five years earlier.

FROM THE AIR I could really appreciate the beauty of the Kruger Park and, yet again, the immensity of the challenge we faced.

The park had a total perimeter of about 1 000 kilometres. I needed to see for myself what was going on at the various ranger posts and out in the bush, in Kruger's four regions.

The Air Wing, with its two helicopters and a fixed-wing Cessna, was clearly an essential part of our anti-poaching effort. However, the aircraft were also used for counting game, darting animals for capture and relocation, and other conservation-related tasks. I made it my business to get to know the pilots, and to explain how I wanted them to work from now on. Prior to my arrival, if a section ranger wanted use of a helicopter, he or she would call them and they would say yes or no. That was no way to manage a high-value asset such as a helicopter.

The pilots were extremely professional and dedicated, but they had never been seen as part of the bigger picture, and nor did they expect that. I explained to them that from now on requests for air support would come via the ops room, such as it was, and that the decision would be made there. The pilots, in turn, needed to keep us up to date with their movements and availability.

'So, I am dog tired after days of flying,' a pilot said to me, 'and now I must report to the ops room? Do you really expect me to do that?'

I nodded.

We flew low along the Lebombo Mountains, following the ridge-line, with Mozambique to the east and the rest of Kruger and South Africa to the west, on one of my self-organised reconnaissance sorties, this time with Ken Maggs. There, in front of us, clearly visible, was a fresh carcass. The pilot put the chopper down and we all climbed out to look.

The rhino lay on its belly, almost as if it was sleeping and might get up at any minute – the vultures had not even found it yet. It had been killed by a waterhole, shot in the head as it began to drink. We scouted the area and found the poacher's hide, where he had cut some branches to camouflage his position, and had lain in wait, during the night of the full moon. The horn was gone, removed cleanly with a knife. I would learn about the modus operandi of poachers – a skilled one could remove the horn with a blade; an amateur used an axe, the noise of chopping often heard some distance off.

We took off and carried on. The pilot spotted vultures and we deviated to take a look. There were three older carcasses, so we landed once again. The white rhino is so placid and docile that even an amateur is able to get close enough for a killing shot and this trio had been slaughtered before they even realised what was happening.

The stench was overpowering. I was in shock and I could tell that the others with me were watching the brave general, looking for a reaction. I know the odour of death, but I had smelled nothing like this before. It was a pungent, repulsive, clinging and evil smell that matched my mood right then. How futile, was all I could think. Why have you killed these animals?

We radioed in the discovery of the carcasses. I looked around me, my hands on my hips, surveying the terrain. We were so close to Mozambique – the poachers would have travelled to the border with absolute impunity, safe in the knowledge there was no one to stop them on their way, and that they would most likely find rhino just inside Kruger. Our park was like a supermarket to them – pick and paid. They know rhinos must drink every day, so all they have to do is stake out a waterhole. How, I wondered, would we regain the initiative, or, rather, had we ever had it in the first place? Which of the holes in this leaking dam was I to plug first?

Again, I surveyed the carnage, trying to make sense of it. This was what happened when greed meets poverty. Rhino horn was worth $65,000 per kilogram in South East Asia at the time, and a good-sized set of horns from one animal could weigh in at six to nine kilos. Even though poachers would only get a fraction of that, there was no question of why they were risking encounters with dangerous wildlife and rangers to kill these creatures. I have hunted in my life, not often, but when I do I take a moment to feel for the animal whose life I have taken, and take some solace from knowing it will be consumed. The waste of this type of killing brought on a quiet rage, which I did not let the others with me see. Inside, however, I was the moer in. What are you doing, coming here to our park and doing this to us? I let the anger burn inside me, channelling it, making me even more determined to fulfil my mission.

THE CHOPPER SET down at Letaba Rest camp, overlooking the broad river of the same name. Dainty little brown bushbuck, habituated by generations of tourists, picked their way between the rondavels. People were dining at the restaurant, picking out elephant and waterbuck in the distance through their binoculars.

A group of about 30 rangers was waiting for me in the auditorium of the nearby Goldfields Elephant Hall, with its life-size statue of one of the great animals out front. I walked in, an interpreter with me in case one was needed. Again, I felt embarrassed – I called myself an African, but could speak no indigenous languages. I sized up the crowd as I stood in front of them. They were quiet, with an air of polite attention, but I could tell some were also trying to assess me. Others were more distant, as if there was nothing new or useful I could tell them. As I began to address them, telling them about myself, I could see that although most listened carefully, none was enthused.

Who is this madala talking nicely to us now? their eyes seemed to say. I felt an outsider, not because of the colour of my skin, but because I was not one of them; I had not come from their ranks. I tried to convey how important their job was, and what I would expect from them.

'We are going to do things differently from now on,' I said to them. 'There will be additional training.' Here I was, telling them they would need to do more work, learn more things, while they still went about their existing duties.

When I was done, we took a break outside, where I was able to mingle with the rangers. One, a sergeant, and a natural leader judging by his bearing, made his way over to me.

'You tell us our job is important, and we will be supported,' he said, squaring up and towering over me, 'but we are not being supported.'

Some of the others, emboldened, gathered around him. 'Tell me what you mean,' I said. I was not intimidated; I was here to learn and I preferred that a man would tell me straight what was wrong, rather than the indifference I'd sensed in the room.

The sergeant called to two rangers. 'Come, stand in front of the General,' he said. One ranger, a woman, wore a uniform that looked like a light, mottled khaki, almost camouflage; the other's shirt and trousers were green.

The ranger pointed to the man in green. 'We are not getting our uniforms on time, when we ask for them, and when they do first arrive, this is the colour.'

I nodded.

'This,' he pointed to the pale-coloured uniform the woman was wearing, 'is what this same green uniform looks like after just three washes.'

I looked at the evidence before me. I was almost speechless. I took a picture of the rangers with my phone camera.

'Three washes,' the sergeant said again. 'What do you say now, General?'

I looked him in the eye. 'If this is the sort of support you are getting, then I will do something about it.'

PRETORIUSKOP, in the far south of the park, had been chosen as Kruger's first site for tourist huts. Its elevation made it cooler than the surrounding Lowveld bush, and kept it out of the malaria zone. I was feeling anything but cool, though.

A ranger held up a brown boot. It looked shiny and new, but when he took hold of the sole, near the toe, he peeled it back so that the whole underside of the boot came away.

'It is not even rubber,' he said, sneering, 'it's plastic.'

I was ready to blow my top, but I kept myself in check. As with the uniforms, I told him I would follow up, but I had to be careful not to overextend, nor promise something I was not absolutely sure I could deliver on. It was clear that the rangers felt as though nothing was ever followed through, and they had been continually let down.

The long strike, I had since learned, was not incited by one particular event or grievance, but rather a long list of festering issues that bubbled up from a lack of communication and a sense of abandonment, which led to discontent. Add to that, the rangers had to deal with regular media reports about their 'failure' to curb poaching.

It was little wonder, then, that their quarters were not exactly in inspection order. When I visited the rangers' posts I found litter, buildings in need of painting, and a broken generator. Some of the rangers had their families with them and there were cooking pots and other personal items just lying around. Their uniforms were old and torn, or new and faded; their boots were dirty; and a gate was hanging askew, supported by just one hinge.

At the Mooiplaas Ranger Post, near Mopani Rest Camp, and at other posts I visited, I found that that some of the newer rangers, the recruits from the previous year, were living in old tents, because there was no permanent accommodation for them. In some cases, whole families were living under canvas.

This made me even more the moer in; there might have been building programmes on paper, but clearly there was a lack of urgency. Also, no one was communicating with the rangers, telling them what was going to happen from one day to the next. There were not even enough rifles for every ranger to have his or her own weapon.

I stood in front of a tent at Mooiplaas, anger boiling up inside me as I spoke to Section Ranger Joe Nkuna: 'I promise you that I will see to it that this is addressed and I will communicate the progress to you.'

The new recruits had been deployed without proper command and control and, as a result, there was a distinct lack of focus. Bad habits were already creeping into their daily routine, undermining their basic training.

I approached a group of rangers sitting in the shade. None stood. As rangers, we did not salute, but a person was expected to stand straight, to 'brace up' in the presence of a senior officer. This did not happen. Later, I told the section ranger how I expected his post and his men to look, and the courtesy I, and their other leaders, should expect without having to ask for it.

'How,' I asked the ranger senior leadership group, 'can I expect a man's rifle to be clean if his clothes and the place where he lives are dirty?'

One of them pushed back. 'But we are not military,' he said. 'This is not the army, General.'

He was right. I was conscious that I had to ease the corps into change, not bully them. What I wanted was for them to be able to do their job to the best of their ability and, whether they liked it or not, their job had changed.

In the past, rangers worked on eradicating alien plants, fixing fences, tackling erosion and building dams. Law enforcement might have been 10% of the workload. Now, however, poaching was an urgent, overriding priority, taking up 90% of their time. I needed to know, for their own safety, that if I went to a ranger post their radios would be working, their vehicles in good order and their rifles clean. First, however, I had to find enough weapons for them. On the plus side, the grassroots ranger structure I inherited was sound. The 22 sections, within the four regions, were each commanded by a section ranger. He or she was responsible for everything that went on in the section, from law enforcement through to tourism and management of the wildlife and habitat. In the sections, each covering about 100 000 hectares, the section ranger was the king, or queen, with delegated authority to make the decisions necessary to achieve our mission. I sensed, however, that what was lacking was sound leadership from above.

I thus decided, on my own, even before developing my detailed strategy, to convert the entire ranger corps, and those in the field in support of it, into an anti-poaching unit. Even the pilots would now become 'ranger pilots'.

Back at Skukuza, I started asking questions, locally and in Pretoria. The bureaucrats in SANParks soon became sick of me.

'When will we get new uniforms?' I demanded.

'When will you find or build housing for my rangers who are living in tents?' I said in another call.

On regular visits to Pretoria, I stalked the corridors of Groenkloof, undeterred even when I was shunted from office to office. 'Where is the ammunition for my rangers? When will we get more rifles?' 'Why are you raising your voice with me, General?' I was asked more than once by a bureaucrat.

It was maddening. I was supposed to be sitting in the strategic chair, directing the fight against poaching, yet here I was harassing civil servants for uniforms and boots. Half the time I didn't even know who I should be beating up – someone in Skukuza, or someone at head office in Pretoria. We should have been supported, with equipment and resources pushed out to us; instead, I found myself constantly pulling, continually asking for clothing, rations, rifles and ammunition – it was like pulling teeth.

Everyone in the organisation knew I had the backing of David

Mabunda, but so many of the people I dealt with hated me intruding in their comfort zone. Often, the attitude I encountered was one of 'Who do you think you are?'

At a management meeting in Skukuza I held up my cell phone, to show attendees the picture of the rangers in the mismatching uniforms.

'I understand you have to follow processes,' I said when the procurement system was explained to me, yet again, 'but give urgency to it at the same time!'

I HELD a joint planning session with the regional rangers and senior staff. For two and a half days we sat in the small conference room at Skukuza, me writing on a flip chart. I have always preferred to plan on paper.

'This is your opportunity to give me your views,' I told them. I have often said that people do not care to listen until you show them you care. While I listened to their grievances and their suggestions, I also looked for ways in which I could improve their lives and the living conditions of the rangers.

The air conditioner in the meeting room was broken and it was stifling. Using a marker pen from my battered old green canvas army pencil bag, we worked through a SWOT session, looking at strengths, weaknesses, opportunities and threats, as they applied to my mission, of consolidating and para-militarising the ranger corps. Our strengths began with our people. The rangers knew the terrain intimately and, by virtue of their day-to-day work, were good trackers. They knew how to shoot, because their job also required them to protect themselves and occasionally euthanise animals. These were basic skills that could be built on. We had some air assets, but these, I thought, could be expanded. I was only beginning to learn of our weaknesses.

One of the key things to address, early on, was command and control. The ranger corps had traditionally reported to the General Manager of Conservation, Dr Freek Venter. However, their day-to-day support and management were handled by the tourism services based in the four regions.

I quickly learned that the current structure did not sit well with the section rangers. They told of sitting through endless meetings where tourism managers debated new colours for the curtains, or the appropriate number of knives and forks for a tourist rondavel. When the rangers did get to have their say, they found that some managers did not even have a basic understanding of a section ranger's duties or challenges, and would sometimes act irritated and dismissive when the rangers pushed for urgent decisions and requirements.

Two lines of reporting were cumbersome at the best of times, but in the face of a crisis it was impossible. The rangers had traditionally worked with the seasons, burning the veld and looking after roads in the winter, and taking things easier in the wet summer. They adopted what I called a 'shorts and slops' attitude, reflected in their dress and bearing. By contrast, they now faced an enemy who did not sleep, and who ramped up his activities over school holidays and long weekends. Full moon was also a favourite time for poachers, because it was easier to track and shoot rhino.

When it came to opportunities, I began to consider how technology could help us. On the day my appointment had been announced at Skukuza, in conjunction with the news about the reward from Yusuf Abramjee, South African aerospace company Denel had shown off a drone, and told the media how it could be used to track poachers. There was already a buzz about the use of such devices. I needed to consider anything that could help.

Every day I learned more about the poaching problem and the challenges I would face. The threats were many. From what I could gather, about 75% of incursions were from the east, from Mozambique. It seemed an almost lawless environment on that side of the border. In poverty-stricken villages, poachers operated with impunity and carried an almost Robin Hood-like status.

There had always been a fence along Kruger's 350-kilometre eastern boundary, but some adaptations had been made after the proclamation of the Great Limpopo Transfrontier Park in 2002. This forward-thinking initiative, promoted by the not-for-profit Peace Parks Foundation, called for the removal of barriers – physical and political – to the movement of game between South Africa, Mozambique and, to the north, Gonarezhou National Park in Zimbabwe. In the northern section of the extended park, 80 kilometres of the Mozambican boundary fence were removed to promote the movement of game, and the southern section had been allowed to fall into disrepair. Many people were already calling for the re-erection of a 'Berlin Wall' type of fence to stem the flow of poachers into Kruger.

Rangers faced a number of risks. First, there was the threat of being killed or wounded in action by an armed poacher. Secondly, if a ranger shot and killed a poacher, he or she immediately became the subject of a murder investigation, so they would need on-call legal representation. Thirdly, there was the threat of mental illness from repeated exposure to combat and seeing people and even rhinos killed. There was also the stress of a ranger being alienated by his or her own community, some of whom would be sympathetic to the poachers.

As well as the external threats, from Mozambique and the South African communities to the west of Kruger, where poverty and unemployment were also a problem, there were enemies within. Right from the start I was hearing about corrupt staff, including rangers, who were either poaching or supplying information to criminals. These 'snakes', as I began calling them, had to be flushed out.

In addition to equipment, the rangers would need training in order to fulfil the mission of becoming a paramilitary force capable of defeating poachers. In the meeting I stressed the term 'para'. A military force comprises platoons, companies and battalions, with supporting heavy weapons, such as machine guns and artillery. That was not what we had in mind for the rangers. Rangers mostly operated in pairs, moving quietly through the bush or waiting in observation posts and this low signature allowed them to observe poachers before they themselves were seen. We needed to enhance their existing skills, and develop tactics and techniques through training that would allow them to defeat the armed bandits they were up against and to survive in the bush. While I would not be deploying heavy weapons, we did have the Air Wing and canines and the promise of technology to provide support.

I did consider a plan, at this early stage, to enlist the army's help in a big way. I came up with a proposal to convert 7 SAI, the infantry battalion at Phalaborwa, into a light infantry unit with a specialist capability in anti-poaching. My vision was that its 800 members could combat wildlife crime in the Lowveld, which was home to many private game reserves, as well as the Kruger Park. I knew from my time at Phalaborwa that the base was huge – it had been designed to accommodate large intakes of more than 1 000 recruits for national service at a time – so there was space to conduct tracking and other specialist training that soldiers would need to become effective anti-poaching operators. Even though this would have dramatically increased the numbers of individuals at my disposal, neither SANParks nor the army could countenance such a radical change of thinking.

The lack of equipment and support for rangers in Kruger extended even to an inability to supply rations to remote ranger posts – food was being pilfered along the supply line before it reached the rangers and their families. This, it seemed to me, was one of many issues that contributed to ranger dissatisfaction. I had also met with the 25 shop stewards from the various unions in Kruger and knew it was a catalogue of these types of issues that had led to the general strike the park had just endured. Any one of the problems, from late rations to a broken generator, could easily be fixed, but the fact that there were so many issues spoke of systemic problems. I had seen from my visits to the various posts that conditions were tough, but this need not be the case.

As well as a lack of support, there was a lack of discipline and pride, evidenced by the state of the living areas and the response I had received – or not received – from rangers lounging about, or unwilling to meet my eye. I would lead from the front, setting an example in my dress and bearing, but we also needed to instil pride in the rangers themselves. In my eyes, they were the heroes of this struggle – they just needed to believe it.

We broke the mission down into long-term goals and the objectives we would need to meet to achieve the goals. The missing factor was command and control to ensure the sustained and intelligent deployment of the potentially formidable ranger force and all its associated resources.

It was one thing to announce to the media that we were going to 'take the fight to the criminals', another entirely to put that into practice.

4

'I s your name Johan Jooste?' the technician asked.

'Yes.' With the sensors attached via a strap around my chest, and clipped to my fingers, I became conscious of every nuance in my body language and breathing. I was convinced I could hear my own heart beating.

'Have you ever told a lie?'

To deal with the issue of 'snakes' – the corrupt rangers and other staff within our ranks – I suggested that lie-detector tests become mandatory for all rangers. The CEO agreed and I fully expected a backlash from the unions and staff. Symbolically, I volunteered to take the first integrity test. It was a confronting experience for anyone to go through, but I had decided it was essential.

I was shocked by the results. There were just too many red and amber flags coming up, even amongst the leader group.

Human resources and the legal people from SANParks were quick to caution me that the integrity testing could not be used as grounds for dismissal or prosecution, which I fully understood. However, I now knew who I should keep my eye on, and where future investigations might be carried out.

With the input of the rangers at the initial planning meeting, a plan was forming in my mind, but I needed help, urgently. I was losing 'friends' by the day in Pretoria as I continued to pester people about our supply-chain issues. Many in head office had never learned nor embraced the concept of servant leadership, in which the leader focuses on the growth and well-being of the workplace or community. Instead, they were infected with what I called the Groenkloof Virus, an insidious malaise that attacks and then slows down initiative, more often than not in the name of 'good governance'.

A philosophy for action and business I heard many years ago told me: 'Think big, start small, act now.' I printed the words out and stuck them above my desk to remind me daily of what I needed to do. I was acting fast, but there was so much to do that it felt as though I did not even have time to think.

I BEGAN THE STRUCTURAL TRANSFORMATION.

'Since you are appointed now, what is my role?' Ken Maggs asked.

'I want you to be my chief of staff,' I said. 'What does that mean?'

'The chief of staff gives continuity, and ensures the day-to-day running of everything we do, including logistics and operations, not focusing on just one thing. This will help us create a firm base.' I told Ken I expected him to fill in for me when I was away, and this he did on many occasions. Soon after appointing Ken as chief of staff, I made the Air Wing part of the ranger corps, with the chief pilot, Grant Knight, part of my command group. Next, I allocated the job of policing Kruger's entry gates to a new 100-person protection services unit under Victor Nxumalo. By bringing in security officers to check staff and tourists' vehicles and paperwork, I could free up more field rangers to go on patrol. Also in the command group were Mbongeni Tukela, in charge of ranger support; Bruce Leslie, who commanded the special rangers; and Kobus de Wet, who headed up ECI, our criminal investigation division. Don English, the regional ranger of Marula South, was also part of the command group, because he was based in Skukuza.

I started the process of expanding ECI by 50%. Under the leadership of Kobus, we transformed ECI from a small organisation, previously responsible for crime-scene investigation and individual cases, into a crime intelligence outfit, in an effort to inform the operational planning process with in-time intelligence and information on poacher tactics.

I also obtained funding to double the number of Bruce's team. Highly trained and experienced, the special rangers were our elite, like the army's recce commandos; they were also involved in intelligence gathering and semi-covert operations.

I took over the ECI conference room at the airport and turned it into an operations room. With its 12-seater conference table, it was really too small for a fully-fledged joint operations centre, but it was the best I had to work with.

'But what about our nice conference room?' one of the staff asked after I'd made the announcement. 'Where will we have our meetings now?'

'You can have your meetings outside, under a tree,' I said.

As a former military commander and business executive, I knew well the old adage from the Chinese general and military strategist, Sun Tzu, about intelligence: 'Military intelligence is the key to war; without it, you cannot win.'

Fortunately, David Mabunda had also realised that intelligence would be a critical success factor. He and I decided we should contract Marius Roos's company, Pathfinder, to work in Kruger. We had the legal people draw up an agreement. However, when we tried to get that through, it initially boomeranged on us. David used his delegated authority to step in, and instructed that a deviation be made from normal procedures; this was allowed under legislation. Within a month I could add the Pathfinder package of an analyst, ops-room operator and two to three investigators at any one time. This was serious capacity, which I now had to embed in an already anxious environment. This was one of the human elements of change, bringing new people into an environment where, quite frankly, immature professional jealousy was a factor.

I also contracted three ex-rangers on small salaries to give specialist support. I needed Arrie Schreiber, a specialist in area integrity management, to help get to the bottom of the exact state of the rangers, without relying on the opinions of those inside the corps, or outdated reports. The other two rangers would offer support at flash-points within the park while we were building capacity.

But I still needed one more specialist to run operations integrated with intelligence, and in my mind this would have to be an experienced ex-military person who could live in the park full time. Gerard 'Otch' Otto was a former Special Forces colonel, divorced and living in the bushveld housing estate, Marloth Park, just across the Crocodile River on the other side of Kruger's southern border. Otch had called me on the day my appointment was announced, the previous December, offering his services and I had told him I would get back to him once my feet touched ground. I called him in February 2013 and told him that if he was still interested in meeting me, then he should come to Berg en Dal Rest Camp in the far south of Kruger to see me.

Set amidst the hills that, along with the river, formed a natural boundary of the park, Berg en Dal was in prime rhino country. Otch reported and we shook hands; from his firm grip to his straight-backed bearing, he was still a military man. He was about my age, and in good shape. Nearly two metres tall and built like a rugby forward, this grey-haired warrior, like many former South African military men, had been serving as a contractor in Afghanistan and Iraq. Currently, though, he was out of work.

Otch had risen through the ranks to become a full colonel by the end of his time in the army. He and I had been on the command and staff college course together and he had ended up in charge of the army battalion in the Kruger prior to the change of government in South Africa. He knew the park and knew how to plan and run operations.

'I need a senior staff officer,' I told him, 'but I can't use a term like that – it's too military. The position will be called the "mission area manager". I need someone to set up a JOC and help me with operations, intelligence and planning.'

'I'm interested, General,' he said.

I laid my cards on the table and told him I could not pay him much.

'Tell me why I should appoint you,' I said.

He looked me in the eye. 'If you appoint me and use me for three months, you will not be able to work without me.'

I knew that as an ex-Special Forces operator, he would be confident, but I had to roll my eyes at that statement. 'Bliksem, but that's very bold.'

Otch smiled.

This was the man I needed. 'I'm going to have a battle to appoint you,' I said, knowing Mabunda had gone out on a limb to appoint one old white man already, 'but I'm going to do my best. In the meantime, you can help me move ahead; I want a full military appreciation of the situation in Kruger – our own forces, terrain and the enemy threat.'

'Yes, General.'

Otch began working straight away, from his home. He had completed an art diploma when he was younger and was a talented painter. I knew his flair for design and graphics would also help me in preparing punchy PowerPoint presentations, which I would use to brief government and other stakeholders.

Back at Skukuza, I briefed senior management on my decision to appoint Otch. To say they were lukewarm about the idea would be an understatement. Several members of the senior leader group were dead against it. During his time as the military commander of the Kruger battalion, a ranger's wife had left her husband and married Otch; they subsequently divorced after 10 years and he was a bachelor again. I stuck to my guns and reminded everyone that I was hiring him for his skills and experience as an operator and a planner.

I finally received approval from Abe Sibaya to appoint Otch and a contract was drawn up. We found him accommodation in the staff village, initially a room in the house used by the Pathfinder intelligence operatives.

Otch worked like a beaver, panel-beating our small meeting room into more of an ops room. There were screens to provide electronic data displays; paper maps on the wall; an organogram of a poaching organisation, showing their hierarchy, and where they came from; our orbat, or order of battle, and where our forces were located; and poacher infiltration routes and flash-points. Of course, there was also my trusty flip chart with many pages and pens.

I set him to work writing standard operating procedures in his 'spare' time. 'There's no documentation of how things work in this place,' I told him.

He was a paradox. He was the first to admit that I could not take him into a meeting where politics or black economic empowerment was to be discussed, but he worked closely and constructively with the Xitsonga and Siswati-speaking women who acted as our message-takers, talking to the rangers in their respective languages, and the radio operators, to improve the flow of communications.

He instituted a system whereby they filled out different slips for various incidents, such as shots fired, or tracks discovered, so that all the relevant information was recorded. He championed his people, pushing back on me to ensure there was career progression for them.

'This radio operator must want to be president one day, General, not listening to a radio for the rest of his life,' he insisted.

I was not a fan of holding regular meetings just for the hell of it, but when I had an issue or a number of things to discuss or seek advice on, I called my senior leadership together. There was always a point to these meetings and I sometimes used them to get a more personal or inspirational point across. I had picked up that Otch's fast-paced changes were causing some mumblings behind the scenes about him – and me.

Before we got down to the business of the day at a meeting soon after Otch's appointment, I rose to my feet at the head of the table. 'I get the feeling some of you are uncomfortable with Otch,' I said, scanning their faces. 'I did not appoint him because he was some old army tjommie of mine. The last time I saw him was in 1984. Please stand back from any personal feelings and work with him.'

There were nods and I was pleased to see that within a few weeks many of those who had been against his appointment were now working well with him, and some had even become friends. A few, however, were the type of diehards who would always resist change.

I managed to secure funding to build accommodation for those on duty at the ops room, including a room for a pilot and a hut for the mission area manager. Frequently, some colleagues and I would braai and have a few drinks, the latter of which I always considered part of the meal.

However, whenever Arina visited I was so jealous of our time together that I made sure I spent as much of it as I could with her in the evenings. Arina had begun overseeing some renovations to our house in the staff village. She had plans for a garden but, as with the dog, was disappointed when she learned we could not bring certain plants into the park because they were classified as aliens, and therefore prohibited.

With the members of the command group, we began developing our concept of operations, more often than not while braaiing as our days were filled with begging for equipment and setting up the ops room, in between the staff dealing with contact after contact. The CONOPS would form the basis of a full-fledged strategy.

First, we agreed, we needed to 'protect'. This meant establishing a firm base from which to conduct our operations. As our borders were impossibly long and porous our firm base was not a place, but rather people – our ranger corps. We would protect them by ensuring they were properly trained, equipped and motivated.

Second, we would react. We had to. Our adversary was proactive and we had to first respond to him and, hopefully, disrupt him before he could act. It was estimated that there were six incursions by three-man poaching gangs into the park per day, with as many as 12 separate groups active at any one time. In order to react we needed to be mobile, with the ability to deploy helicopters, fixed-wing aircraft and more vehicles, perhaps including quad bikes and all-terrain vehicles. Our rangers needed to be fit, in order to pursue poachers over great distances, and they needed to hone their existing tracking skills. We also needed to be mobile in our thinking, persistent and unpredictable, avoiding routine at all costs. We could not fall into the trap of sticking to a routine. One factor I wanted to address was the fact that to date the vast majority of ranger patrols were conducted during daylight hours only, and our helicopter pilots had neither the training nor equipment to fly at night.

At the same time, we needed to become proactive. We needed good intelligence to find out where the poachers were launching from and who their middlemen and kingpins were. We could do this by using humint – human intelligence, including informer networks and technology. There was an array of gear on the market, from night-vision goggles and camera traps to thermal-imaging equipment and various alarm systems, but it had to be effective and user-friendly.

EASTER at the end of March in 2013 was a busy time in the Kruger Park. Families from Joburg and Pretoria and further afield, as well as foreign tourists, filled the reserve to capacity. The rains had eased and the days were clear and warm.

Having given me time to find my feet, Arina had joined me at our home in the staff village. There was still so much to do, but for the first time since January, I was able to get some of my family out to Skukuza. Ilze could also visit us in this wildlife paradise for the first time. It was wonderful to have a break, and for a couple of days, at least, we could appreciate the plus side of living where we now did.

The day after Good Friday, as I was enjoying a glass of wine and watching my braai fire die down, a tourist was sitting at the restaurant at Olifants Camp, high up on the cliff looking out over the river. At about 7 pm the visitor saw a flash of light in the distance and alerted the staff, who contacted Section Ranger Dalton Mabasa.

Just as I was about to put my chops on my nicely prepared coals, my phone rang. It was Dalton.

'General, we have a chopper down.' As a military commander, I knew what it was like to lose men under my command, but nothing can prepare you for those words.

It was a South African Air Force helicopter, so I notified Joint Operations Headquarters in Pretoria then started calling everyone within our organisation who needed to know. I then logged an air request for a helicopter flight and, before dawn on Easter Sunday, I gave my apologies to the family and drove the short distance to the airport, across the low-level bridge over the Sabie River, as fast as I legally could. I was at Skukuza Airport at first light, along with some of the key staff and an SAPS member. A SANParks helicopter was waiting for me.

Since my first round of visits to all the ranger posts I remained conscious of not making a nuisance of myself by taking helicopter trips unless it was absolutely necessary – this was one of those occasions. We flew to the crash site and landed.

An area about half the size of a rugby field had been burned and in the centre all that was recognisable of the South African Air Force Agusta A109 helicopter was the tail section and the remains of the engine. There were five bodies, charred and shrunken by fire. Dalton and his rangers were at the site.

Everyone on board had been killed in the crash, which was later determined to be an accident. The flight crew, pilot Phil Chabalala and flight engineer Gene Ruiters, were carrying three passengers from 5 Special Forces Regiment based at Phalaborwa: Captain Jakes van Rensburg, Sergeant Paulus Ndishishi and medical orderly Lance Corporal Bheki Petros Cele. The three Special Forces operators had been on an anti-poaching patrol and the helicopter had been doing some dummy drops, a deception tactic that involved the helicopter landing and taking off from multiple locations, pretending to drop off or pick up phantom patrols. This would make any poachers in the area think we had several teams out in the bush.

While we were on the ground radios hissed to life. It was Richard Sowry, the section ranger for Kingfisherspruit, an area in the central part of Kruger, between Skukuza and Olifants, on the border of the Timbavati Private Game Reserve. Richard reported that a rhino had been shot in his section. That was significant – it was the first time the poachers had struck west of the main tar road that ran north–

south through Kruger. I decided to head to the scene; there was nothing I could do for the five brave souls who had died in the service of their country.

With the image of the bodies of the military people still fresh in our minds, we flew to where Richard was waiting, bearing witness to another horror.

The rhino was still alive. Richard had just got there himself and we approached the animal. It had been shot, but its ears were twitching. As we moved closer, I could hear the swish, swish, swish of each exhaled breath from its nostrils. Its big chin was resting on the ground. The front of its face had been hacked off, exposing blood and bright white bone.

This was Easter Sunday – a holy commemoration of resurrection, sacrifice and hope.

Richard turned to me. 'Shall we go to social media with this, General?'

The scene we were witnessing was horrible, confronting. This magnificent animal had been left to die in pain, presumably so as to avoid a second shot giving the criminal's position away. People would be shocked if they saw this on social media, perhaps sickened.

'Do it.'

Richard hauled out his phone and took the pictures. When he was done, he put his phone in his pocket and took up his R1 assault rifle and put the rhino out of its misery.

Section Ranger Steven Whitfield radioed in; his rangers had just made another contact with a gang of poachers. Like Robbie Bryden and Don English, Steven – a big but softly spoken guy – was also a second-generation ranger, with the bush in his blood. Steven said he needed the helicopter, as well as Richard Sowry and his dog.

Richard was an early proponent of using dogs to track poachers and, while not all of Kruger's rangers believed in the value of canines, he was convinced they could add value. Of medium height and solid build, Richard was an innovator and, unlike some rangers, very tech-savvy. We all got on board and the pilot took off for Tshokwane, where Steven was based.

At Tshokwane, I had to disembark to make room for Steven, who would oversee the chase from the air. I stayed at the ranger post, waiting for the hunt to end and the chopper to come back for me. I monitored progress on the radio – there was a heavy chase going on, with the helicopter searching from above and the dog team and rangers bashing through the thick bush on foot in the hot weather.

I was so angry. I had pumped myself up, beginning to think I could make this work, and bring about change. I knew full well the challenges of an insurgency war, which was exactly what we were fighting here. It could not be fixed in the 1980s by bringing in more helicopter gunships and tanks, and now it was the same here. We had lost the initiative.

Word came back from Steven that they had managed to catch one poacher, who led them to the carcass of another slaughtered rhino.

Back in Skukuza my family was doing its best to enjoy Easter Sunday without me. Meanwhile, I sat there on the stoep of the ranger post, feeling utterly helpless and hopeless.

Across the border, our adversaries taunted us – literally.

I received a report from rangers in hot pursuit of a poaching gang. They chased them right to the border, to the dilapidated fence and the road that marked the line between South Africa and Mozambique.

'They laughed at us, General,' the ranger in charge said to me during a debrief. 'As soon as they crossed the border, they stopped and started waving at us, yelling insults. One fired his rifle in the air. They know we cannot chase after them.'

Our intelligence told us that the poaching kingpins drove their foot soldiers right to the border, sometimes in broad daylight, and dropped them off. There was no one on that side – not rangers, nor police, nor military – even trying to intercept them.

On social media, armchair experts called on us to change our rules of engagement, to implement a shoot-to-kill policy and allow us to conduct hot pursuits across the border. Others yet again demanded the fence be re-erected along the length of the Kruger's eastern boundary. What any military person would have explained to such 'strategists' was that any obstacle, such as a fence, was no good on its own – it needed to be covered by fire and observation. I had neither the manpower nor the technology to cover the 350 kilometres of border with Mozambique, let alone Kruger's total perimeter of 1,000 kilometres.

EARLY ON, not long after my posting as chief ranger had been announced, I was home in Pretoria for a weekend and went to church at the NG Kerk in Centurion. I was on duty there, welcoming people, when Chris Serfontein and his family came up the pathway. 'Congratulations on your new appointment, General,' Chris said as we shook hands.

A few years younger than me, his hair still dark and his body lean, Chris had served 21 of his 27 years in the army in Special Forces. Unlike in Hollywood and fiction, it is often those of medium height, seemingly unassuming and quiet, who fill the ranks of many elite forces. Chris was extremely articulate and had a serious intellect.

He had left the army in 2010 as a colonel; as well as commanding the Special Forces School at Murrayhill, north of Pretoria, he had worked for the CSIR, overseeing high-tech projects for Special Forces. After leaving the military he took a civilian position at the CSIR in charge of development and planning.

'Jong, I must talk to you after the service,' I said.

'If there is anything I can do to help, General, I am ready.'

Later, I called Chris. I brought him up to speed and invited him to come visit me in Kruger. 'Chris, I need a technology roadmap,' I said to him when he came out to the Lowveld.

'Where is your CONOPS, General?'

I sighed. 'I'm working on it. Please understand, though, that this is not a typical military situation and I have to apply my mind and make sure we have the right information – even more so if we plan to deploy technology.'

The strategy I was formulating would be pioneering – there would be few, if any, case studies for the large-scale protection of an area the size of Kruger. This was like trying to plan the defence of a country almost the size of Belgium against an intense and consistent threat with a 400-member paramilitary force.

I needed Chris to start analysing what technology I could and should employ in support of our fight, even before I could work out how to pay him. He already had a full-time job at the CSIR, so what I was asking him was to find a way to do my work in what spare time he had, until I could formalise our arrangement. His technology roadmap would feed into my CONOPS, which would then form the basis of a strategy.

All this would take time – and money. In my outline CONOPS, I also listed 'fundraising'. I knew that many of the measures I would want to implement would be expensive and that SANParks and the government were not a bottomless well. On the plus side of the balance sheet, I knew there were NGOs and philanthropic organisations in South Africa and abroad that wanted to help.

Before I could even start purchasing equipment or gadgetry, I needed to pay for the technology roadmap and I knew it would not come cheap. I approached the SANParks Honorary Rangers (SHR), a corps of dedicated part-time rangers who raised money for projects in the country's game reserves.

'You want how much?' Janssen Davies, the SHR national chairman, said to me, eyes wide, when I went to them seeking funding for the roadmap.

'One million rand,' I repeated.

'One million rand for a piece of paper?'

I had to explain that I was enlisting some of the finest minds in the nation to address the technological needs for the fight against rhino poaching and that Chris had already been working for nothing.

In order to attract more funds, I knew I would have to put myself 'out there' in the media and on the world stage in order to garner support for our fight. For an old soldier, engaging with the media does not come naturally – I know many who would rather face enemy bullets than television cameras. However, I knew also that communication would be key to CONOPS and strategy. I had the media and the government breathing down my neck, looking for answers and solutions, but if I was going to be successful, I needed their buy-in.

AT SKUKUZA AIRPORT, the ops room – the embryonic JOC in the former conference room – was up and running.

We had moved on from the aimless daily briefings, which simply listed the numbers of rhinos killed. The staff now monitored all events associated with poaching from one central location and were able to prepare a daily Kruger National Park (KNP) situation report, or sitrep. Yes, we listed fresh kills and carcasses discovered, but we also began estimating the numbers of poachers in the park, the likely number of weapons and incidents. An 'incident' could be a confirmed sighting or contact with poachers; the discovery of tracks; locating poachers' temporary camps in the bush; or hearing a shot fired. In order to be as accurate as possible, we had to be conservative. The correct use of available software was now helping us record our stats and display the information visually.

We applied analysis and intellectual rigour, examining trends and using this information to influence our deployments and strategy. Full moon was, traditionally, a time of increased poaching activity, but poachers could be influenced by the economy, as well as the phases of the moon.

The ops room and ECI staff noted, for instance, that there was a spike in poaching on the weekend before the end of the month, when people ran short of money before pay day.

As well as the hardcore poaching gangs walking in from Mozambique, there were 'part-time' poachers, who would drive into Kruger from the South African side of Kruger, kill a rhino to supplement their income, and then head back to work on the Monday.

We had inherited a runaway train. Such was the demand for rhino horn that all our intelligence and reporting told us one thing:

the number of poaching incursions, whichever side of the border they originated from, was increasing.

While I continued my battle with head office to sort out our logistical supply chain, I now had enough information to start implementing the changes I knew were needed inside the KNP. The CONOPS had identified early on the need for a streamlined system of command and control. As chief ranger, I started to exercise my new authority.

I ordered manageable numbers of rangers to be redeployed from the north of Kruger, where there were fewer rhino and fewer contacts, to the south. I also deployed the special rangers (SRs) unit to flashpoints.

Up until this time the SRs had been based at Skukuza and near Phalaborwa, and deployed in two-man teams, in response to contacts and other incidents. Now, however, the poaching hotspots in the park were so big and busy that I allocated areas of responsibility to the SRs. I had them deploy into the bush, with a headquarters element in a tent with a radio, and 'froze' the area in which they were working, making sure no other rangers entered that part of the park to avoid 'blue-on-blue' incidents where rangers might fire on each other.

There was some pushback to this change in traditional tactics, but I had to proactively match the threat in specific parts of the park in order to avoid a massive slaughter of rhinos in these critical areas.

The two Marula regions were home to 70% of the park's rhinos – which, in effect, amounted to more than 25% of the total number of rhinos left in the world. There was resistance and grumbling to me moving rangers from one part of the park to another because this was not the way things had been done. However, I was able to bid for extra funding to pay allowances to rangers now forced to live and work away from their homes. Also, while I was making strategic decisions, I was more than happy to leave the tactical implementation of our plans to the section rangers in the affected areas, and this went down well.

Back in the JOC, I worked through the graphs and the maps; they painted a stark visual picture of the problem and our shortcomings, but the strategy was firming by the day and I had started taking the first steps towards my eventual goal of creating the best anti-poaching unit in Africa.

New boots and uniforms started to arrive, and instead of every ranger section doing its own thing, we now had proper operational planning for the deployment of rangers: centralised coordination, with decentralised execution, which still allowed for initiative on the ground.

But still the number of rhinos being killed continued to rise.

5

'When will the numbers come down, General?' the Chairman of the SANParks Board asked, leaning forward and staring at me, as I addressed a meeting of the board at Groenkloof in June 2013.

I stood in front of the members and clicked on the next slide of my PowerPoint presentation. Unlike the first made-up briefing I had done for the SANParks Board, based largely on what I had read in the media, I was now armed with data and intelligence, which had been gathered and analysed by my ops room, and could now form the basis of my strategy.

The month before, at Mokala National Park, near Kimberley, I'd had my first opportunity to present my strategy to the SANParks Exco. It had gone down so well that it had been decided there and then that I should deliver the same briefing to the board at their next meeting.

I was able to present my strategy for para-militarising the ranger corps and taking the fight to the criminals. I started by stating the mission, even though that, aside from para-militarising the rangers, was still vague. I determined that what the government wanted was to get poaching numbers down to an 'acceptable level' – whatever that was. The question I had been asked summed up the impatience: When will the numbers come down?

Using a slide showing an inverted pyramid, I explained what was within my remit and control. My rangers and I were at the bottom of the pyramid, where I had circled what we could target, namely "the poacher in the park".

'What we need,' I said, 'is a "whole-of-government" – and international – approach to target the other players.'

These were, in ascending order of importance: the local courier who took the horn from the poacher; the national courier who collected the product from a number of local dealers; the exporter/importer; and, finally, the consumer in South East Asia.

Within South Africa itself, I said, we needed a "whole-of-society" approach to the problem of poaching. There were several players locally, in addition to the various government departments, and agencies, including: private game reserves on the edge of Kruger with their own private security resources; NGOs – it was often stated that there were as many rhino charities as there were rhinos being killed; business, which could play a part in funding the fight; the wider South African population as custodians of our natural heritage; and the communities on the border of the park that were also home to poachers.

I talked the audience through my 'think big, start small, act now' philosophy and what I had been doing in the park and at head office to better equip rangers, improve integrity through the use of polygraph testing, and improve command and control. I worked through the principles of my CONOPS: protecting – consolidating our ranger corps and freeing more of them up for anti-poaching by installing a new protective services unit on the gate; reacting – becoming better at responding to incidents; and being proactive, through increased patrols and being unpredictable in our approach.

'My grand strategy is to clear the park from the outside,' I told the board.

It was clear that no matter how good the ranger corps became at detecting and arresting poachers, the war against rhino poaching could not be won just by focusing our efforts inside Kruger.

'We need to form alliances with our neighbours in the private game reserves in South Africa and the concessions across the border, as well as with the government and agencies in Mozambique.' We also needed to work with the communities on our border, I said. At a government-to-government level, we needed South Africa to work with countries such as Vietnam and China to encourage demand reduction and law enforcement. At the local level, we needed stiffer penalties for rhino poaching and access to a full-time law court at Skukuza, where cases could be heard. This would save rangers time, not having to travel to give evidence in cases, and avoid a situation where angry community members and poachers' relatives were harassing and intimidating rangers and prosecutors.

I spoke of the need for a fully resourced JOC, where SANParks, the police and the military could all work together, jointly. At that time, we were still operating out of our makeshift operations room. The army was continuing to deploy an infantry company, military police and support personnel, and there was air-force liaison. The police maintained crime-scene investigators, detectives and a canine element.

As part of the strategy, I used a map to illustrate how the park's four existing administrative regions would be overlaid with three operations zones for the purpose of implementing the strategy. These would be an Intensive Protection Zone (IPZ), a Joint Protection Zone (JPZ) and a Composite Protection Zone (CPZ).

I explained that the Marula South region of the Kruger Park, between the Sabie River to the north and the Crocodile River to the south, would become our IPZ. It was here, where the concentration of rhino was greatest, that we would focus most of our manpower, resources and technology.

On the same slide, I pointed out the broad strategy for the rest of Kruger. The Marula North region would be a JPZ, where our effort would be focused on joint planning and execution based on human intelligence and communication with partners in the private reserves to the east and west of the park. The two northern regions and the main part of the Mozambican side of the Great Limpopo Transfrontier Park, the Limpopo National Park (LNP) would be under a CPZ, where cross-border cooperation and local community involvement were key.

Next, I gave my views on technology. 'We must use "brown-earth" technology, not "blue sky".' Rather than be dazzled by new innovation, we needed to employ technological solutions that would be embraced by our ranger corps. While younger rangers, with their smart phones, were more tech-savvy than their seniors, there was a reluctance by many of them to embrace any new device or system that could not be seen to be immediately providing them with some benefit – even if it was useful, say, for gathering and recording intelligence and data – or if it required significant extra effort to maintain. I was expecting Chris to have our technology roadmap finished by the fourth quarter of that year (2013).

'Technology makes things possible,' I said to the audience, 'but only people make it happen.'

Again, I reiterated that Kruger could only be cleared from the outside and I looked forward to the day when, with improved intelligence, we could target and bring down organised criminals before a poaching gang even entered the park.

My presentation over, I surveyed the room. 'Are there any questions?'

'When will the numbers come down, General?' the chairman asked.

SLOWLY, better rations and specialist equipment, such as night-vision devices, started moving downstream through the supply system to the rangers.

As part of my strategy of protecting my support base – the rangers themselves – I needed to ensure they were well trained and equipped with the skills they needed to defeat a motivated, cunning foe. In order to do this, I struck up a relationship early on with the Southern

African Wildlife College (SAWC). We prepared and facilitated the approval of a five-year agreement between the college and the Kruger Park and a very productive relationship ensued.

Based just outside Kruger's Orpen Gate, adjacent to the Timbavati Private Game Reserve, the SAWC was established in 1996. The college had been set up with funding from local and international donors, its mission to give students the knowledge and skills in all relevant musterings to conserve and protect wildlife and the environment. The college offered courses in, amongst others, nature conservation, resource management, responsible resource use and 'Protected Area Integrity'. This last part of their curriculum was of particular interest to me.

On Kruger's doorstep, we had a ready-made academy that had trained field rangers from many African countries. Of interest, also, was the fact that the Peace Parks Foundation (PPF), founded by the wealthy philanthropist, the late Dr Anton Rupert, together with the World Wildlife Fund and other NGOs, were providing some of the funding for the college. PPF was also interested in the promotion of the protected areas across the border in Mozambique.

Training was an area of great interest to me. Most of my time in the army had been spent not on operations, fighting the war, but rather on learning and teaching. I went to the college to see what they offered, and I was impressed. We needed help in a number of training areas, from ranger selection to basic and advanced training. Also high on the list of priorities were weapons handling and marksmanship. In addition, we would need to conduct advanced first-aid training, especially the treatment of gunshot wounds.

I started negotiations with the college, which led to the creation of a memorandum of understanding for how they could assist us. Even while doing so, I still did not know if I would be able to get the funding I needed to carry out our ambitious training programme. In the meantime, I decided I would seek and use donor funding to at least get the process underway.

We contracted the SAWC to provide a ranger training centre, based along the lines of our existing facility at Sand River in the

Kruger Park, which included accommodation, storerooms, a kitchen, mess area, classrooms and a rifle range. The courses they would offer would begin with a seven-day ranger selection module and a 10-week Basic Field Training Programme.

Importantly, I specified that the new basic training course contain elements that were crucial to our current fight against rhino poaching. Firstly, it would need to include an introduction to tracking. Our older rangers were good trackers; some had grown up in the bush and perhaps, as children, had even taken part in hunting with dogs or other means. Over the years of working in Kruger in a nature conservation role, they had learned to track animals. Many of our younger rangers, however, tended to come from a more urban environment and had no tracking skills; I was convinced that the key to success for our rangers was being able to detect and track poachers on foot.

When assessing the risks to our rangers during preparation of the CONOPS, the ECI staff and I had also identified the sometimes harrowing and time-consuming legal rigmarole rangers went through when apprehending a poacher and, especially, when they fired their weapon and a poacher was killed or wounded. We made sure that right from the start, in the basic training course, rangers received introductory training to the law and legal processes. One of the first steps I had taken towards this was to engage Kruger's existing on-call lawyer, Advocate Coert Jordaan, from Nelspruit, to prepare and facilitate the legal module on the course. Trainee rangers would also receive basic first-aid training.

Moving on from the basic course, the SAWC would offer a two-week patrol-leader course and one-week team-leader course. This was important; I had already identified the need for more junior leaders to command the new recruits who badly needed real leadership to ensure a sound foundation for their careers and the daunting task at hand.

Also on the syllabus was a two-week extended clandestine patrol course for all rangers. As I'd already observed, a normal patrol pattern saw a pair of rangers going out into the bush for a day and then coming back. Overnight patrols, when they happened, were referred to as 'camping' – I soon put a stop to that sort of language.

For my rangers to be successful they had to work the same way as the poachers did – moving at night, staying out in the bush and operating from remote locations. If two-man patrols could move silently into an observation post, patrol from it during the day, and man it quietly at night, they would have a far better chance of detecting and surprising a poaching gang.

At the section ranger level, I had the college organise customised training, including a Protected Areas Planning Course. In line with our need for better command and control and collection of intelligence and data, section rangers also needed to be able to collect and analyse data. We needed to be able to map where incidents and rangers were at any one time. On one of my earlier visits to a ranger post, I asked to see a map of the area.

'We know where the observation posts are,' a ranger said to me. 'We don't need a map.'

'Yes, but I do!' I said.

By contrast, when I flew to Section Ranger Tinyiko Chauke's Woodlands Ranger Post in the north of the park, west of Shingwedzi Rest Camp, she greeted me and took me to the map of her section in her office, and proceeded to deliver a briefing that would have done any army officer proud.

'My rhino are grazing here, here and here, General,' she said, indicating the locations on the map.

Her reference to 'my rhino' warmed my heart, as did her professionalism. I made a mental note to keep an eye on Tinyiko; I sensed she would soon be ready for bigger things.

In the parts of the park being hardest hit, such as Houtboschrand, I could see the rangers' sense of frustration and concern. 'Sir, they are coming from the east,' said Section Ranger Rendani Nethengwe, pointing towards Mozambique, 'and the west, and even from the north via the Letaba Section. It is impossible to block them everywhere.'

The rangers' tracking skills needed to move beyond identifying and following spoor, to Tactical Combat Tracking. Poachers used a number of ruses to fool anyone trying to follow them, such as wearing specially made shoes with the hooves of animals, such as kudu, stuck to the soles, or placing socks over their shoes to disguise distinctive tread patterns. A poacher was actively trying to avoid being tracked by using a variety of skills – skills that our rangers had to learn.

Much of this training had to be conducted against the backdrop of ongoing operations. Our memorandum of understanding with SAWC stated clearly that trainers would have to fall in line with ongoing operations and that rangers would not be taken out of the field to conduct training. Rather, the instructors were expected to form part of the section for the duration of training, and could very well find themselves coming into contact with poachers.

One of the key instructional staff who impressed me was Colin Patrick. Quietly spoken and as polite and unassuming as the boy next door, Colin was a true professional. It was in watching him train that I learned 'bush literacy' and a little of the art of tracking. More than that, however, Colin set an example of resilience.

He taught our rangers that tracking was far more than reading spoor. It was about discipline, and pride in finding a track and having the strength and fortitude to carry on, in the harsh African bush, until the quarry was caught. Colin stressed the importance of team-work and supporting each other.

This was tough training, and many rangers, especially some of the more experienced hands, initially resented it. However, I insisted that everyone go through the tracking modules. I knew full well that not every ranger could be a class-A tracker, but the training also revealed those who were the best at the job and, in time, I was able to select those individuals for use in hot pursuits and followup operations.

As well as tracking, our rangers needed to learn basic patrol, immediate action, and fire and movement skills to cover each other as they advanced towards contact, as well as the rules of engaging an enemy – when they could shoot – and the rules for evidence collection.

As the training regime was implemented, I could see signs that the new training was being carried through to operations. From the ops room, we started to see section rangers submitting weekly patrol plans and developing their own strategies to protect their areas, and a dramatic increase in night operations.

At headquarters, we now had oversight of what was happening throughout the park and we could allocate resources – helicopters, men and dogs – to the areas where activity was greatest. Command and control of the ranger patrols was still devolved to the section rangers, but they were slowly becoming part of a planned and coordinated overall effort to stop the poachers.

The command group had to keep the wheels rolling even as we implemented the many changes needed to convert the ranger corps into a paramilitary machine. Ken Maggs often had to act in my absence, as I had anticipated, and Mbongeni not only fixed the support and logistics, but also oversaw the commissioning of the new Protection Services division.

The regional and section rangers likewise reinvented themselves, submersing themselves in warrior mode. While still endeavouring to uphold all their traditional conservation-based tasks and functions, the majority of their time was taken up by anti-poaching operations or training. All of this was done, admirably, with few additional resources, and at the expense of family time.

Our rangers were getting better at finding and apprehending intruders, but our own figures told us that the tide of poaching was not retreating – it was turning into a tsunami. We were, however, taking the fight to the criminals and we were turning their own skills and strengths against them.

IT WAS GOING to be a full moon, a 'poacher's moon', on the night of 24 May and I was at the SANParks Honorary Rangers' indaba, their annual general meeting, at Berg en Dal Rest Camp in the south of Kruger.

The formalities over, I looked forward to evaluating the part-time rangers' potjiekos. Talking to these committed volunteers in such a pleasant setting, I picked up not only a real warmth, but also a good sense of the valuable support they provided.

My phone rang. I could see on the screen that it was Ken Maggs. 'Andrew Desmet's been shot,' he said.

Tall and solidly built, with a toughness behind his blue eyes, Andrew had been on patrol, with an army unit in support, in the Houtboschrand area, where he was section ranger.

Andrew's military colleagues tried to organise an air-force helicopter to evacuate him, but none was available. Our Air Wing was contacted and Charles Thompson, one of our ranger pilots, took off with Ken and Dr Peiser on board. It was late in the day and Charles took off knowing that his courageous rescue mission would involve night flying – something the pilots did not do at that time.

Allergic to bee stings, Andrew always carried several EpiPens with him. He injected himself with three shots of Epinephrine – adrenalin – to keep himself conscious as he waited 90 minutes for the helicopter to arrive. Once on board, Gary Peiser gave Andrew morphine to ease his pain and Andrew passed out.

Initial media reports claimed that Andrew was shot by a poacher, but the truth was that he was, unfortunately, the victim of friendly fire. One of the soldiers on the patrol had accidentally discharged their weapon. Andrew was flown to the Mediclinic at Nelspruit. According to his doctor, Andrew should have died of his wounds, but he clung on to life.

Andrew underwent emergency surgery, in which three of his ribs were removed. He ended up spending 10 weeks in hospital, five of those in intensive care, and underwent several more operations. A Facebook group was set up for people to show their support for Andrew and pray for his recovery; it attracted thousands of followers. Andrew had very nearly made the ultimate sacrifice, but his personal story also spoke of the incredible pressures rangers were under on a daily basis. 'Work takes up a lot of our time and because of rhino poaching you work long hours and weekends,' he told the local newspaper, The Lowvelder.

He added: 'It's not our job, it's our passion. We take this ongoing war very personally.'

BACK IN MAY, when I gave my strategy briefing to Exco at Mokala National Park, I was approached by Dr Mvusy Songelwa, Managing Executive of the Parks Division. She was responsible for the 21 parks other than Kruger, including six containing rhino.

'I was taking notes during your briefing,' she said to me at the time. 'Will you come and brief our six rhino parks and help guide us?'

Two months later, in July, I returned to Mokala for the work session Dr Songelwa had organised to discuss security for the other parks that were custodians of rhinos. Mvusy had impressed me, as did her park managers.

On my previous visit I had arrived at Mokala after dark, but showing up in broad daylight, I was very surprised to see, was like visiting a farm. I opened the unattended entry gate myself, drove my rental car in, and then closed the gate behind me. As I drove through, I spotted a couple of rangers mending a fence; they smiled and waved at me. There was no access control, no layers of security, no sense that within this perimeter was a commodity that criminals would risk their lives to kill – rhinos.

I, on the other hand, was jacked up after spending six months trying to organise a strategy and a campaign against poaching. What I discovered at the conference was that Mvusy and her park managers were eager to learn, and ready for action. Clearly, they did not want to find themselves in the same situation as Kruger, and wanted to take action – now.

Over the following day and a half, I talked them through my strategy, what we were already doing in Kruger and what I hoped to achieve. We listed everything they needed to address as a matter of urgency: access control at the parks' gates, equipment, centralised control rooms, the establishment of a K9 capability, integrity testing, advanced training for rangers, extended clandestine night patrols, the setting up of informer networks and gathering intelligence, and forging alliances with local police, other authorities and neighbours.

We extended the planning right through to the drawing up of a budget and the relevant staff were given the job of formalising our workshop into a strategy. I left feeling positive and energised. However, only time would tell if the plan for these other 'rhino parks' would be finalised and, more importantly, put into action.

'THE LEADWOOD TREE has survived where others have disappeared from the landscape,' I told the audience of dignitaries and rangers assembled at Letaba Rest Camp in Kruger. 'Often alone, the leadwood stands tall where other trees have succumbed to the elements.'

It was 31 July 2013, World Ranger Day, under a clear, blue perfect Lowveld winter sky. In new boots and uniforms, our men and women had put on displays for their audience, demonstrating a mock contact and capture of poachers, their use of new all-terrain scrambler vehicles, and their marksmanship.

Standing at the microphone, I was reading from the creed we had come up with; we had settled on the iconic leadwood as a metaphor for the strength and resilience needed to become a ranger.

'Hard and resilient, the leadwood stands face into the wind, resisting storms, drought and fire. Should an elephant push it over, the leadwood will recover provided a single root touches the soil and then once again stand tall to face the elements.'

Andrew Desmet, looking pale and thin after his weeks in hospital, was in the audience. Like the tenacious leadwood, he had survived and would go on to make a full recovery.

I had the attention of the rangers seated before me. Unlike the scepticism or polite indifference I had encountered on my first visits to this and other ranger posts, I now saw men and women who were engaged and proud to wear their new, neat uniforms.

'Like the leadwood, the rangers of the Kruger National Park have survived for more than a hundred years,' I said. What every one of them – and their colleagues who were out on patrol in the bush as we celebrated this important day – knew, was that the Kruger was facing its worst crisis in a century.

'They stand tall against their adversaries. The rangers are resistant to hardship and set good examples at all times. Their hearts are pure and large and their spirit even larger.'

I saw the smiles on their faces. It was true, the hearts of the overwhelming majority of them were pure, but in their ranks, too, were the snakes, the corrupt few who would betray their comrades and the natural heritage of their nation. With the benefit of the lie-detector testing, we'd begun investigating people.

'The rangers will survive; they will adapt and overcome trials and tribulations until the end. Protecting Kruger, ranger and leadwood stand side by side.'

By this point, about six months into my new command, I had the confidence to be able say and mean what I said in reciting the leadwood creed. We were a long way from victory, and still had no clear concept or guidance as to what that meant or would look like, but I had lived up to my promise to myself, of thinking big, starting small and acting now. We were already seeing changes and making progress, as evidenced by measures such as the arrest rate.

These men and women before me were my base, the foundation of my strategy, and we needed to protect them. One of the ways to do that was to strengthen their sense of pride and purpose, and to recognise the sacrifices they had made. That was what World Ranger Day meant to me.

Next, I invited the senior leadership team to the front of the marquee and each took a length of rope. We tied these together, making a continuous loop, showing that together, united, we were stronger than if we were continuing to operate the old way, with a confused – or non-existent – chain of command, and each section operating independently of the other.

To reinforce this, I had Derick Mashale, the regional ranger for

Marula North, read out a pledge to the rangers: 'We as the command group of the Kruger National Park Ranger Corps pledge to lead the Corps as servant leaders – servants of the people in this organisation who, in their turn, serve our natural heritage so well and who have accepted the challenging task of anti-poaching with typical Ranger commitment and skill. We salute you all – also our colleagues from other Parks as we all pledge to serve with honour, dignity and pride.'

Abe Sibaya, Managing Executive of Kruger, was sitting next to me. He leaned over and said: 'You know, your rangers are impressive.'

It was gracious of Abe to say that, because that day I had already been the cause of some embarrassment for him in front of our boss, David Mabunda. When Dr Mabunda arrived at Letaba I greeted him and introduced him to Otch.

From the look on David's face as he shook Otch's hand, I knew he was the moer in. I suddenly realised that no one had told Dr Mabunda that we had appointed Otch. I thought to myself: That's what you get from dotted reporting lines. Mabunda quickly asked Abe for a word in private and I could see from Abe's face, even though I couldn't hear the words, that he was being dressed down by the head of SANParks.

David had exhausted much of his own political capital with the SANParks Board and Exco by appointing one white man, and I had now done the same thing by employing Otch on a short-term contract. I knew I needed the best man for the job, and I was prepared to bear the consequences.

I took to the stage again. 'Whilst we are proud of every ranger and thankful for the contribution of every ranger every day, my colleagues will now remind us of those who did it exceptionally well and serve as an inspiration to all of us.' I then introduced two rangers I believed were doing an exceptional job: Rodney Landela and Tinyiko Chauke. Rodney read out a speech in Shangaan and Tinyiko then repeated it for the benefit of those of us who spoke English.

'On behalf of all rangers, I acknowledge the rangers in our parks who over the years have made severe sacrifices in their selfless dedication to our cause,' Tinyiko said.

She paid tribute to those rangers who had made the supreme sacrifice and died, and those who had been injured in the execution of their duties while in service.

'We are so glad that Section Ranger Andrew Desmet can be with us today,' she added.

'Many were injured by animals. We are thankful for the recovery of Corporal Dzambukiri, alias "Sjambok", after a snake bite three weeks ago.' This was a timely reminder that rangers face real dangers in the environment in which they work.

'Viva!' Tinyiko spontaneously held up a fist and the crowd responded with a roar, 'Viva the rangers!'

'Viva the rangers!' the audience yelled.

Section Ranger Thomas Mbokota urged everyone to get to their feet and led the crowd in singing and clapping. The rangers began toyi-toying and, yes, even an old platinum-status, former general got up and started dancing, badly, but with a wide smile.

6

I felt proud of my rangers on their special day but, while I could allow myself to feel some small sense of achievement, I was not at all at ease.

The number of rhinos being killed was still escalating, but we had put the brakes on the increase. The rate of incursions was growing at a far higher rate than the number of rhinos poached, so we knew that, if anything, the problem of poaching was getting worse, although we were getting better at dealing with it. This was a very difficult concept to 'sell' to my political leadership and the media. The curve, however, was finally turning in our favour.

The rangers had demonstrated their skills to the dignitaries and looked sharp and disciplined in their new uniforms. We had organised for them to have a proper three-course buffet of note and they had appreciated that, as well as the attention of the head office people from Groenkloof.

I had enjoyed seeing them grow into their new-found confidence. They had put on a good show, but I knew that behind the demonstrations there had to be solid skills and tenacity. I reviewed the results and scores from the SAWC training courses and could see that marksmanship and other important skills were improving and that the college was already moving toward delivering the more advanced follow-up courses.

Despite the tragedies of the helicopter crash over Easter and Andrew being shot by a soldier, we had maintained our record of zero losses to poachers. A ranger had been wounded in a firefight, but fortunately his comrade with him had recently undergone an advanced first-aid course as part of the enhanced training programme; he was able to treat the gunshot and the wounded ranger had recovered and returned to duty. The first-aid training was one of many meaningful contributions by a small but dynamic needs-driven NGO, Stop Rhino Poaching.

There were couple of reasons for our enviable record. Time after time, our rangers were able to detect poachers by their spoor, or evidence of their temporary camps before the poachers spotted the rangers. Another indicator of success that we were able to track in 2013 was an increase in the number of arrests and contacts that resulted from rangers picking up spoor and then following up, rather than chance encounters in the bush or poachers being detected by other means. Our people were becoming better at tracking and had the fitness and stamina to capitalise on that.

Rangers had to maintain a high level of alertness, always, and they were getting better and better at approaching poachers quietly. Often, by this time, these contacts were happening at night. Something as subtle as the glint of moonlight on the metal barrel of a poacher's rifle might give him away and then our rangers had to react in a split second, challenging the poacher and then closing in on the gang.

What helped was maintaining the traditional two-man patrol system.

'These poachers are aggressive once they get a horn; you need to be operating at section strength,' an army Special Forces officer said to me, giving me his view of the situation as a military man. I had to disagree with him. A 10-person army section had a much bigger footprint and made a lot more noise than two rangers moving quietly through the bush. A poacher gang might be three people, and yet our people were consistently surprising the enemy.

As such, they needed crystal-clear training and understanding of their ROE, or rules of engagement. The rangers were told to use the minimum force necessary to stop, detain and arrest a poacher. This also applied to the use of tracker dogs; handlers needed to ensure that the dog could be controlled and if it bit down on a poacher then the dog was commanded to release as soon as possible. Our legal representative Coert Jordaan made it clear that the dog was not to be used to 'punish' the poacher, and all injuries had to be documented.

If a ranger's life, or the life of a colleague, was in imminent danger of an unlawful attack, and no other means, such as minimum force, were available, then a ranger could shoot a poacher.

'Don't die with a gun in your hand,' I told my people, on many occasions. 'If you must defend yourself as a last option, then do so.' The ROE allowed for rangers to fire warning shots, but there were clear guidelines for these as well. Rangers had to be sure that there was no risk of accidental collateral damage when firing a warning; for example, they were not to fire into the air, in case their bullet hit an orbiting helicopter, or caused damage when it fell to earth some distance away. When firing into the ground they had to ensure they had full visibility of where the bullet struck.

They had to be conscious of the possibilities of ricochets, and were reminded of the fact that a bullet can bounce off water.

While warning shots could and were used to deter poachers, compel a man to drop a knife or other weapon, for instance, it was made clear that the potential disadvantages outweighed the advantages. Rangers were told that if their bullet was found somewhere it shouldn't have been then it could be traced, ballistically, to their rifle.

Section rangers were encouraged to regularly quiz their people on the ROE, as often as twice a week, to make sure everyone knew the rules. Every time a ranger fired his or her rifle, for whatever reason, even if it was an accident, the incident had to be reported. A measure for success in a contact was if very little happened. The ideal, for us, was for our rangers to detect the poachers first, surprise them, and then arrest them. We were not out to kill people or to test our mettle in combat.

Our rangers learned to read not only spoor, but also poachers' habits. If they came across a poachers' camp and there was the remains of a fire, then they knew the intruders were either relaxed, lazy or inexperienced – or all of the above. Such men would be easier to track and catch than, say, the wily poacher who stayed up without a fire, or who used a knife instead of an axe to silently remove a horn.

With the benefit of training and discipline, a ranger could walk through the night and then silently move into an observation post. From there they could watch and detect.

If contact was made and the poachers made a run for it, our people then had the fitness and stamina to give chase. This, however, was never easy. In the thick African bush even an unfit person will get away if they have a good head start, and if he believes he is running for his life.

I stressed that what we wanted – the ideal situation – was a 'full house' after every contact. We wanted to catch the poacher or poachers with their equipment, including their weapon and a rhino horn if they had taken one; we wanted the chain of evidence correctly recorded; and we wanted the poacher uninjured. Emotions some-times ran high, particularly if a poacher had shot at a ranger, but we could not risk a criminal case being thrown out of court because a suspect claimed he had been beaten or otherwise badly treated by a ranger.

As per my instructions in the memorandum of understanding with the wildlife college, training at all levels incorporated a legal element. Rangers were instructed in how to bag and tag evidence and the importance of not disturbing a crime scene.

Each ranger carried a pocket notebook, and they were encour-aged to take photos of the scene of any crime. Hand-held GPS devices were used to record the latitude and longitude of each scene, as well as evidence, if it had been left or placed some distance away from where the arrest was made. In training and role-play, they learned how to question a suspect.

'First of all, show me your ID document and your permit to be in the park,' a ranger would say to a poacher, or a trainee acting in that role. By immediately establishing that the suspect had illegally entered the country and/or the Kruger Park, they would have proof of the person's first offence.

'Where are you from?' 'Who dropped you off?' 'Whose number is this on your phone?' These were all questions that rangers were trained to ask poachers. A poacher's phone could be an important link to middlemen higher up the chain. Our people learned how to properly and safely search a suspect, and were reminded of the importance of seizing their passport or ID document.

They were taught how to write a statement about what had happened at the scene of a crime; for instance, whether they had taken a poacher into custody or killed or wounded him. They were taught the basics, to take down the who, what, where, when, why and how of what had happened. In particular, they had to record details of shots fired; injuries sustained by poachers and rangers and the causes thereof; resistance of arrest by poachers; and details of anything a poacher said in the course of the initial interview conducted by the ranger.

The statement was the start of the chain of evidence that would ultimately enable a prosecution. This could allow poachers to be charged with other offences, such as possession of a firearm, as well as poaching.

While all this might sound like the job for the police, it was done as much to protect our rangers and their rights in the event of subsequent police investigation as it was for the purpose of assisting the police to secure a conviction. Part of their training also involved learning how to deal with the police, as the rangers, too, would come under questioning and investigation if shots had been fired.

They were taught to read through their statement before handing it over to the police, to sign it, and to take a copy of it, even if just on their cell phone. Do not make verbal statements, they were told; do not sign anything that was not 100% correct, and do not speculate on the causes of injuries or other things of which they were not sure.

Above all, they were reminded that a statement, once given, could not be withdrawn.

Our people were taught to make meticulous notes of evidence seized, even though the police would be doing the same when they arrived. Rangers were instructed to take pictures of the soles of poachers' shoes and of the tracks they had made in the ground that the ranger may have followed. Coert Jordaan stressed that this type of evidence, though circumstantial, could be vital in ensuring a conviction.

In effect, as well as turning Kruger's ranger corps into a para-military anti-poaching unit, we were also training them in the arts of investigation and crime-scene recording. Often, due to time and distance and the frequency of incidents, rangers were the first and last responders on the scene, so they had to record and collect evidence that would be crucial to subsequent prosecutions. Like so much else going on in their lives, this was a quantum leap from the job they had been doing just a few months or years before.

One grey area that arose during the course of the struggle against poaching in Kruger was what to do if a contact had occurred and a poacher then fled the scene. If, say, the poachers had adopted a threatening stance, with a rifle, or fired a shot at a ranger, and the ranger had returned fire, there was a legal opinion circulated that stated a ranger would be within his or her right to shoot that poacher during a pursuit.

Over the next couple of years, I would have several meetings with the police and lawyers over issues such as these and the way rangers were treated in the aftermath of a shooting incident. At the time of me taking command, the police's standard procedure was to automat-ically open a murder docket if a ranger shot a poacher and killed him. We were later able to have those procedures changed, when the police agreed that when a poacher was killed an 'inquest docket' would be opened, as would be the case in a manslaughter or self-defence case; the ranger would not be arrested, and the ranger's rifle would not be seized.

After weighing up the legal opinion on firing at a fleeing poacher, even if the criminal had been shooting at our rangers, I also made a command decision: No ranger may fire warning shorts, or fire at a fleeing poacher, I ordered. It simply was not worth the risk of one of my people being convicted of murder.

OTCH HAD TAKEN on the job of designing what would become our new Mission Area Joint Operations Centre (MAJOC) building.

He had used his other talents to draw up plans and an artist's impression of the new centre, and on the day he planned to brief me he had marked the outline structure and its internal rooms on the ground adjacent to the airport buildings using a bag of baking flour. By the time I got there, however, a troop of vervet monkeys was already eating his plan off the ground.

As part of the ongoing improvements to the ops room and our standard operating procedures we had also redesigned the park's radio network. Earlier, at one of our leadership meetings, I posed a hypothetical question to everyone in the room.

'If you had unlimited funding,' I asked the team, 'what would you buy first?'

'New boots,' said one ranger. That, we were working on. 'More dogs.'

'Another helicopter.'

I then turned to Otch. 'I would spend all the money on the communications backbone,' he had said. 'If you have that, you can plug in everything else.'

Previously, Kruger had one, big radio network, but in cooperation with the park's technical staff, we divided the communications network into the three protective zones we had designated for the park. The IPZ, for example, now had its own network.

When I arrived in Kruger, it was impossible for the ops room to talk directly to a helicopter pilot while the aircraft was in flight. Because the chopper would generally be carrying a ranger, we would talk to him or her, by radio, and they would relay messages to and from the pilot, or we would send a text or WhatsApp messages if there was phone signal in the area. This was not acceptable simply because sometimes it was difficult to even hear the ranger over the noise of the helicopter, or they were busy talking to their rangers on the ground.

Through my contacts in the Defence Force, we arranged for the military to bring their ultra-high frequency trunking system to the park. This allowed us to use the military's tactical network, which enabled multiple users, on the ground and in the air, to be on the same channel.

I was also able to get us an ASCO, an air-force Air Space Control Officer, who assisted the JOC with the command and control of all air assets flying missions at any one time. The ASCO was based at the airport in a customised air-conditioned container, with its hi-tech communications equipment. This added value and helped share the workload of the already busy ops room. In addition, we put trackers on our aircraft so that we knew exactly where they were at all times.

UNTIL THE DEDICATED JOC could be built, space was at a premium at the airport, so I was still based in my small office in the park head-quarters, adjacent to Skukuza. At least by now I had managed to get a proper uniform, as had my rangers. I wore long green fatigue trousers, sturdy brown boots and a green shirt with the sleeves tailored short.

My phone rang – it was the ops room.

'They've spotted a live rhino in Mozambique, General,' said the messenger.

I immediately climbed in my Amarok bakkie, a much-appreciated sponsorship from Unitrans Volkswagen via the Unite Against Poaching NGO, and headed straight to the airport. It was midday, the temperature had climbed and the air was heavy with humidity and the promise of the summer rain. I had no time to stop and look at hippos, crocodiles or browsing elephants as I crossed the Sabie River.

The ops room was humming as usual, operators taking calls and a couple of staff standing by the radios. As well as our dedicated staff and contractors, Honorary Rangers also sometimes did duty, manning our nerve centre.

I was given the radio for the Composite Protection Zone network, covering the far north of Kruger.

'Marius, it's General Jooste, over,' I said into the handset.

Marius Renke, the section ranger based at Shingwedzi, which extended to Mozambique and the Limpopo National Park (LNP), across the border, came on the network.

'General, Billy Schoeman says they've spotted a live rhino across the border in Mozambique.'

'Copy that,' I said to him.

I thought about the significance of the news. Billy was the operations manager of the LNP. The fact that we were talking to Mozambique was at least a positive sign of the progress we were making in forging alliances with Kruger's neighbours.

When the Great Limpopo Transfrontier Park, the Peace Park linking Kruger with the old Mozambican hunting concession then known as Coutada 16, had been proclaimed, the fence along that section of the border had come down. Rhinos from the north of Kruger had migrated across the Lebombos, but they had been hammered and were once again thought to be extinct in the LNP.

One of the reasons poaching was a problem in the LNP was that the park had been proclaimed while there were still people living within its borders. There were plans to relocate these people, who lived in very basic conditions, but for the time being they supplemented what meagre incomes they had with poaching.

Marius was on the radio to Billy at the same time, and was being updated on the whereabouts of the lone white rhino. I had come to Kruger with my urgencies and overriding priorities, of what needed to be done, but here was a reminder of what we were fighting for. One animal, still alive, against the odds.

There was more news: the rangers in Mozambique had picked up signs that there were poachers in the same vicinity as the rhino, and appeared to be actively tracking it.

'If that thing's still there after nightfall,' Marius said, reminding me of what we all knew, 'there'll be another horn on its way to Asia by tomorrow.'

The moment was not lost on any of us in the ops room, or on the ground. It had been a while since a live rhino had even been sighted across the border and we now had a chance to save this one, or at least give it a shot at survival.

How far should we go, I asked myself, to save one rhino? While I deliberated, the ops room staff went into a quick planning session on what needed to be done and briefed me. Shingwedzi was more than 200 kilometres from Skukuza, in the far north, and it would take the chopper two hours just to get there. A helicopter burned R14 000 worth of fuel and maintenance costs per hour of flying time, so this round trip would cost about R56 000, with no guarantee of success. Added to that concern, we would be sending a South African helicopter into the airspace of a sovereign country – we would need permission, probably at a high level, from Maputo.

We called in Chief Pilot Grant Knight, and he called the South African Civil Aviation Authority (SACAA). Even though there were formal agreements regarding movement in the transfrontier park, aviation authorities still had to be advised and permission given. Grant stressed the urgency of this request and SACAA gave its approval. Next, we needed written authority from ANAC, managers of Mozambique's national parks and reserves, to actually move a rhino out of their country and into South Africa.

While Billy and his leader group worked their way through their channels, I gave the green light for Grant to take off – he would fly the mission himself. With a Kruger veterinarian and a special ranger on board for support, Grant headed north.

The pilots – or aviation rangers, as I had re-designated them – were so bloody good. They pushed the envelope, flying low to capture game, bringing veterinarians in close enough to fire a tranquiliser dart, and now also scoured the bush for poachers. More than once, poachers had fired on the helicopters. After taking part in a pursuit, the pilot might very well have to land and take a casualty on board, a poacher who had been shot.

I had seen these young men standing on the tarmac with hosepipes, washing the blood out of the back of their aircraft.

I stared at the map on the wall showing Kruger and the adjoining LNP. Peace Parks were not just about removing fences. The programme had brought three governments with disparate agendas together in order to work for the good of wildlife and conservation. It was a winning recipe for transnational cooperation. If the organisation had succeeded in allowing fences to come down and tourists to cross from one part of a game reserve to another across a border, then surely that same framework and goodwill could be harnessed to help save the rhino?

Marius came back on the radio, his voice calm: Billy had advised that approval had been given for us to save the rhino. We monitored progress from the ops room. Grant landed at Shingwedzi and picked up Marius, then flew east, to the border – now, they needed to find that rhino.

Grant thought fast as he flew, coming up with a search pattern that would make the most of the remaining daylight. Finding the rhino was just their first challenge – once they spotted it, they would have to find a way to get it back into South Africa. The old fence between the two countries was still in place in this section of the park, although there were gaps; Grant had to identify these to give him somewhere to steer the rhino towards.

Time dragged as we listened, from far away, then there was the message we'd all been waiting for. The team on board the chopper had found the rhino, but it was running in exactly the wrong direction, deeper into the LNP.

Using the skills he'd developed over many years, Grant flew ahead of the rhino and descended, just low enough for the animal to realise that there was something in the air above it, but not close enough to panic it. If the rhino panicked and went into a full charge it might exert itself, with possibly fatal consequences. Grant knew from past experience that if the rhino bolted there would be no stopping it – he could land the helicopter in front of it and the animal would simply plough on.

Having found the wayward creature, Grant now had to reconnoitre a route back to South Africa, avoiding obstacles such as dongas and waterways, to give the rhino a clear pathway. He returned to the rhino and, with patience and perseverance, was able to get it to turn and move westwards.

Grant later recounted that while those on board the chopper were giving him well-meant advice about which way to turn and what to do, he was chilling out by listening to his Chris de Burgh playlist through his headphones.

Once the rhino was finally across the border, Grant deliberately sought out an obstacle, a shallow river. His aim now was to get the rhino to go into the water and wade across; he wanted the rhino on the other side of river so that once the helicopter left there was less likelihood of the rhino turning and heading back to where it had just come from. Grant brought the chopper down lower now, deliberately urging the animal into the water. It worked and the big creature waded and splashed his way across and then carried on, deeper into the Kruger Park.

'The rhino's crossed back into Kruger, General,' the chief pilot said over the radio.

There was no back-slapping, no high-fiving, but those of us in the ops room had just witnessed something special. Cooperation, rather than confrontation, had just saved one animal from almost certain slaughter, for now.

It was a beginning.

THE DEPUTY CHIEF of Police of Hanoi, the capital of Vietnam, stood beside me as we stared down at the carcass of yet another dead rhino. As always it, was horrible, the whole front of the animal's face hacked off.

The chief was visibly shocked. 'When we arrest a dealer in our part of the world, they tell their customers that they do not kill the animal,' he said. Most people in Vietnam, it seemed, do not know about the looming extinction of the species.

Vietnam is a key market for illegal rhino horn. Largely shut off from world markets during its protracted wars with France and America, the Vietnamese people had endured years of economic hardship as their country recovered from decades of conflict. In recent years, however, the country had undergone something of a boom, emerging as one of Asia's fastest growing economies.

With its high proportion of ethnic Chinese people, traditional Chinese medicine had always been practised and respected in Vietnam, but its more expensive potions, such as rhino horn, had, until recently, been a luxury not even the wealthiest Vietnamese could afford. That had all changed.

Our adversary was nimble and clever; the middlemen and marketeers of rhino horn were constantly changing their strategies and sales pitches to keep prices and demand high. There had long been a myth that rhino horn promoted sexual virility. In fact, it had been more traditionally 'prescribed' as relief for fevers and headaches. Any lingering belief that it did help male potency was probably knocked out of the market by the advent of Viagra.

One falsehood that was perpetuated and took hold in Vietnam was that rhino horn was a cure for cancer. There were media reports that a Vietnamese government minister put his recovery down to his use of rhino horn. Of course, there was no scientific basis to the claim, but it was yet another example of how information, and the media, could have a direct impact on a conflict being waged half a world away in Africa. Demand increased.

The charity Rhinose had contacted me, asking if I would be interested in meeting the Hanoi Police VIP and showing him around if they could get him to South Africa. I said yes. As part of my strategy, I had specified that we had to clear Kruger from the outside and that meant forging alliances not only within South Africa, but internationally. We also needed to start using the media to get our messages across, locally and abroad. It seemed like the chief's visit would tick many of those boxes.

After taking him to see the rhino carcass, we arranged to have dinner at the Protea Hotel. Set just outside the park on the edge of the Sabi Sand Game Reserve, at the Paul Kruger Gate, the hotel was popular with tourists and locals. The officer was resplendent in full uniform, as was I. We had agreed on this together, at his suggestion.

'I want to stand out, be visibly identified with your cause,' he said to me.

Two aides were with him as we followed the long wood-deck walkway to the boma dining area adjacent to the Sabie River.

The deputy chief was a macho oke, with the dress and bearing of a military man. We ate from the expansive buffet and he enjoyed the traditional singing and dancing by a local Shangaan performance group.

'What do you think of calls to legalise the trade in rhino horn?' I asked him, over a glass of red wine in the open dining area, a fire burning nearby.

This was a thorny issue. In preparing my strategy I had to look at all the options and keep an open mind. As I had already identified, this war could not be won with only boots on the ground. The chief was one of my early attempts at forging international alliances and I was interested in his views as a stakeholder.

'Here in South Africa, you talk about legalising the trade, while in Hanoi I am working the streets trying to stop people selling rhino horn,' he said. He waved a hand in the air. 'For a decade you have been telling us "Thou shalt not trade" and rapping us over the knuckles for not doing enough, talking to us like children. Then tomorrow you say: "It's OK to trade!"'

I could feel and understand his frustration. It was a crucial lesson that whatever happened as a result of the growing debate over legalisation of the trade in rhino horn in South Africa would have flow-on effects around the world and that there were other stakeholders who needed a say. There were many who touted legalisation and commercial farming of rhino horn as the magic bullet to stop the illegal killing.

Whenever Rhinose brought delegations from Asia to South Africa they also included celebrities, banking on 'star power' to help spread their conservation messages. A Vietnamese actress, well known in her country, accompanied us on the deputy chief's visit. Over dinner, she used her phone to post pictures of her visit to Kruger, including the carcass of a slain rhino. I watched in amazement as her posts attracted millions of likes while we were eating. It was a good lesson in the power and reach of social media.

I had started using a hashtag in all of my communications: #4therhino. I was in favour of doing anything, exploring any initiative that would help us help rhinos.

THE SENIOR POLICE officer and I parted on good terms. It was late September and I was readying for my first break since taking up my new posting in January.

Arina had tried working from our house in the Skukuza staff village, but our internet connectivity was not good and, as a result, she ended up spending more time than we had originally expected in Pretoria. The dogs appreciated her attention, and I had been consumed by work. Even when we were together, she had become used to me opening my laptop as soon as we had finished our evening meal. At 5 am my alarm would go off and, after a quick run, I would leave for my office or the ops room.

Our evenings, too, could be interrupted. On one of her visits I was tending to the braai as Arina toiled away in the garden, still working at dusk. She was intent on knocking our yard into shape.

'Love!' Arina hissed at me.

I turned from the mesmerising flames and saw my wife, reversing on foot towards the stoep; I went to her, and backed up myself as she pointed to the cause of her alarm. There in the bush, just a few metres from where we had been standing, was a leopard, now slinking across the road, disappearing into the gathering darkness.

We had planned a two-week break to Golden Gate National Park in the north-eastern Free State. As the date approached, we were like school kids, so looking forward to seeing each other again once Arina had travelled down from the Highveld. We packed the car and set off. Heading down the R40, through Hazyview, we made it as far as

White River, about a hundred kilometres from Skukuza, when my phone rang. I pulled over to the side of the road to take the call.

'General, did you take the chief of police from Hanoi on a tour of the Kruger Park?' David Mabunda asked from his office at SANParks headquarters in Groenkloof.

'Yes.' There had been some media interest in the visit and I thought it had gone well.

'Did you take him to see a rhino carcass?'

'Yes,' I said, wondering what the reason for the call could be. 'Why?'

I explained to David the background of the visit, and how Rhinose had approached me.

'General, there are protocols that have to be followed.'

At this point I climbed out of the car to continue with the call. It was clear that, in the eyes of the government, I had done the wrong thing by inviting the representative of a foreign country into the park. More particularly, the fact that the visit had resulted in media coverage was the cause of the problem. Mabunda was in trouble for not letting Minister Molewa know about the visit and for not seeking her approval, and now I was in trouble.

'OK, General,' David said at last. 'Now that I have all the facts, you can leave it with me. Enjoy your holiday.' I could tell Mabunda was not happy, but the good thing about him was that he was mature enough to not hold grudges.

Arina and I carried on. It was not until we were far from the Kruger Park and had reached our destination that I started to realise how extremely stressful the preceding months had been. I knew that I needed to rest, and that the bonds of my marriage needed tending.

I had left Ken Maggs in charge in my absence, and I knew that he would call me if there was an emergency or something that needed my urgent attention. Even so, and even as Arina and I enjoyed the natural wonders of Golden Gate, every day I checked my phone for the daily sitrep. The situation report now not only listed rhinos killed and carcasses discovered, but also contacts with poachers and incidents, such as the discovery of tracks or a poacher's camp. I had always prided myself that I could live my life in boxes. If

I had a problem, I could excuse myself from whomever I was with or whatever I was doing, and sort it out, then get back to the business at hand. It was a skill I had developed as an army officer and as a leader.

But this was different. I tried to force myself to check in only once a day, if I could, and to then quickly deal with anything that I thought needed my attention. It was no good. I could not keep this problem, this fight, this so-called war in a box.

Back in Skukuza, Liezl and Grant travelled from Cape Town to visit Arina and I. It was wonderful to have them there, especially knowing how they appreciated the simple natural beauty of the place we lived in.

Arina was cooking dinner one night; Grant and Liezl were in the kitchen chatting to her when my phone rang.

'General, just letting you know the helicopter is safely back from its mission,' the ops staff member told me.

'Thank you,' I said. I could not complain about being contacted by the ops room after hours; they knew I had to be informed of key events such as this, and that if I was not notified, they would hear about it the next morning.

I ended the call and overheard the conversation in the kitchen. 'Dad is looking stressed,' Liezl said.

'You know men,' Arina said, 'and especially your father. They don't talk, but he's admitted to me this is the most challenging task of his life. I don't know everything, but it pains me to see how he has to face not just the poaching scourge, but all the external challenges on a daily basis.'

I closed my eyes for a moment as I sat there in the lounge. This thing was taking over my life.

7

Turbulence buffeted the SA Airlink Embraer passenger jet and lightning lit up the late-afternoon sky as we circled Johannesburg's OR Tambo Airport, waiting for a break in the weather so we could land.

As an ex-military man, I hated being late, but our flight from Skukuza had been delayed. It was late November, so the thunder and lightning of a Highveld storm was not unexpected. The weather matched my mood. I opened my laptop and checked the notes I had made for the keynote address I was supposed to give. I never write prepared speeches, but I found that having some bullet points down on PowerPoint slides in large type was enough to help get my message across without having to put on my glasses. I made some last-minute tweaks. I checked my watch; If we ever get there, I said to myself.

We landed, at last, and walked briskly through the parkade to the hotel shuttle-bus station. We boarded the black van to Emperors Palace. Thankfully, the casino and hotel complex was only a couple of kilometres away. All the same, we were late and Arina was waiting in our room – she had checked in hours earlier.

When our group entered the banquet room, packed with attendees for the 2013 Rhino Conservation Awards hosted by the Game Rangers' Association of Africa, proceedings were well underway. An announcement had already been made, I was told, that our group was not going to make it, so there was some spontaneous cheering when we walked in.

The field rangers with me, who had all been nominated for awards, had quickly changed into their best attire: gleaming, pointy-toed patent-leather shoes, smart shirts, suits – this was a big deal for them. I had made sure that the time-consuming process of nominating rangers for awards and then organising the logistics to get them to Johannesburg had been followed through. It was worth it. The awards, I believed, were an important plank in securing my base, instilling pride and a sense of achievement in my rangers.

Also with me was Dr Sam Ferreira, the head of large mammal research in the Kruger Park, and Regional Ranger Don English and Section Ranger Steven Whitfield. Don had won an award the previous year in recognition of his tireless efforts and his large number of contacts with poachers. If there was such a thing as a front line in our war, Don's Marula South region was it. Certainly, it was a big red dot on the heat map in the ops room.

I was welcomed to the head table and quickly introduced to the patron of the awards, His Serene Highness Prince Albert II of Monaco, and the two key sponsors, Chinese businesswoman Xiaoyang Yu, and a representative of Hasselblad cameras. I also met, for the first time, Fundisile Mketeni, the Deputy DirectorGeneral of the Department of Environmental Affairs.

We were just in time for the official speeches and presentations. The SANParks Honorary Rangers, as an organisation, received an award in recognition of the millions of rands' support they had provided to parks in the fight against rhino poaching, through training, equipment and manpower. From very early on in my tenure, the Honorary Rangers had been there, willing and able to help with the fight. They had provided everything, from chest webbing for rangers to accommodation for a pilot and a dog master at Skukuza. Our Kruger contingent did well, picking up a number of awards and, via their nominations, gave an indication of the different fronts in the fight against poaching. Sam Ferreira received the gold award for science and research, for his studies of the workings of illegal syndicates, security effectiveness, monitoring techniques and poaching prediction models. At the time of receiving this honour,

Sam was working on no fewer than 24 different research projects related to rhino poaching.

'Despite several near-death experiences,' read the nomination for Don English's category, 'he keeps on improving on his achievements.' Following on from his award for courage in the field in 2012, at this ceremony Don picked up gold in the Best Intelligence Gathering category, in recognition of the intel and informer networks he had established. He was in the thick of the fight in southern Kruger and his results were outstanding.

Described as 'one of the most experienced and respected rangers in the Kruger Park', Team Leader Wilson Siwela received the coveted Best Field Ranger award for 2013. Wilson was a truly inspirational figure, a man who led from the front and did not hesitate to engage armed poachers. He had been involved in the arrest of many poachers and was already the holder of the Kruger Cross for Bravery for taking on a gang of five armed poachers in early 2011.

Coming in second to Wilson was Section Ranger Steven Whitfield, who not only coordinated and took part in actions in his part of Kruger, but also learned to fly a Bantam ultra-light aircraft, which he used to follow up on poachers and patrol the bush. Rangers Albert Maluleke and Amos Mzimba tied for third place. Both were experienced operators who had been in many contacts with poachers, but Amos was also honoured for his work with his canine comrade, Killer, a Belgian Malinois tracker dog. One of the first anti-poaching dogs to be employed in the park, in 2011, Killer's fame would grow in the coming years.

Fundisile spoke before me and I was the last to approach the lectern, a little uncomfortable about giving the keynote address after a man who outranked me. Fundisile had expressed appreciation for the effort the rangers were making and I wanted to amplify this. My key aim was to use the speech to recognise rangers' efforts. I started by explaining why it was so important to protect and save the rhino, how these iconic creatures were part of our natural heritage, and was at pains to stress, early on, that we were not yet winning the war. Once again, I had the difficult task of conveying the fact that while the number of rhinos being killed continued to increase, it was against a backdrop of a dramatic surge in incursions.

I spoke of the increase in demand and the value of rhino horn. South Africa, I said, now had to accept the true cost of protecting this species; we were, in effect, victims of our own success in bringing rhinos back from the brink of extinction the first time around.

As well as the cost of ownership, I raised other issues that we, as a country, and the audience, as rangers, needed to address. We needed to improve our access to intelligence around poachers and their networks; we also had to accept the very real possibility that what we were being asked to do was going to be too little and too late. They were sobering words, but this audience was no stranger to the scope of the problem and they knew all too well the sacrifices they were being called on to make.

At this point, Mozambique was no more than a note on a couple of PowerPoint slides. I had intended to mention the country as only one 'issue', and to later talk about the need to engage with stake-holders on the other side of the fence.

But then, as I closed off, I felt the frustrations and emotions of the previous months rise inside me. I thought of the carcasses I had seen, the orphaned rhino calves, and the poachers who stopped for a cigarette and to hurl insults at our rangers once they crossed over the border into their home country.

'How is it,' I asked the audience, in their suits and evening dresses, their eyes on me, 'that Mozambique allows these armed bandits to illegally enter our country repeatedly?'

It was a rhetorical question and I had not planned to use the speech to attack a sovereign nation, but my blood was boiling. Heads in the crowd were nodding and there was a murmur rippling through the audience. Perhaps they, too, were not expecting the by-now very prominent, yet still not fully embedded general to be quite so controversial.

'How is it that these people can be allowed to plunder our natural resources at will?' I asked.

The crowd broke into applause and there were calls of support from the floor. I glanced over to where Fundisile was sitting, close to the podium. He had a pensive look on his face and while I did not think he was angered by my remarks, it did seem to me that they had made him slightly uneasy. Of course, he could have been thinking: 'So this is the little shit about whose employment I learned via the media ...'

I gripped the sides of the lectern tight, and realised that every one of the men and women in the auditorium who had put their lives on the line could relate to every word I was saying. This was not a time for political correctness, nor diplomacy – that time would come. This was a time for talk of war.

MOZAMBIQUE, Mozambique, Mozambique.

It preyed on my mind as I, like hundreds of thousands of tourists, traders, travellers and thieves every year, gritted my teeth and plodded through the intricate, convoluted rituals of an African border crossing, at the Komatipoort–Ressano Garcia frontier post.

Touts offered to ease my way through Customs in exchange for a discreet payment, as insurance brokers clustered like vultures on a kill, waiting to sell me a policy and change rands into meticas. Everything imaginable – legal and illegal – passed through this hot, steamy border town on the banks of the Crocodile River. Mining trucks filled with ore from South Africa queued on the N4, flanked by sprawling sugar-cane estates. Somewhere in the rusty bakkies or backpacks of foot-travellers could be illegally mined gold, drugs, diamonds and rhino horn.

This was not just a crossing between two countries, but also a transition zone between different cultures. Although Portugal had given up her colonial possessions after a coup in the motherland in

1975, the evidence of the former colonisers was everywhere to seen as soon as one joined the queue for immigration. The English and Afrikaans, crisply ironed uniforms and 'relative' efficiency of South African Home Affairs gave way to Portuguese and officials in Eastern Bloc-style military fatigues, wearing berets at a jaunty angle with an AK-47 slung over one shoulder. The Russian-designed assault rifle, with its distinctive banana-shaped magazine, even features on the national flag, a reminder that independence and the current regime had come at the cost of armed struggle and a protracted civil war.

All our intelligence was telling us that the vast majority of rhino poaching – about 75% – originated in Mozambique. I had played to the crowd at Emperors Palace when I talked about armed invasion, but I knew I needed to be more diplomatic now that I was actually in the country I had publicly named and shamed. If I was to follow and implement my own strategy, to clear Kruger from the outside, then I needed to forge alliances with key players in Mozambique and support them, rather than just cast stones.

I drove on the South African-funded highway – a gift from President Nelson Mandela who had married Graça Machel, the widow of Mozambique's revolutionary-era leader, Samora Machel – acutely conscious of the speed I was doing; stories of the country's over-zealous traffic cops were legendary in South Africa. I was also very mindful that if my 'Platinum Status' might have raised some eyebrows in SANParks, it could very well raise the ire of some officials in Maputo, the Mozambican capital. The apartheid era government and military, of which I'd been a senior member, had supported the opposition forces during Mozambique's bloody civil war.

Maputo, too, still clearly bore the stamp of Portugal, from the grandly ornate Catholic Cathedral to the sidewalk cafés and the music blaring from shops and minibuses. The traffic was chaotic, the air rich with the smell of peri-peri chicken sizzling on roadside braais.

There were seven different government bodies charged with law enforcement in Mozambique and we had to deal with them all: the Fauna Bravia, the popular name for the conservation police; the

Guarda de Fronteira, military border guards; provincial police officers from Maputo and Gaza provinces, which covered the area bordering Kruger; various departments of the National Police; and ANAC – a Portuguese acronym for the National Administration of Conservation Areas – which was their equivalent of our SANParks. As well as these, I also needed to liaise with state and privately funded anti-poaching units and local communities across the border.

At my first meeting with representatives of many of these government bodies, my hosts were fashionably late. When they arrived, the senior police officers, accompanied by interpreters, were cordial and welcoming, with fruit juice and biscuits laid out for us.

The conversation was stilted as we waited for translations; every now and then an officer would interject, in Portuguese, while the interpreter was talking, further confusing things. I knew I needed to be patient and not pushy. This was an introductory meeting and I did not expect to be able to resolve everything, or even just one issue here in Maputo.

I raised the issue of poaching bosses transporting their men to the border of South Africa and Kruger unchallenged. I couldn't help myself. 'How are you allowing this to happen?'

There was silence while my question was translated. Officers looked at each other, sipped their juice or took another cookie.

'There are so many incursions,' I said, filling the void. I had to be polite and not point my finger at them. But the elephant – or, rather, rhino – in the room could not be ignored.

At another meeting, an open forum for conservation stakeholders organised by the US Embassy in Maputo, I again bemoaned the plundering of South Africa's national resources.

'You've got to support us,' I told the audience of about 50 in my closing remarks. 'This park is in your interest; you have concessions to the east of us so it is not as if you are divorced from us. The existence and well-being of Kruger is in the interest of Mozambique.'

When I finished, a tall, older Mozambican man – like me, a former general, I learned – stood up from the crowd and took me to task.

'Why are you blaming us only?' he said, forcefully. 'Your facts and stance are one-sided. You care more for animals than you do for people, who are needy and poor. What are you doing for the communities that live alongside these parks?'

It was not my job to engage with or uplift communities in Mozambique, although it was clear that more needed to be done on this front, but his response did give me pause for thought and I realised that I needed to rethink my position. I could not just walk into another country and speak my mind so plainly, especially in an open forum.

People have different views; we saw ourselves as custodians of nature in Kruger, but to people living in poverty in Mozambique, the wildlife reserves on their doorstep were a potential source of food and income.

IT WOULD BE wrong to suggest, however, that no one in Mozambique cared.

Dr Carlos Lopes Pereira, head of law enforcement for ANAC, had been a tireless champion of conservation. He too, however, was challenged by the realities of the situation in Mozambique.

Responsibility for the border lay with the Guarda de Fronteira, while prosecutions were the remit of the police. The army was also present throughout the country and did not take kindly to civilians in the administration telling them what to do.

While the law enforcement agencies quibbled about who was responsible for what, the poaching bosses acted as a law unto themselves. I travelled with Carlos to Massingir, the hot, dusty town on the eastern extremity of the Limpopo National Park. Here, a long, low dam on the Rio des Olifantes, our Olifants River, marked the edge of the LNP. Massingir was experiencing a mini building boom, not because of the waves of tourists that had been expected and not really yet materialised, but because of rhino poaching.

Carlos and I sat in a meeting, sweltering in a little room in the transfrontier park's head office, and it seemed like all the odds were against us. The town had an air of forgotten destitution; its people had nothing, zero options or potential for advancement. For many, poaching was their only ticket out of poverty.

Yet, here and there were budding mansions with terracotta roofs sprouting satellite TV dishes, and ornate cast concrete pillars out the front. The poaching bosses also flaunted their wealth in their actions. They would pay for the funerals of the men our rangers had killed, and dispense gratuity payments to grieving relatives.

For a successful gang, there was a bag filled with the equivalent of a minimum of R100 000 in cash when they came back with a couple of horns.

Carlos pointed out the houses of the kingpins in Massingir and, on a later trip, the businesses in Maputo that had been set up with money illegally earned from the blood of rhinos. The poaching bosses' reach was extensive and there was no doubt they had their protectors. Carlos was as frustrated as I, and as committed to turning things around.

Amazingly, poaching was not even against the law in Mozambique – specifically, there were no penalties for killing wildlife. Carlos was working on this, and a bill was being introduced into parliament the following April to make killing wildlife illegal. It was also important, I believed, that we secure an extradition agreement between Mozambique and South Africa.

Where there was cooperation, it was at the very grass-roots level, on a ranger-to-ranger basis, such as the report that had alerted us to the existence of the last living rhino on the other side of the border. I reminded myself of the sign above my desk in my office: we needed to think big, in terms of changing legislation, but also start small, with our allies in the bush in Mozambique, and act now.

THE CONFLICT I had served in on the frontiers of Angola and Namibia was known as the Border War. The irony was not lost on me as I sat in the co-pilot's seat of the helicopter, flying towards the Lebombo Hills. To put the fight in Kruger into perspective, I now pointed out when I did my many presentations to stakeholders that the number of contacts in the park – firefights between poachers and rangers – was now greater per year than the number of contacts at the height of the conflict in South West Africa. The number of poachers being taken out of action was increasing, but still we had yet to suffer the loss of a ranger to hostile fire.

The man I was flying to the border to meet was, according to the media, a mercenary. Lionel Dyck had been a colonel in the old Rhodesian Army and had stayed on in the military to serve his new political masters after Zimbabwe gained independence in 1980. As a Zimbabwean Army officer, he had worked with the FRELIMO forces in Mozambique to support their political and military enemy, RENAMO. Ironically, the Rhodesian military had backed RENAMO in the early days of the civil war, as had South Africa, albeit covertly. Dyck's company, DAG (the Dyck Advisory Group), had been working in Mozambique rendering security services and advice and removing landmines, and had also been involved in anti-poaching. We touched down and I checked my watch. We were behind schedule.

A table had been set up under a tree and Lionel was there, with a few of his staff and his mostly black rangers. I'd heard of him, but this was the first time I had met him. He was about my height and older than me, beyond his mid-seventies. He was balding, not a gram of fat on his body, and he had eyes that had seen it all.

'How long do I have with you?' he asked, getting straight to the point.

'I'm running late. Maybe 10 minutes,' I said. I was taking a tour of the border, trying to meet as many people as I could from the private reserves bordering Kruger on the Mozambican side. A number of concessions had been let by the Mozambican government to promote tourism and hunting, and many had been taken up by South African individuals and companies, including the Singita group of luxury safari properties.

Dyck cast an eye over me, just as a combat officer might size up a general visiting the field. 'When I was serving in the army, senior officers would tell me I had 10 minutes to brief them. Now, I'm not in the army, but you're still telling me I've got 10 minutes.'

Lionel – or Colonel Dyck, as he preferred to be addressed – seemed overly abrupt as we chatted, but I knew he was super efficient at what he did. DAG was running anti-poaching operations in the Sabie Game Reserve, the long, narrow strip of privately owned land just across the southern section of Kruger's eastern border, north of the Komatipoort–Ressano Garcia border post. This was a hunting concession, part owned by a wealthy Arab sheikh.

I asked the Colonel for his assessment of anti-poaching operations further north in the LNP, the area of land that had formed the Great Limpopo Transfrontier Conservation Area.

'It's the Wild West up there,' he said. 'No effective anti-poaching units, and the poachers are running riot.'

He said that if a meat poacher was picked up then the park rangers would be assaulted by locals, who treated the poachers like heroes. Also, there were still people living inside the park, eking out a living by subsistence poaching or venturing across the border into South Africa. Rhino were now extinct in the Great Limpopo Transfrontier Park, and poachers were concentrating on either bush meat, or elephants, for their ivory.

There were rhino in the Sabie Game Reserve, but this sliver of land was well patrolled by Colonel Dyck and his men. He had raised money abroad, mostly in America, to fund his own helicopter, and he and his experienced operators were a force to be reckoned with.

What he did tell me was that his men often picked up the tracks of poachers transiting through the Sabie Game Reserve on their way to Kruger in search of rhino. He was keen to work with us to catch these intruders. I immediately thought that I would like to see him expand his operations in Mozambique, but for now I was happy for him to brief me.

Chatting with the Colonel and others, I found that little to no information was being shared by operators in the field on either side of the border, and when it was, it was in the same ad-hoc manner that had been used in Kruger prior to my arrival.

'We need structure, Colonel,' I said, 'and clear lines of reporting.' He was on board completely, and as a pair of former military men, we both knew what had to be done. And so we kicked off Operation Lebombo, a concerted coordinated effort to improve communication and share information on a frequent, regular basis. By feeding information on the movement of poaching gangs and incidents, we could track gangs heading to and from both sides of the border.

This then allowed us to plan and conduct joint operations, working together, but on each side of the border road. While we could not accede to the frequent insistence by members of the public for us to conduct 'hot-pursuit' operations, this new level of cooperation at least meant that poachers could not arrive at or depart the border with impunity, as they had in the past.

Colonel Dyck told me a story, though, that highlighted the persistent problem of entrenched corruption in Mozambique.

'We had one case where we picked up a poacher who was also wanted for murder in South Africa,' Colonel Dyck said. 'My guys caught him in his vehicle, took his rifle off him and handed him over to the police. However, the police said they didn't want him, because he was too big, too important, so we flew him to Maputo in our helicopter.

'Three days later,' he continued, 'one of my operators was driving along and saw a vehicle broken down on the side of the road; when my guy got out to offer to help, he saw it was the poaching boss we had taken to Maputo. When we asked him what he was doing back here, free, he said, "Nobody puts me in prison."'

Further to the north of the Sabie Game Reserve was Karingani Game Reserve, where a number of concession holders were also ramping up their anti-poaching capabilities. Ellery Worth, a South African running a unit of rangers, initially had to send his men into the field with paintball guns, loaded with balls of pepper spray, as local laws initially prohibited him from arming them with military-style rifles.

Carlos Lopes Pereira was working hard behind the scene to have the firearms laws amended to allow anti-poaching operators to be better armed. Like others involved in anti-poaching on private reserves, both Ellery and the Colonel faced the challenges of getting landholders and senior management to spend more money on security, while confronting ruthless armed poachers and their bosses head on in the bush. The odds were stacked against them, but I believed their increased effectiveness would be crucial to our success in Kruger.

I had to be careful when opening the channels of communication with authorities and others because that this new approach came with some degree of risk. The dedication of many local police officers in Mozambique impressed me, and I could empathise with the frustrations they shared with Carlos.

Sometimes in Mozambique I would be in a meeting, in a room with eight or more police officers or other officials, and I would get the distinct impression that I could only trust half of them. When sharing details of our patrols and operations, we had to mindful that our plans might be leaked to the poaching bosses. On balance, though, it was worth it.

Operation Lebombo was a lesson in multi-party engagement. What was key, I realised early on, was that I needed to be patient and realistic, and to work with our Mozambican partners to set common goals.

Importantly, we needed to bring them along with us and make them part of the team. In the far north, I launched Operation Capricorn in similar fashion, with staunch allies like Anthony Alexander and Billy Swanepoel in full support. Sharing of intelligence, joint planning, vigorous and hands-on execution were the modus operandi with the LNP. This was in response to the public outcry to rebuild the fence and literally 'fence them out'.

Our informal meetings on the border continued. Sandy McDonald, CEO of the Sabie Game Reserve, would also be there, arranging logistics, such as erecting a tent or gazebo for the meeting. At other times, he, the Colonel and I would sit in the shade of a tree and discuss future operations and dissect recent contacts. Often, there would be a fire already going and we would burn some meat and drink some Cokes under the clear African sky.

Section Ranger Rendani Nethengwe, who had told me almost despairingly in my early visit to his post about how he was being assailed by poachers from all sides, took me aside while we were waiting for one of these informal border meetings to start. For a change, we had some quality time in which to chat; we sat in the shade of a tree.

'Originally I was unsure about what you wanted to achieve and questioned many things,' he said to me candidly. 'But I must tell you, now I not only understand, I appreciate what you are doing, General.'

IN QUICK TIME, Colonel Dyck's operators were feeding information into our ops room. They contacted us by WhatsApp, if there was signal, but they were also now on our radio net so they could report incidents directly to us, just as our rangers did.

The Colonel's men patrolled their 'inland' fence on the eastern side of the Sabie Game Reserve every morning and when they picked up tracks, probably made by poachers entering the night before, they would radio the information to the ops room. There, the staff would record the information, scramble to get a helicopter and deploy rangers on our side of the border to act as a stop group. If our rangers were chasing poachers and they crossed the border into the Sabie Game Reserve, the poachers could not expect a warm welcome from Colonel Dyck and his men. They carried real rifles, with real ammunition, and if placed in a position of danger they were not afraid to use them. With their organic air support, in the form of the Colonel's chopper, they ran a mini fire force, able to respond to incidents and tracks in their small reserve at a moment's notice.

In a very short time, the simple process of getting people to talk to each other started paying dividends and that stretch of the border, about 40 kilometres long, became a place no smart poacher wanted to pass through.

With the cooperation of Colonel Dyck's teams, we had effectively increased the size of our overall effort, begun the process of clearing the park from the outside and added to our intelligence-gathering capability. With the help of our allies across the border, we were now taking the fight to the poachers just as I had promised, boldly, in that first media conference. Rather than complaining about Mozambique and throwing our hands up in frustration at our inability to carry out hot pursuits, we had enlisted some very effective allies to do the job for us.

It can be done, I told myself.

8

D rone fever was infectious and it had taken hold of officials, journalists and NGOs.

'Please, General,' the representative of an overseas company begged me on the phone, 'let me show you our UAV.'

'All right,' I sighed, 'come on Sunday. I'll arrange access for you to the ops area at the airport. I'll meet you there.'

From the very first day of my appointment, UAVs – unmanned aerial vehicles, commonly referred to as 'drones' in the media – had been touted as the answer to all our poaching woes. I had stood in polite silence and watched a demonstration of the South African-made Denel Dynamics Seeker drone as it patrolled along the Sabie River during the media show. Nothing I saw that day, or after, convinced me that drones – or any other one piece of technology – was that 'silver bullet'.

That did not stop the arms and aviation companies and military veterans from around the world from trying to convince me otherwise. Yes, UAVs had been successful in conflicts such as Iraq and Afghanistan in providing live feeds of battles to commanders far away, or launching deadly missile strikes, but that was not what we needed here in the Kruger Park.

'All the videos I see on laptops are of drones filming pipelines, fences and roads,' I said to one peddler, 'and you show me how you can zoom in on the number plate of a car. Rhinos don't have number plates. Can you spot a man hiding in the bush?'

'Infrared', I was told, was the answer, but I already knew that it had limited effectiveness in a place such as the Kruger Park. Infrared (IR) technology identified a human, animal or other object by its radiated heat, but the rocky soils of our part of Africa retained the heat of the day long into the night, making it very hard to discern a human from the air against the backdrop of the ground. A human's IR signature might be visible, say, between midnight and dawn, when the soil temperature cooled, but a termite mound bustling with underground activity would also show up as a glowing red blob to further confuse matters.

For a drone operator watching a small screen or computer monitor, it was almost impossible to spot a poacher hiding in the bush. If a poacher was spotted by a drone or ground forces, then a potential UAV needed the fuel or battery life to stay with the target, until a reaction force of rangers could respond. These challenges were too great for anything available and affordable to us in Kruger.

However, I was under considerable pressure to keep listening to the sales pitches of the drone sellers. Politicians loved these gadgets and so, too, did the media. In addition to aerospace companies 'pushing' drones on me, I also had to deal with donor 'pull'.

I realised early on when formulating my strategy that funding would be a major challenge and that I would need to call on the corporate and NGO sectors to help fund the technology, training and equipment we needed. Donors, I soon realised, were easily seduced by 'sexy' high-tech solutions, such as drones, and I needed to help manage and curb that 'pull'; I would find myself suggesting more practical, less flashy priorities – things such as food for tracker dogs, and vehicles for response teams.

On the Sunday morning after I had spoken to the latest overseas drone seller, I drove to the ops room from my house in Skukuza. Sunday was just another work day for me – poachers never took a break. I was working between 80 and 90 hours a week, not because I was unable to delegate, but because as well as running a 'mini war', I had to reply to more than a hundred emails a day. I had to guard against falling into the trap of pushing myself too hard; the risk was that I would lose a sense of my real priorities and not allow myself enough rest. Any military commander knows that if you don't rest, you make mistakes.

Pulling up at the airport, I headed out to the tarmac. The drone was there, with its visibly concerned salesman. After a few hours of standing in the harsh African sun, pieces of the aircraft were falling apart, as the glue holding them together had melted.

DURING ONE OF the first planning sessions, when developing the concept of operations, I wrote on my flip chart my aims for the employment of technology.

I took a marker pen from the old green canvas bag. 'Old school is cool,' I said tapping the chart. Some things just had to be written and seen.

Firstly, I wanted to improve our situational awareness, to use a range of systems to tell us how, when and where poachers were entering Kruger, and what their movements were once they were inside the park. Technology could also, I hoped, give us in the ops room eyes on where our people were and what they were seeing and hearing in the field.

'Connectivity' had been the next word I wrote on the chart. Modern technology was largely digital and the Kruger, a vast area of wilderness, was by no means covered by cell-phone signal or even effective radio communications. In one respect, this helped us – if poachers could not use their phones, then they could not receive reports of where rhinos or security forces might be. On the other hand, it limited our employment of certain technologies.

I needed a summary of the different types of sensors we might employ in and around the park, and I identified early on that, as with our strategy, we would need a layered approach to the use of technology. High-tech systems and devices could help us secure and monitor our perimeter and access gates, and could also feed us information about what was happening in our area of operations – the Kruger Park. I also noted that technology would be a key part of our strategy to set up an IPZ, the Intensive Protection Zone, south of the Sabie River.

Technology had been included as a key plank in the national rhino strategy in 2012, the year before I started at Kruger, but very little had been done about it. Industry had been awakened and had been bombarding the park with solutions, but the technology roadmap, which I had commissioned Chris Serfontein to write, would specify what we needed technology to achieve. As much as I believed in technology as part of the solution, I had to be careful to avoid being seduced by it. The golden rule was to make sure we knew what we needed before we fell into the trap of buying what we wanted.

Through the planning and implementation of our technology requirements, I had to continually remind myself of the saying I often repeated in presentations: technology makes things possible, but only people make things happen.

Another guiding principle I followed and impressed on would-be suppliers was that our technology needed to be 'brown earth' not 'blue sky'. I wanted systems and solutions that were proven, those that my rangers could not only learn and understand easily, but also embrace.

Most rangers, because of their backgrounds, were not especially tech-savvy. The younger ones had no problems with smart phones, but older ones needed to be convinced of the value of a new system and that the technology was there to help them. Whatever physical assets we introduced needed to be robust enough to deal with the harsh African climate and the possible interference of animals, and they needed to be relatively easy to maintain. The rangers, I soon learned, wanted all the benefits that technology could bring, but did not necessarily have the time or the inclination to learn how to use and maintain it. This would not be just about introducing magical new hardware or software; I would need to consider our flesh-and-blood rangers, our 'wet ware'.

Fortunately, I was experienced enough not to be seduced by technology as a single solution for any part of the task of safeguarding Kruger. I was also well aware of the pressures put on sales representatives in the arms and aviation industry to land a new client, particularly one that generated widespread media coverage.

Whenever I received a call or an email from yet another arms or tech company about their latest product, I immediately passed it on to Chris Serfontein. Until the funding arrived – the Honorary Rangers eventually came through with the one million rand I had requested for the roadmap – Chris would work in his own time, at night and on weekends, to review the submissions.

'It's like I'm doing a master's thesis in military technology,' Chris joked. Every time I sent him a proposal he would research it, online and through other sources, to see what similar and competing systems were out there, how effective they had been, and whether they met some of the criteria we had already set for our needs, based on our early planning. He would then give me a recommendation as to whether we should move to the next stage of allowing the company to present to us.

Chris weeded plenty out, but I still sat through PowerPoint presentation after presentation, watched endless corporate videos and listened to earnest guarantees that this latest piece of gadgetry was the answer to all my woes. The industry was aggressively marketing its new products, not just to us in the Kruger, but also to well-meaning NGOs. Both these players also lobbied government intensely.

'Why won't you speak to these people, General?' a politician would ask me. 'They're offering you a free trial of their technology.'

Managing this process was time-consuming, but I was also wary of not allowing my technology fatigue or scepticism to miss out on a sound solution. So, in between dealing with incidents and contacts and directing and planning operations on the ground, I spent valuable time listening to sales pitches.

. . .

IN THE BUSH, three men, rifles by their sides, sat around a campfire, keeping their voices low as they chatted. In the air, 200 metres above them, an unmanned aerial vehicle, or drone, cruised through the night sky, looking for them.

In the ops room at Skukuza, CSIR staff and I watched on as the drone operator stared intently at his screen.

Some of the technology options we had been considering had advanced from the 'pitch' proposal stage to evaluation. I was conscious of the need to 'act now', even if I didn't have funding immediately available, and I had ceded to the enormous pressure on me to at least trial a drone.

The CSIR and I had gone back to industry with our specifications of what we wanted a drone to be able to do for us. We heard back from many companies, but offered a South African operation the opportunity to put one of their more advanced, fixed-wing UAVs through its paces in a trial.

Doing some testing of our own, we had decided that any UAV we used must be able to operate at night, when poachers are most active, and that the targets on the ground must not be able to hear it. For that reason, we had worked out that most drones would have to fly at an altitude of 200–400 metres above ground level.

For the purposes of the trial, the CSIR evaluation team had marked out 500 x 500 metres of bush in the Kruger Park that would be patrolled by the UAV. The three men at the campfire were thus rangers, playing the part of poachers in the night. We also had more of our people out simulating other types of activity, including walking in the bush, and lying under a tree, hiding or sleeping. Our aim was to see how many of the 'pseudo poachers' the operator could identify, and whether the platform was better suited to, say, detecting people on the move.

The drone found none of them.

What the team and I came to realise was that the Hollywood image of drones and their effectiveness was vastly different to the harsh realities of the African bush. Much of the success or otherwise of UAVs was linked to budget. The wars in Afghanistan and Iraq had shown that UAVs could pinpoint individuals, but there was no comparison between, say, a US Air Force Global Hawk UAV – basically an un-piloted jet aircraft – and the drones we could hope to afford. The drones in our budget would, at best, be restricted to a payload of one to two kilograms, which severely limited the type, number and sophistication of the sensors and cameras they could carry.

A comprehensive scientific trial of UAVs over nearly a year, allowing us to cater for all seasons, weather, vegetation and terrain, gave me the information I needed to brief our minister on the real situation regarding drones. This enabled her to be prepared for the industry onslaught when she went to the next cocktail party where she would inevitably be bailed up by a drone salesman.

One thing we quickly learned was that whatever technology we employed in the fight to save rhinos would cost big bucks.

WHEN IT CAME to monitoring Kruger's borders and the movements of poachers once they were inside the park, there was an array of technology – both new and old – to consider.

Poachers, like most people these days, used cell phones. While these devices could be handy for us to stay in contact with each other, they also allowed our adversaries to communicate with their middlemen, as well as people inside the park who were able to feed them real-time information. Our rangers already knew that a poacher's phone could provide intelligence vital for tracking other members of their network, and for securing a conviction.

Existing technology allows for cell phones to be tracked and we were more than happy to investigate this as a potential weapon in our arsenal. There was a range of offerings from various companies in different countries, and we invited a company from the UK to show us their wares. This was a field not even Hollywood could keep up with or do justice to in the First World.

This state-of-the-art technology was also tried and true, and was employed by governments around the world for counter-terrorism operations and the fight against organised crime. We were given permission to conduct a trial and the results were amazing. First, we tested vehicle-mounted applications of tracking devices that picked up cell-phone users in the immediate area. Even without listening in on conversations, we could use this system to find someone in the bush using a phone.

When we took the system and its monitor into the air, in one of the helicopters, the screen lit up with 30 000 hits, picking up tourists, staff and people living on the fringes of the Kruger Park. Of course, we were not allowed to eavesdrop on any conversations, though the technology certainly allowed that.

This particular technology was too good to be true. When we put out feelers to government, we were told that the State Security Agency was the only government body that could legally employ such a system in the nation's interest, and that there was no prospect of us getting the legislation changed to catch rhino poachers. It was disappointing, but we had to accept that such rules regarding the protection of privacy was one of the features of living in a liberal democracy.

More down to earth, literally, were ground-based sensors that would detect movement when poachers tried to enter the park. This was true brown-earth technology and showed enormous potential. We looked at seismic sensors, and trialled a system that would alert us when a fence was tampered with or someone – or something – was moving through a sensitive area. We had to be aware that animals such as elephants could set off these sensors, which could also be activated by extreme weather, such as lightning or heavy winds. It seemed to me that seismic sensors might be good for securing a smaller area, such as a boma housing valuable animals, but less so when monitoring a remote stretch of fence line. Another system that showed great promise was a buried magnetised cable that could be run along a stretch of the perimeter of the IPZ. This system was sensitive enough to pick up a poacher's rifle, bullets or machete as he crossed the cable. A power source, located in a shipping container, was needed to maintain an electric current through the cable in order to keep it magnetised, and this required regular maintenance. A challenge might be to get rangers to commit to monitoring and maintaining the cable's power. They needed to be convinced that the extra time and manpower needed to keep this system – or any other – running, was worth it, in addition to their existing workload.

I was interested in radar. US and coalition forces engaged in the war on terror in Afghanistan and the campaigns in Iraq had been making use of WASS (Wide Area Surveillance Systems), as well as airborne systems mounted in helium-filled balloons, known in the American military as 'aerostats'. These employed long-range cameras, with laser sight designators to scan for insurgents on the move and approaching bases. I wanted the CSIR to investigate these systems, but there was some pushback about the effectiveness of radar in the bush – nevertheless, I made sure they kept it on their list.

CHRIS and his team at the CSIR had completed the plan by October 2013. The roadmap identified the range of technologies appropriate for Environmental Asset Protection, or EAP, a term we coined at the time, and gave clear guidelines that would inform our decision-making.

From that point on, we were in a position to start inviting proposals and welcoming focused demonstrations – in addition to trying to deal with the many others being pushed or pulled towards us.

We started planning our acquisitions and 'wish list' with an emphasis on 'force multipliers' – a common military term that meant we could ensure a greater impact while using the same number of rangers; a force multiplier could also allow us to become more proactive, the second part of our strategy after we had consolidated our ranger base.

My first dealings with industry were tentative from my side, because I still had no budget to develop, procure or maintain any specialised equipment or systems. In essence, my requests for proposals boiled down to two key planks of the strategy we had identified early on: enhancing connectivity and situational awareness. Improving these would allow us to bring in other technology and resources to secure the proposed IPZ in the south of the park. I needed buy-in from my higher headquarters for this concept, but did not know that I was about to get the chance. In September 2013, I was called down to Addo National Park near Port Elizabeth to consult with them on anti-poaching. While I was there, I took a call from David Mabunda. He had arrived at a SANParks board meeting at Tsitsikamma National Park, expecting to find me there, but I had not been invited. He told me to get there, straight away, and so I drove to the stunning park at the mouth of Storms River.

Before, during and after the meeting I fielded questions from board members and other senior management about what I had been up to over the preceding nine months. My initial push to have everyone in Kruger undergo a polygraph was controversial and my demands for greater accountability and better supply chains had clearly rankled some senior leaders who took this personally. The spectre of racism reared its ugly head again when I was asked why I favoured employing people on short-term contracts. In the meeting I again picked up on some underlying conflict between the board and the Exco.

However, I came away from the meeting encouraged that the board understood my strategy and supported the zoning concept – specifically the IPZ and the associated technology roadmap.

'It is good to see another level of thinking since General Jooste came on board,' board member Professor Graham Kerley had said during the meeting.

I got in my rental car and drove back to Port Elizabeth where, having achieved my aim of getting support for the technology plan, I relaxed over a lovely fish dinner, with white wine, of course, as part of the meal.

Working within the bureaucracy, this was a new experience for me, I reflected, as I ate alone. I had the overt support of Minister

Molewa and top management, and a high public profile thanks to the media – even though I was only a contractor. I knew my place, but I was prepared to leverage things in my favour. I knew I was walking a tightrope over a crocodile-infested river and there was no shortage of people who would be happy to see me fall.

However, I now had approval in principle for the technology plan and it was time for me to hit the road. I would take our fight onto the world's stage, in the hope of finding enough money to make our technological dreams a reality and, in the process, save some more rhinos.

9

W erner Myburgh, the CEO of the Peace Parks Foundation, came to visit me in Skukuza and we hit it off immediately. I'd already identified Peace Parks as a fine example of an existing structure we could tap into to help coordinate the fight against poaching.

PPF was the driving force behind the creation of the Great Limpopo Transfrontier Park and now that landmark initiative was under threat. We were already seeing people calling for the fence between Kruger and the Limpopo Park to be re-erected because of poaching.

Between 2001 and 2003, with financial support from PPF, Kruger had darted and relocated 111 elephants from the South African side of the park to Mozambique. Kruger's ecologists feared that in the absence of culling, elephant numbers were growing at an unsustainable rate and translocation was an option. Of the 25 elephants relocated in 2001, three bulls and a breeding herd of seven returned to Kruger, although one of the bulls later went back to Mozambique. In time, nature took a hand and the bush on the other side of the Lebombo Mountains, left untouched by megafauna such as buffalo and elephant for decades as a result of poaching and civil war, proved too attractive for Kruger's elephants – they began moving into Mozambique of their own accord. As of 2022, there were an estimated 1500 elephants living in Mozambique's Limpopo National Park.

The rhinos that crossed into Mozambique from the north of Kruger, however, had been hammered, leading to our frantic efforts to save the last known animal by chasing it into South Africa.

Werner and I hit it off immediately. He was young and dynamic and PPF was growing exponentially under his leadership. Werner immediately grasped the scale of the crisis we were facing and offered to mobilise PPF in support of us – it was a significant moment. PPF already had the contacts in Mozambique to help us get things done, and they had a well-oiled fundraising machine.

Werner explained that he was heading to the UK and Europe to approach the Dutch and Swedish Postcard lotteries in search of funding for a raft of Peace Parks initiatives. The lotteries, extremely profitable ventures, also gave money to charity. Werner told me that PPF had been investigating a number of measures aimed at devaluing rhino horn, including infusing horns with dye, which would colour the keratin from the inside, and a mild poison. Rather than trying to kill users, the aim was to make them think twice about buying, and therefore reduce demand.

'Can you maybe add an appendix to your proposal,' I asked him, 'so that if they fund your projects, they might have money for some of ours?'

He agreed and I put together a spreadsheet of what we needed, including training, vehicles, kits for rangers, and a house for a dog master at Skukuza Airport so that we could always have a dog and handler on standby, close to the helicopters.

I realised SANParks would not have the funds to execute my strategy, so I planned and executed international fundraising trips of my own. With a sense of déjà vu, I packed my bags and left South Africa for the first of many overseas trips. This time, instead of developing business and selling military vehicles, I was on the road to raise money and support. In the UK, I met with the environment minister and the Department of Environment, Food and Rural Affairs. I visited

NGOs and was invited to speak at a conference where various well-meaning individuals pontificated on what we should be doing to save the rhino.

Nodding and with a look of polite engagement, I checked my phone during yet another long-winded presentation. While these earnest people talked, we had lost three more rhino in a single day.

'Can we try to formulate and enact one decision that will ensure urgent and short-term impact?' I asked, when it was my turn to talk. The concept of 'think big, start small, act now' was lost on this crowd. 'Time is running out for the rhino in Kruger.'

On a positive note, I made contact with the Royal Foundation of Prince William and Prince Harry in the UK and, according to their staff, it seemed the Royals were very supportive. The young princes' visits to Africa had been well publicised in the past, and, as military men, I hoped they might appreciate the nuances and seriousness of the conflict we were involved in half a world away. Only time would tell.

I firmly believed, and often said, that leaders are merchants of hope. It is easy to lapse into the negative, as I had done at the Game Rangers' Association Rhino Conservation Awards, lambasting Mozambique, and I had to remind myself, often, to stay positive. At yet another speaking engagement in London, I made it very clear that the world had been in this position in the past, and that my country had taken a stand once before.

'The world has rhino,' I told the audience, 'because South Africa saw to it that we have rhino. These are our rhino and our responsibility, and that also involves the resourcing of our campaign.' Yes, I was abroad looking for money, but I also wanted to make it clear that we had a plan, and we were not looking for an open-ended blank cheque.

I was back in South Africa and it was five o'clock on a November morning, the sky already lightening at this time of year, the outside air warm. Hippos honked as they returned to the Sabie River after a night's foraging. Rangers and poachers had been out searching for their respective prey.

Before setting off on my morning run, I checked my emails on my iPad to see whether there was anything that needed urgent attention. Dear General Jooste, I would like to make contact with you when I am next in South Africa, the sender wrote. It was short and to the point, not much more in the body of the message, but it was the name that leapt out at me.

Howard G Buffett.

This was a total surprise to me, but I recognised the name immediately, as I had heard about the man and his Howard G Buffett Foundation (HGBF) on my visit to America. Howard was the middle son of multibillionaire investor and business magnate Warren Buffett, the tenth wealthiest man in the world. Howard had made his mark in his own right, through business and the well-publicised philanthropy of his foundation.

The HGBF was active in many parts of the world, but especially in Africa and Central America, supporting initiatives aimed at improving agriculture, nutrition, water and conservation. Buffett himself had travelled to some 130 countries to learn more about the world's problems and help find solutions. In addition to being a businessman and sheriff in his native America, he was also a farmer, photographer and author, having penned several books on conservation and environmental issues. He had served on the National Geographic Council of Advisors and the World Wildlife Fund National Council.

I replied immediately and, just as quickly, received a reply from Buffett, saying he would be in Johannesburg on 22 December; we arranged to meet over dinner at The Butcher Shop and Grill in Sandton.

HGBF had already set up a local body in South Africa, the Nature Conservation Trust, and I called them to try to gather some information in preparation for the meeting.

'Should I bring our fundraiser with me?' I asked the woman who answered the phone. I had dealt with senior military officers, politicians and media personalities, but I was unsure of the protocol when meeting a billionaire philanthropist. I had travelled to the UK with the SANParks head of fundraising, so thought that might be appropriate.

'If you want to annoy this man,' the woman on the other end of the phone said, 'come as if you're asking for money.'

In December I flew from Skukuza to Johannesburg and caught the Gautrain to Sandton and checked into the Radisson Blu Gautrain Hotel. At 6.30 pm sharp, dressed for the occasion in sports jacket, pressed trousers and shined shoes, I walked into the restaurant on Nelson Mandela Square with my iPad tucked under my arm. The maître d' showed me through to the private dining room the Buffett Foundation had booked.

Buffett looked like a friendly, amicable next-door neighbour. There were six other people around the table, one of whom, Chris Marais, I recognised. Chris was a former SANParks executive who had founded the group Leadership for Conservation in Africa. LCA was active in about 16 African countries, encouraging socioeconomic development in communities bordering flagship game reserves, including the Kruger. They reasoned that the communities living next to national parks were, in many cases, among the poorest of the poor in rural Africa and that it was difficult to get them to care about protecting wildlife when they were living hand to mouth. Howard Buffett, along with many other high-powered businesspeople, sat on the LCA board.

The drinks waiter came to our table. I'd done some research on Buffett and knew that he was a teetotaller, and, when I looked around the table, I noticed no one else had ordered alcohol.

'Is one allowed to have a glass of wine?' I asked the host.

'You may,' Buffett said.

He talked, and I listened, making my glass last. He told me he had visited all 54 countries on the African continent, and been held hostage three times. He explained some of the projects his foundation was currently working on, and asked for my opinion on some of them. It was interesting learning about the foundation's work, which also covered conflict resolution. It was not until dessert that I was invited to speak.

Using the iPad, I talked him through our strategy and my plan to divide the park into zones. The Intensive Protection Zone (IPZ) in the south was where we needed to concentrate the technology we had been assessing. He seemed interested, and asked some questions.

'I'm not promising you anything,' Buffett said, 'but how much do you need for all this?'

I'd been told not to go into the meeting with my hand out for money. While I was aware of the estimated costs of the systems and equipment we needed, I was not 100% prepared to be put on the spot like that.

'Ten million US dollars,' I said, and added a silent little prayer. We finished the meal and then, as we were leaving the restaurant, he took me aside.

'I am promising you nothing,' he said again, 'but I have a board meeting on 2 January. If you can get me a funding submission by then I'll take it to the meeting.'

CHRIS SERFONTEIN, like many in South Africa, had finished work for the year and was with his family, enjoying the beginning of a summer holiday in the parks in the Western Cape.

'Chris,' I said on the phone when I called him that night, 'by 1 January Howard Buffett is expecting a proposal from us.'

I had given him a heads-up about my meeting and now I was asking him to take time away from his family after I had already tied up many, if not most of his nights at home over the year while he evaluated dozens of proposals and worked on the roadmap.

'No problem, General,' he said.

I was humbled. I had been chosen for this job, in part, because of my military experience, but now I was seeing the true character of a person who had lived their life in service, and the strengths they bring to any task or challenge. Chris did not, for a moment, ask for more time, or make excuses.

In the lead-up to Christmas and immediately after, we worked by email and phone, consolidating our wish list of technology and assets and costing it in as much detail as we could manage. We submitted a proposal for vibration sensors on fences in the south of the park and a subterranean magnetic cable more than 30 kilometres long; we also put in a proposal for cell-phone tracking technology – I thought I could get government approval for that as we were not proposing to listen in on conversations.

'Mr Buffett's willing to fund research into technology as well, if it can be deployed on a major scale to benefit conservation,' I told Chris.

Should our shopping list of technology be filled, we would be better at detecting incursions. If that happened, we needed to be able to rapidly deploy rangers to intercept the poachers. We looked at our mobility needs, including more all-terrain vehicles and 4x4s. In the meantime, the war continued unabated. Christmas brought only increased demand for rhino horn in Massingir and the other poaching villages across the border in Mozambique. Between exchanging calls and emails about the Buffett proposal, I flew with Arina by helicopter to all of the ranger posts in the park over 24, 25 and 26 December.

Chris Marais, who had been at the dinner with Buffett and had a longstanding relationship with the philanthropist, also agreed to help. Begrudgingly, I left Arina at Skukuza and drove to Pretoria where he and I did some joint preparation at his home over 30 and 31 December.

Chris and I worked late on New Year's Eve to finalise the initial proposal, and I drove back to Skukuza to join Arina on the morning of 1 January.

I sent the proposal to Howard Buffett and he then told me to put to put together a detailed project plan to submit to the board of the HGBF in mid-February. In early January, I was able to enlist Charl Petzer, from the CSIR, who assembled a team to write the more in-depth proposal.

Charl, a tall heavyset man in his mid-fifties, with a solid engineering background, was just the man to lead a team who would translate my technology concept into real terms. I knew, however, that the long periods he would have to spend in Kruger doing this would not be easy as he was a devoted family man.

Charl and his team, which fluctuated between four and six people, spent a few weeks in the park in order to gather all the facts they needed and discuss concepts. They also interacted with the ranger leadership, specifically those from the budding IPZ. In Groenkloof, the team thrashed out some joint-planning initiatives with the financial and procurement staff. The team went about their work in a very professional manner, toiling around the clock, confirming our requirements. The plan they came up with was nothing short of a masterpiece set to meet all the expectations of the HGBF project manager.

Three quarters of the way through preparing the project plan, Charl came to see me.

'I have good news and bad news,' Charl said to me.

'Go on,' I said.

'General, the good news is that the plan will be complete in time, but the bad news is that we're way over budget.'

'How much?'

'It will cost us $13 million.'

Charl had already warned me that $10 million may not be enough, but I had told him to 'make a plan'. Now that I was faced with the reality – that we needed $3 million more than I had first suggested to Buffett – I broke the news to him and, while he was clearly irritated, he was not dismissive. The ball was now in their hands for a final decision.

One morning in late February, my cell phone rang at five in the morning. It was Buffett.

'I'm giving you a grant,' he said.

'Thank you.' I held my breath, remembering his annoyance at my miscalculation.

'You didn't ask for a helicopter, but I'm giving you one. I'm giving you $17 million.'

. . .

THINGS MOVED QUICKLY. Just over two weeks later, Buffett flew to South Africa and a function was held at Standard Bank's headquarters in Rosebank. There he handed over a cheque for R255 million. Astonishingly, Buffett had once again upped his donation from the US dollar equivalent of $17 million when he last called me to about $23 million.

'I want you to trial an aerostat as well,' he said, explaining the additional amount. I was over the moon.

The handover presentation was a gala occasion, with plenty of media coverage for the largest single donation ever to SANParks for rhino conservation. The Finance Minister, Pravin Gordhan, was there, as was our Minister for the Environment, Edna Molewa.

'Today, no more than 4 000 rhino are found outside of Africa, while the continent is home to an estimated 25 000 of these ancient animals,' Minister Molewa told assembled dignitaries and journalists. 'South Africa is home to more than 80% of the world's rhino population, a testament to our country's successful conservation practices. It is this successful restoration of the rhino population since the 1960s that makes South Africa the single-most important country in the fight for the survival of the rhino.'

The minister was a force to be reckoned with. Like Mabunda, she had gone out on a limb to endorse my appointment and I was called several times to her home to brief her in person. Although she had her critics during her career, she was, at heart, a woman of great strength and courage. During the apartheid years, she had suffered and been imprisoned – she was nursing an infant child when she was arrested. When she gave media updates on the rhino struggle, it heartened me greatly when she referred to me in media interviews as 'our General'.

Here, in the Standard Bank building, she had also paid tribute to those in the past, in the time of the regime she had fought against, who had brought the rhino back from the brink of extinction once before.

'We would like to assure you, Mr Howard Buffett, that we are determined not to lose this fight,' Minister Molewa said. 'We, as South Africa, certainly do not intend to capitulate and lose the battle for the survival of key members of the iconic Big Five.'

The minister said that a multibillion-rand problem, rhino poaching, needed a multibillion-rand solution. This was a good start.

However, even as the cameras flashed and the good news was transmitted around the world, I knew there were tensions behind the scenes. There were some on the SANParks Board and in Exco who did not want to accept the money from Buffett, and a key board member was not present for the announcement.

The wording of Clause 8 of the agreement between the HGBF's local body, the Nature Conservation Trust (NCT) and SANParks had been the cause of much of the negativity.

It read: 'NCT may terminate this Agreement at its sole discretion at any time by notice to SANParks if Major General (Ret.) Johan Jooste is no longer employed by SAN Parks and/or is no longer able to direct the use of these grant funds to support the Intensive Protection Zone grant for SANParks. If this Agreement terminates pursuant to this section, SANParks must immediately return any Grant funds in its possession which have not been expended for the purpose of this Grant prior to the date of NCT's notice of termination to SAN Parks.'

Even though this was, in fact, well-established good-business practice around the world – to hold one person responsible – the clause was like a red rag to a bull to some, who saw this as a kind of 'white collusion', unduly benefiting me. I knew from the start that there would be no glory for me, no medals hanging on trees for easy plucking. Although Buffett and the NCT had meant no harm, they had inadvertently made my life harder, fuelling jealousies and suspicion.

As a compromise, my name was deleted and replaced with the broader term, 'key personnel in charge of the anti-poaching unit', as a face-saving exercise for others. Even so, this clause would later prove to be one of the major obstacles to getting cooperation from SANParks and the job done in Kruger.

However, I was appointed as chair of a committee to oversee the spending of the grant money. Suddenly, I had the funding I needed to embark on the most expansive and technologically advanced Environmental Asset Protection (EAP) plan in Africa. This amount of money was an unheard of donation to conservation in southern Africa and a fantastic start for our technology programme.

As soon as the ink was dry on the cheque, I facilitated two months' worth of intensive work sessions in Kruger for the CSIR

EAP team, the ranger leadership group and certain industry representatives. The CSIR had appointed Charl Petzer to head up the new EAP team. We all worked hard to reach consensus on the types of technology we would need, and how it should be installed and employed.

There were, however, still challenges to overcome, among them the laborious procedures for procuring the technology and finalising our specifications. At the same time, I knew I needed to bring the rangers along with me, to show them the benefits new technology would bring.

The context and objectives were still clear, as we stuck to our basic approach. We focused on connectivity and situational awareness and refined that into surveillance, early-warning, detection and tracking subsystems, deployed in layers from as far as possible outside the park, up to the perimeter, internally at choke points and around key rhino populations.

We started putting the Buffett money to work, installing a microwave communication system in the IPZ where there was little or no 3G mobile coverage. Having our own 'network' meant that the various sensors we were installing could talk to the ops room and we could communicate with each other. Improved communications would lead to improved response times.

We issued a tender for a fence-mounted seismic detection system on what was left of the eastern boundary fence, along the southern section of the border with Mozambique, on the flank of the IPZ. Any poacher who touched the fence would send instant alarm signals to the ops room and to rangers' smart phones or tablets.

A trench would be dug along the western boundary of the IPZ and a magnetic sensor cable buried underground. According to the operators, this would detect a pocketknife to within 10 metres' accuracy and also send an immediate warning.

Around the same time as the Buffett initiative was launched, Werner Myburgh called me to tell me that the Dutch lotteries had agreed to fund my wish list, which he had appended to the Peace Parks' funding proposal. I now had another R35 million to spend on rangers, mobility and accommodation. In early 2014, work began on construction of the Mission Area Joint Operations Centre, the MAJOC, the building Otch had laid out with baking flour, much to the delight of Skukuza Airport's resident monkeys.

It was a start.

DAVID MABUNDA FLEW to Holland to accept the donation from the lottery, but that didn't worry me, because I was packing my bags again. Once more I kissed Arina goodbye, and headed to the United States of America.

I had reached out to the US Embassy in Pretoria and been very ably assisted by Holly Waeger Monster from the economic section, and Eric Killoran from defence cooperation. Along with the South African Embassy in Washington, they helped put together a packed schedule for my visit in April 2014. Holly would accompany me as a liaison officer.

In Washington I had a working lunch with Jon Jarvis, the director of the US National Park Service. In the evening, I had to sit through another UAV presentation, but I had much more on my agenda for this visit.

South African Ambassador Ebrahim Rasool came to my hotel for breakfast and offered his support, and that of his staff. This was a wonderful gesture on his part and I really felt as though I could make some progress with that kind of backing. I knew that to some extent I had gone out on a limb, as a comparatively junior cog in the machine of government, to approach a foreign government, so it was good to see I had some official backup.

At the US State Department, I met with the deputy assistant secretaries of the Africa Bureau, Environment Bureau and the International Law Enforcement Bureau. Most of the meetings I attended were overwhelmingly welcoming and positive, but later, at a US Fish and Wildlife Service round-table meeting, I found myself being lectured by a bureaucrat who purported to know all about Africa. He lamented the problem of 'the Big C: corruption'.

'It's almost impossible to help Africa, because of the Big C,' he said.

'Corruption is worldwide,' I pointed out to him, when it was my turn to address the round table, 'and while we are in your country, how can we forget the Wall Street crash of 2008, and the recall of tens of thousands of cars in Europe because of Volkswagen's misrepresentation on their emission stats.' Corruption was not some African-centric disease, but rather a manifestation of greed and the pursuit of profit over law or ideology and that was by no mean restricted to the continent of my birth.

I visited the Federal Bureau of Investigation (FBI), the United States Agency for International Development (USAID), and the George Mason University Terrorism, Transnational Crime and Corruption Centre in Arlington, Virginia.

After meetings with five different congressmen on Capitol Hill, Holly took a call on her cell phone. When she finished, she told me she had just been contacted by the South African Defence attaché, a brigadier from our embassy in Washington. Holly passed on a message: I was forbidden to visit the Pentagon, where I had been invited to explore cooperation and support, given the US footprint in Africa. From South Africa, we had arranged for me to meet with various offices of the US Department of Defense, including the Defense Security Cooperation Agency, the Office of the Secretary of Defense, the Africa Centre for Strategic Studies, and State Partnership Program at the Pentagon Conference Centre in Washington.

It was a sour note on what had been an otherwise very positive trip, especially as the ambassador had taken the time to welcome me personally. Politics, it seemed, was rearing its ugly head again back home in South Africa.

At a fundraiser in Washington, my message to the NGOs, government agencies and philanthropists of America was simple: 'A relatively small contribution from this country can make a huge difference, especially if applied on the operational level, where we see little of it.'

Mindful of the sweeping generalisations I'd heard about Africa and corruption, I asked the audience: 'Are we so difficult to do business with?'

When I returned to South Africa, I learned through various sources that one of the state intelligence organisations had opened a file on me. Clearly, there were people in government concerned about an apartheid-era general trying to line up meetings with the US military.

I confess that I was guilty of not going through official channels when organising meetings with international government agencies and politicians. As a former army officer, I knew full well the importance of procedures, correct staff work and chains of command. However, too much talk and a lack of a sense of urgency were partly to blame for the situation we were now in. By contrast, I had people in the private sector and governments around the world only too happy to throw their doors open and put their hands in their pockets to try to help the rhinos.

But from the corridors of power in Pretoria I was getting a clear message – people were asking: 'Who the hell is this oke and where is he getting his money from?'

A chief director from DIRCO, the Department of International Relations and Cooperation, summoned me to Pretoria for an official appointment. I was given a firm but polite dressing down and told to follow official channels in the future when liaising with foreign governments and their agencies.

But the people I was most worried about were the board and

executive of SANParks; although they knew what I was up to, I also had to be mindful that there was infighting between them. I was no stranger to minefields and I took my official warning on the chin; I was reminded of an old saying from my army days: 'If you can't take a joke, you shouldn't have joined.'

Howard Buffett flew to South Africa for a visit in mid-2014 to receive an update on how the various technology projects were unfolding and to indulge in his passion for wildlife photography. I arranged for a chopper to take him and Anne Bolton, the chairperson of the board of the HGBF, to view three gruesome rhino carcass scenes.

One, in particular, was a terrible sight. Just like the one I'd seen with Steven Whitfield, and many others before and since, the poachers, having wounded the rhino with their first shot, had severed the animal's spine with a blow from an axe in order to immobilise it. I showed Buffett how the poor thing had lain there, shaking its huge head from side to side as it breathed its last, ploughing a furrow in the blood-soaked earth.

He snapped away with his camera, recording the horror of this war and its mute victims. As always, it was impossible not to be moved in some way, no matter how many times one bore witness to this type of crime, which seemed as brutal as it was pointless.

Buffett returned to the luxury lodge in the Sabi Sand Game Reserve, just west of Kruger, where he was staying. That evening I was hosting a function for the police at the Skukuza Golf Club, a popular hangout for Kruger Park staff and visitors alike. My phone rang; it was Buffett.

'Anne and myself have realised today that what you need is another helicopter,' he said. 'Buy it, and send me the invoice.'

10

What kind of man plunges an axe into the back of a wounded animal to sever its spine and not put it out of its misery?

From the earliest days working on the CONOPS and the strategy, we had done our appreciation of the battle space and that had involved an assessment of poachers and their tactics. That process never ended, as we continually sought intelligence on the foot soldiers, the middlemen and their bosses.

Because they came from varied backgrounds and had different levels of experience, it was difficult to come up with a profile of a 'typical' poacher. They might be a dirt-poor Mozambican, dressed in rags, or a 'weekend' poacher from Bushbuckridge or Hazyview in South Africa. Hardened criminals, car hijackers or armed robbers who took down cash-in-transit vans had also been known to take to rhino poaching, seeing it, on balance, as a safer way to make several thousand rands than coming up against armed security or the police in the city.

Those who had grown up in the rural areas of Mozambique were natural bush men. From the time they were boys they would have been used to walking, say, a 30-kilometre round trip through the bush to get to school or to a store, or spent time in the bush herding cattle. They navigated by the stars, land beacons such as prominent features, and the glow of lights from towns bordering the park. The poachers never had the luxury of – or need for – GPS or a map, but there were times when they were assisted by former SANParks employees who knew the lay of the land and where to find rhinos. Walking at night was second nature to them and they were tough – they had no rain jacket, no tent, no stout boots.

I often used the contentious phrase that law enforcement in conservation required an iron fist in a velvet glove. It was a reminder to myself that while I was busy turning the Kruger ranger corps into a paramilitary force, the rangers were not soldiers at war – their prime aim was not to kill, but to prevent rhinos from being killed by using the minimum force necessary. We had to be careful not to fall into the trap that so many armchair experts had succumbed to on social media, insisting that poachers be shot on sight. At the same time, we – myself now included – had to face the fact that a poacher might open fire on us without a second thought.

A typical poaching group consisted of three men: a shooter, a carrier and a scout. The bearer might be carrying an axe or a knife to remove the horns, and the group would sometimes also take tinned food, bread, and maybe drugs and/or liquor, depending on how long they planned on being in the park. One member, at least, would have a cell phone for communication with the middleman and perhaps an informant inside Kruger who might be on the lookout for rhinos. The poaching gangs soon learned that our rangers had been trained to demand and search for phones, so prior to being arrested a poacher would often take the SIM card out of a phone and destroy or swallow it. Later, they would use only new SIM cards with no more than one or two calls on them, but these could still be intelligence gold for us, and help secure future convictions.

The poachers would sometimes wear old tekkies or shoes specially modified with the hoof pads of antelope, such as kudu, stuck to the soles to deceive us. They were masters at counter-tracking and would walk backwards, travel over stones, or pull socks or tie branches over their shoes to try to confuse the rangers. Some would take extra soles to stick onto their shoes.

The poachers infiltrated mostly by night and could easily walk about 25 kilometres and set up a makeshift hide to observe the surrounding area for human and animal movement. Water was a dead giveaway in the hunt for rhinos as the big animals must drink daily. Initially, poachers preferred to track their prey by the light of a full moon, but, as we became better organised, they learned that we deployed extra patrols at this time of the month. Poaching bosses took to deploying multiple teams at once, knowing that even with our growing resources we could not hope to plug all the gaps at the border, and that one or two of their teams might well get through.

I brought in the use of deception tactics to help us make poachers think twice about crossing the border or entering particular hotspots. I ordered the rangers and the Air Wing to adopt a 'gunship mode' tactic. This involved a chopper flying high for a while, deliberately making itself visible to any poachers in the area, then dropping down low over a predetermined area, out of sight and sound of any tourists, and which we had checked for animals. A senior ranger and another on board would then fire their rifles on full-automatic at a clearly identified spot on the ground, often a dry riverbed, where the fall of shot could be clearly observed. By shooting up a well-observed piece of empty bushland, word soon spread that SANParks was using 'helicopter gunships'.

Another tactic was to spread a rumour that we were using satellites and could detect poachers moving at night. That wasn't true at the time, but it hopefully caused some concern. In time, however, the poachers learned that these were, in fact, ruses.

Often, the poachers would try to do their shooting in the late afternoon, harvest the horns in the dark, and then run like hell to exit Kruger before the sun came up. Except in an extreme emergency, our helicopter operations were limited to daylight hours, but I was working on a plan to have our pilots trained in the US to fly using night-vision goggles, which we would also have to purchase. When searching a poacher, it was usually revealed he was carrying muthi, the potions or talismans prescribed by izangoma, traditional healers. A poacher would visit a sangoma prior to setting off on a hunt; this was to receive treatments that would make him bulletproof, or allow him to turn to water, or assume the shape of an animal in order to confuse the rangers tracking him.

Rifles could be 'blessed' with symbolic string tied around the stock, or the working parts sprinkled with snuff. Weapons were sometimes bathed in water infused with herbs that would bring good luck. Muthi could be powders or even animal parts – one poacher was found to be carrying a dried porcupine foetus.

It would be easy to dismiss such beliefs – that a person could be made invisible, for instance – as superstitious rubbish, but one only had to look at the experience of war, or even elite sport, to know that people engaged in high-risk, high-reward endeavours – poaching falls into that category – place a high stock in rituals, good-luck charms and religious or spiritual beliefs. As the old saying goes, there are no atheists in foxholes.

A poacher carrying muthi being captured or killed did not mean people stopped believing in the rituals or talismans, but rather that the user had violated the rules associated with the medicine, such as waiting too long to use it, or having sex before the mission. Even captured poachers believed they could purchase additional muthi from a sangoma to confuse the prosecutors or magistrate when their case came to court. For all of this, the poachers paid handsomely, supporting a thriving informal micro-economy.

Some of our rangers would go to izangoma for their own potions to help them in their hunting. Academics commissioned by SANParks to study this business dubbed it the 'invisible arms race'.

I was always amazed at the poachers' survival skills and hardiness; I sometimes quietly admired their mix of courage and recklessness, operating by night in Big Five country, and their grit and determination. One had to remember, though, that what drove these men was the promise of a plastic bag full of cash, which would be split amongst the three. The money they received was a fraction of what rhino horn was selling for on the Asian market, but a potential life changer for a poor poacher.

I could begrudgingly admire them, but I could never forget, nor forgive, the cruelty these people were inflicting on defenceless animals, which are part of our natural heritage, and the impact their actions were having on our rangers and their families.

One Sunday, after attending the service at the NG Kerk in Skukuza, Arina and I were sitting quietly on the stoep, enjoying a cup of coffee, when three full-grown male kudu walked into our garden. They began feeding, hooking branches with their long spiralled horns and pulling the foliage down to their mouths. I sat there, momentarily moved by the simple sight of animals peacefully going about their business, as God had intended.

This was what we were fighting for.

In 2014, we started a campaign within the judicial system for all rhino-poaching charges originating from the Kruger Park to be heard at the Skukuza courthouse.

The court only sat a few days a month, with cases heard by a visiting magistrate, but we were pushing for the court to sit full time. As tough as it was in the bush and the boardroom, fighting poaching and trying to secure funding, the work of seeing the arrest of a rhino poacher through to a conviction and jail time was an enormous task.

Much of the burden fell to two state prosecutors, advocates Isabet Erwee and Ansie Venter, and the team of detectives in Kruger. At any one point, the advocates would each be dealing with a stack of arrest dockets a metre and a half high on their desks, facing up against aggressive defence lawyers, lying poachers and distraught families.

Hearing more cases at Skukuza, rather than having them transferred to courthouses in surrounding towns, made sense on a number of fronts. Rangers who had to be called to give evidence would not be out of the field for nearly as long if they only had to travel to Skukuza and we would be spared the cost of transporting them and accommodating them in other locations.

Secondly, the Skukuza court and its staff were developing a reputation for expertise and effectiveness in dealing with these cases. Unlike a magistrate or judge elsewhere, those presiding at Skukuza could not be so readily hoodwinked by a smooth-talking defence attorney. Lastly, there was the security aspect. Ansie, Isabet and our rangers had all been scorned and intimidated by angry mobs of poachers' friends and family when they attended court outside the park. Ansie's tyres had been slashed, and she had received death threats from poaching kingpins and middlemen. This was a war that was as dirty and murky in the courts and on the streets of Mpumalanga and Limpopo provinces as it was deadly in the bush.

Time after time, however, Ansie and Isabet won their cases, and the poachers, and even some of the middlemen, were put away.

Early in my tenure, Ansie spoke to me about the issue of poachers being injured in the course of their arrest. In training, we stressed that only minimum force should be used, but I knew too that there was a human element at play. After chasing poachers all night, or doing a follow-up operation over many kilometres in the scorching heat of day, and after encountering mutilated rhino carcasses, I could understand how a ranger might fall prey to emotions. This was no excuse for assault, although sometimes a poacher might be injured if they struggled while resisting arrest or trying to escape. Whatever the reason for injuries, defence attorneys were making much of the issue when poachers came to court.

Ansie followed up our first brief discussion of this matter with a phone call.

'General, you know how much I respect you,' she began in a rather formal tone, 'but since I have spoken to you already about my colleagues and me being confronted in court because of injured poachers, I now wish to tell you that this is the last time I'm going to talk to you about this in this manner. The next time my response will be in writing, and there will be consequences.'

'I understand,' I said.

'Please, General, man,' she added, her tone almost sisterly as she beseeched me.

I respected Ansie immensely and it was time for me to act. I sent out a group email making my position on this matter clear, and reinforced it at my next monthly meeting of the leadership team.

'We are a civilised law-enforcement agency that does not take the law into its own hands,' I said, making eye contact with those in the room. 'We will not undo the hard work we have done so far, nor encumber those working with us in the courts. When you arrest someone, you are not allowed to get physical, unless you have no other option in order to subdue a person. The choice is simple: do this job right, or risk a poacher's case being dismissed in court.

Discipline prevailed, and with the help of all, we made this problem go away.

ONE OF THE best-known and most infamous poaching kingpins was Simon Ernesto Valoi, who went by the nickname 'Navara', supposedly because the Nissan 4x4 of the same name was his favourite target during his alleged previous career, as a car hijacker.

Living in a big, gaudily painted house in one of the two villages inside the Great Limpopo Transfrontier Park, Navara was sought out by a German journalist and a Swedish photographer, who were seeking to do an investigative story on the rhino trade.

When the pair showed up at Navara's house, his wife called him and he mobilised a gang of youths, who surrounded the media team and kidnapped them. They were taken to a local police station and then to Massingir. Their reports inferred that the local police were either under Navara's control, or too scared to challenge him; the police, they said, were going to charge them with trespassing. Fearing for their lives, the pair was eventually liberated after the Swedish embassy intervened.

Whatever was alleged about Navara, he remained at large. Reports estimated that he controlled about 15 poaching gangs. Like other alleged middlemen, the word was that he gained patronage and recruits by promising to pay 'large' sums to successful poaching teams, and to cover the costs of funerals and compensation payments to the families of poachers killed in action.

So, although we were succeeding on a daily basis in the field at the tactical level by cooperating with the rangers and authorities on the other side of the border, entrenched corruption and endemic collusion continued to hamper us and the Mozambican police, preventing us from catching the Navaras of this world.

The Mozambican kingpins operated with impunity, driving poaching gangs right to the border, unchecked, in their luxury 4x4s – Section Ranger Steven Whitfield once interviewed a suspect who said he and his men had been transported in a Range Rover.

Corruption was not confined to Mozambique – in South Africa we had our own 'Mr Bigs' and while the media was ready to identify them when they were caught with large sums of cash and firearms, securing convictions for these wealthy, well-connected individuals was difficult. At the foot-soldier level, a group of five SANParks employees had been caught red-handed killing rhinos a few months before my appointment, but their trial dragged on all through 2013 and 2014.

Kruger's rangers were catching more and more poachers, but these foot soldiers could always be replaced. What was needed was better intelligence and more work by the police on both sides of the border in order to collapse the poaching networks and bring down the kingpins.

I knew about Navara, but there was little I could do about him from my side of the border. What I will say is that I harboured some very un-Christian thoughts about that individual.

MARIUS ROOS and his Pathfinder intelligence team had been doing solid work trying to target the poaching syndicates. In early 2014, they had just notched up another success, passing on intelligence to the police directorate of priority crime investigations, which led to the arrest of three Chinese men in Johannesburg, reportedly members of a triad gang.

Funding for Pathfinder had run out at the end of 2013 and Marius offered to work pro bono until I could raise money, somehow, to keep him and his people going. As it happened, Howard Buffett was impressed with the work they were doing and I had included funding for Pathfinder in my submission to the HGBF. Because I had found money for them outside of the SANParks system, it looked as though everything was going to be fine.

One Saturday afternoon, not long after news of the triad bust, I was sitting in the garden of my house at Skukuza, working on the laptop, when my phone rang. It was Abe Sibaya.

'Fire Pathfinder,' he said.

The news was a blow, but had apparently come from the top, from Minister Molewa. There was immediate speculation in the media that Pathfinder had been sacked because they were 'too successful', hinting that highly placed people, perhaps complicit in poaching, wanted the intelligence company gone before the rotten apples were exposed.

In reality, I thought the decision was more based on politics – both South African and internally within SANParks. I had been carpeted by DIRCO for attempting to make contact with the Pentagon; and many in power in the ANC still remembered the days when America tacitly supported the apartheid regime. There were rumours that Pathfinder had links to the US as well, not helped by the fact that Marius had accompanied me on my trip to the US.

Sam Ferreira had been involved with a US academic, with some input from Pathfinder, in analysing cell-phone numbers we had taken from poachers' phones and SIM cards. They had been looking for trends in calls to and from these numbers, not hacking into messages or listening in; however, this research added to a growing perception, by some, that America was 'poking its nose' into our business, or spying on people on the African continent.

On hearing that Pathfinder was to be dismissed, I dug in my heels and went in to bat for them, but I soon figured out that I was fighting a losing battle and needed to save my political capital for similar challenges in the future. Not even an investigation by the SAPS head of detectives, ordered by the ministry at the time of the sacking, could save Pathfinder, even though the findings were resoundingly favourable.

I feared that Pathfinder had not been a victim of its own success, but rather of internal high-level gossip and paranoid speculation. This was more about bureaucracy, jealousy and the ongoing tension between the board and senior management than entrenched corruption.

In a way, that made the decision even harder to stomach. We could have rooted corruption out; politics was here to stay.

The media went into a frenzy and Howard Buffett, who learned of the news in America, was angry. I told him I was revising the funding plan.

'Show me,' he said, 'how you will now have access to intelligence. You can't do this without intelligence.'

He was right. I proposed that we use the money he had earmarked for Pathfinder to expand our Environmental Crime Investigation unit; my plan was to hire former police investigators to bolster the ranks. ECI had been busy investigating corruption and other crimes committed within the park, but I now needed them to take over from Pathfinder, which had begun setting up intelligence and informer networks outside the park. This had led them to the Chinese triad members.

While the quest to become proactive had been dealt a blow by Pathfinder's sacking, on the positive side, this gave renewed impetus to continue to transform and expand ECI, and improve their cooperation with other agencies. In time, their dedicated effort made them indispensable.

At a time when we were finally seeing progress – through increased training, better equipment, improved communications, joint operations with our allies, more aircraft and vehicles, and the introduction of new technology – petty internal politics and jealousy handed the poachers and their bosses, evil people such as Navara, a bonus.

Later, SANParks head office commissioned a private investigator to look into any alleged conflicts of interest or flaunting of regulations between myself, David Mabunda and Pathfinder. We were all cleared of any wrongdoing.

11

The traditional 'sundowner' is as much a part of a safari in South Africa as the Big Five – lion, leopard, buffalo, elephant and, of course, rhino.

The foreign tourists had enjoyed their afternoon game drive on one of the private concessions in the Kruger Park. Late in the dry season the skies are still clear, the air warm, and the bush sheds its green summer foliage to allow for excellent viewing of animals and birds.

Tradition dictated, in the world of the luxury safari lodge, that just before the sun sets the field guide (known as a 'ranger' in the tourism industry) and his or her tracker would stop the vehicle and produce a table, tablecloth, and a cooler box full of drinks and snacks.

On this particular afternoon, the lodge management had arranged a surprise for their guests. Rather than waiting for the ranger and tracker to set up, staff behind the scenes had gone out to a scenic spot in the park and already laid the table. It was groaning with booze, food, ice and glasses.

When the vehicle pulled up at the site of the surprise there was carnage. Plates were upended, and some of the snacks and drinks had been consumed. The ranger, now trying to placate his annoyed guests, might have thought some wildlife had beaten them to the sundowner rendezvous. When a complaint was received at the ops room it took very little investigating to identify who had raided the impromptu picnic: the South African National Defence Force.

I HAD TO BE DIPLOMATIC, and tried my best to remain positive, but the fact was I was getting nowhere when it came to influencing the SANDF's contribution, behaviour and tactics inside the Kruger National Park.

I had been, and always will be, proud to associate with the South African Army. While, as a leader I knew full well that soldiers could get up to mischief, incidents such as the raiding of the sundowner spot were painfully disappointing. They spoke of a lack of discipline.

There were many who thought that my former career in the military would set me up to forge strong links with the military element in the park. For some time, there had been a company-strength task force based in Kruger. By law, the SANDF's rules of engagement did not allow it to engage in anti-poaching operations within South Africa, but it could operate in Kruger simply because poachers were violating our national border by crossing in from Mozambique.

However, right from the start I could see there were going to be problems. The idea of having an overall commander for the anti-poaching effort had been discussed prior to my appointment, but both the military and the police thought the job should have been theirs. So, rather than the army welcoming me with open arms, I was seen as someone who had robbed a serving general of an important, high-profile operational command.

Having worked with and trained many of them during the period of transition when President Mandela came to power, I was lucky that I could count the highest levels of the SANDF leadership as friends, but in the park, at the operational commander level, it was a different story.

I worked with a succession of army commanders, and each time a new company rotated in I would sit down with the officer commanding and try to explain the realities of the fight we were engaged in. I stressed that our successes came from deploying two-person ranger patrols, which relied, more often than not, on their skill in tracking to find the poachers before they found a rhino.

'Your best chance of success,' I told a new battalion commander, 'is to deploy where and how our ground truthing says you should deploy, not blindly according to your doctrine. Flexibility is one of the principles of war.'

I was wasting my breath. These officers had been conventionally trained and saw their mission as one of dominating the ground, seizing and holding terrain, and denying the enemy movement – and rightly so. This was their doctrine, but anti-poaching operations were specialised and required different tactics and techniques.

I tried to encourage the army officers to break their 10-man sections into smaller patrols, or sticks of five men, so that they might move more quietly. Instead, they stuck to their doctrine of setting up platoon bases in the bush, with lights on at night, and sending their soldiers out on routine daytime patrols.

The poachers mocked them. 'We use their fires at night to navigate by,' we were told during interviews. 'We simply walk around their bases.'

There was no way an infantry section could sneak up on a three-man poaching team. Conversely, it was impossible to get the military, even Special Forces, to accept that a two-person patrol was viable.

Our Special Forces were good, but, in their defence, the role and training of elite forces around the world was moving more towards urban and counter-terrorism operations. On top of this reality was a negative perception about training for a counterinsurgency war; that brought up too many bad memories for those in power of the war they had been through and the regime they had fought against. The South African government – and national defence force – saw its role as protecting the nation, not fighting guerrillas. Our reality, however, was that this was exactly the type of war we were involved with: low-level operations against a highly motivated adversary working in small groups.

The figures spoke for themselves. Yes, a poacher would sometimes open fire on one of our patrols, but because of their training, especially with regards to immediate action drills, our rangers were consistently coming out on top. Also, as soon as a gang was sighted, our rangers would have called in support, in the form of a helicopter, more rangers and, increasingly, a dog.

Many rangers and commentators threw glib military expressions around on social media and in strategy meetings all the time. 'You need to own the night,' I would be told. How? I would ask. Unless every ranger had a set of state-of-the-art night-vision goggles, my pilots were trained for night flying, and the army decided to work rather than sleep at night, then this was not possible. Instead, we opted to own a 'slice' of the night, with well-sited observation posts, some night patrols, and the increasing use of technology to detect poachers and predict their direction of movement or next stop.

I argued that the challenge was intelligent deployment, rather than merely more numbers. I tried a different tack, offering to attach my rangers to military patrols. The army reluctantly agreed; however, I then had a near-mutiny on my hands when the rangers, used to notching up successes against poachers, insisted they did not want to work with soldiers.

'They stop too often to rest,' a ranger said to me, complaining about working with the army. 'They will never catch a poacher because they make such a noise.'

Don English briefed me on one operation, showing me the forces deployed in his region. I noticed he had an army unit marked on his map, but he had neglected to mention its role in the operation.

'Why will you not make use of the army?' I asked him.

He looked at me, deadpan. 'Thanks, General, but give me something I can use.'

I felt my anger rise. 'You've got the wrong attitude, Don.'

After the meeting, we argued. I told my rangers to stick with it, to give the military a chance to learn, but, after two months, rangers again started refusing to deploy with army patrols. There was no benefit in me forcing the issue, dragging rangers along kicking and screaming for the sake of inter-service politics. Besides, it wasn't working and I could see the rangers' side. It wasn't Don's attitude that was the problem; it was the army's.

The army also left a trail of complaints from visitors to the park in their wake. We had to deal with reports of speeding vehicles, litter, noise from the bases and after-hours movements. The rangers were, in turn, a victim of their own success; the better they became and the more outstanding their results, the more the army doubled down, out of professional jealousy, and refused to change their tactics. How, the army was asking itself, could a bunch of civilian rangers know better than them?

There was a never-ending tide of poachers and they seemed to have no problem filling the ranks left by their casualties, but if the ranger effort could have been at least matched by some other force, we could have seen immediate results. It wasn't.

I HAD similar problems with the police.

By 2013, the South African Police Service had all but washed its hands of rhino poaching and the Kruger Park, with only a few detached officers on duty in the park. The initial energy and zest that had come when the scourge of poaching was first attacked, along with huge acclaim, was gone.

I set about using every formal and informal opportunity to push for the police to take their rightful role in pursuing poaching as a priority crime. This was essential if we were to clear the park from the outside and bring down the poaching networks, leaving the rangers to focus on the park itself.

Fortunately, Minister Molewa understood the urgency of the matter and lobbied the police minister to bring the SAPS back into the campaign. However, as with the army, senior ranks already had their noses out of joint that I, ex-army and now a civilian, had been brought in over their heads. I saw the worst of professional jealousy, personal judgement and prejudice from senior SAPS members and from the National Joint Management Structures, whose role was to ensure coordination between government departments on wildlife crime. They were too keen to find fault and tried to pin the increase in rhino deaths on the rangers and even me personally.

It was the role of police to investigate crime scenes, but due to a lack of resourcing, there were already about 200 investigations in arrears. We needed the police to process DNA samples and ballistics, and to analyse cell-phone records. I also believed the police needed to do more about crushing crime networks adjacent to Kruger and throughout the country. The fact was that hundreds of rhino horns were moved by road from Kruger to the Gauteng area, and yet interceptions were few and far between. I expected the police to be able to disrupt poaching supply chains, but they were behind on all of these critical indicators.

One very capable senior police officer, however, was Lieutenant General Vinesh Moonoo, the national head of detectives. He could see that the police needed to be doing more in Kruger. Vinesh took a personal interest in what was happening in the park. He didn't believe in meetings and, instead, would come out to the park every three weeks to see what was going on and what was needed. He visited crime scenes and helped the detectives in the park with their work on the ground.

As a result of his interest, he promoted the head of the detectives in Kruger, Francois Vermaak, to captain and gave his team the resources they needed, including vehicles, a travel budget and cell-phone contracts – Vinesh put his money where his mouth was. Very soon, Kruger's detectives became a force to be reckoned with, amassing considerable experience in the investigation of poachers and shooting incidents, and expanding their intelligence network.

Advocates Joanie Spies and Petra van Basten from the National Prosecuting Authority (NPA) contacted me and asked me to join them in a high-level intervention in relation to the backlog of about 200 criminal investigations. Criminal dockets were being opened, but the backlog was getting worse, with tens of new cases emerging each month, and nothing was happening.

A meeting was called at Silverton, Pretoria, with Joanie, Petra, the deputy head of the NPA, a number of police generals, and me. Amongst the police representatives was the head of the Hawks. There was an air of unease in the conference room from the moment we started.

Joanie bravely, and articulately, began by asking how it could be that so few of the cases that had been opened had undergone even the most basic of crime-scene investigations. With more dockets being opened every month, something had to be done about the situation.

A senior police officer countered, refuting the claim that the backlog was so great, claiming that the figures being quoted were being taken out of context. We were being stonewalled.

At that point, Petra leaned back from the table, picked her lawyer's briefcase up from beside her chair and opened it. From the bag she took a stack of 50 dockets, all relating to rhino-poaching cases and all having been opened by the Skukuza Police Station. Petra set the stack of folders on the table in front of her and, one by one, began opening them.

As she opened each docket, the evidence was there – or, rather, not there – to see. Each of the folders was empty, with not even the flimsiest of paperwork that would reflect the depth of investigation needed to secure a conviction.

The police were red-faced. There were mutterings that they did not have the capacity and that the matter warranted further attention.

What a dismal effort, I thought to myself as I sat there watching these two impressive women coolly, yet forcefully, put their case. It was no wonder we were losing so many rhino. Yes, the onslaught of poachers was relentless, but, if the police had been able to match the effort our rangers were now putting in, things could be different.

After the meeting, I hosted tea and sandwiches at the nearby Botanical Gardens. It was a rather quiet and subdued affair, with all of us contemplating what we had achieved – or failed to achieve – and what the consequences would be if the SAPS complained about us skipping lines of reporting and authority by bringing on this intervention.

Joanie turned to me. 'General, no matter what, you have our support from National.' We parted, and I hurried back to Kruger with a five-hour drive ahead of me.

It wasn't long before news of the backlog made it to parliament and the media; tensions between departments became strained, as ministers demanded answers from their subordinates. Friends came into conflict with each other.

I was getting on well with Lieutenant General Moonoo; he would often come to my place at Skukuza on his visits to the park. On one such visit, he opened up with a salvo.

'General,' he said, 'what are you going to do about this backlog in crime-scene investigations? I want to see progress.'

I squared up to him, ready to shirtfront him. 'This is a police responsibility. You tell me what you are going to do about this and I will tell you how I can support you.'

Vinesh admitted they needed help and, taking our dispute indoors, we sat down and talked the matter through. I could see things from the police point of view. If I were head of detectives or the Hawks then, with all of the other crime-related issues in South Africa, I would probably put catching rhino poachers at about number 10 on my list of priorities.

What I tried to stress to Vinesh and others, however, was that the rhino war was bigger than ranger versus poacher. This was a transnational crime, with trafficking in wildlife ranking among the trade in drugs, humans and arms in terms of its value. We needed the police to match our effort, not in the bush, but catching the poaching bosses and stopping South African poachers before they even reached Kruger's fence.

While the police had been in Kruger in force in 2011 when the rhino war had kicked off, the novelty had now worn off. They – and the army – were happy to regurgitate the figures of poachers' arrests (even though it was our rangers who were catching the suspects), but what was not making it to the media, until the current scandal aired, was that there was little or no follow-through on so many of these cases.

Vinesh was doing a good job bolstering the detectives in Kruger, but more was needed. We agreed that even though crime-scene investigation was a SAPS responsibility, I would dedicate ECI investigators to assist with this role. If that meant more poachers made it to court and were prosecuted, then it would be worth it. What happened, however, was that once we took over the crime-scene investigation, our ECI people – such as senior investigator Frikkie Rossouw – became so good at it the police abdicated virtually all responsibility for this crucial part of the law-enforcement process.

The full importance and impact of this job are hard to describe. Each rhino had to be examined. For a freshly killed animal, this involved cutting into the tough skin and then hacking and, literally, wading into the blood and gore of the slaughtered beast. Using a hand-held metal detector, the investigator would listen for the whine of the bullet projectile, which then had to be dug out, bagged and tagged. Bones had to be inspected for signs of the entry wound. If the carcass was not fresh, as was frequently the case, the crime-scene technician had to deal with the almost overpowering stench of decaying flesh and swarms of flies under the unforgiving African sun.

Frikkie himself carried out more than a thousand of these investigations. As well as our own Air Wing pilots, volunteer pilots, such as Tokkie Botes, would have to fly the investigators from crime scene to crime scene, sometimes three or more in a single day. Tokkie had his own helicopter, and the donation of his time and chopper for weeks on end amounted to a contribution of millions of rand in kind.

This was draining work, physically and emotionally, with Frikkie and the others in his team confronted again and again with the undiluted savagery of the war and the killing. They saw rhinos with their whole faces hacked off; those who had died slow, painful deaths; and the calves who had either been killed by the poachers or, more often than not, taken by hyenas on the spot because they were too confused and frightened to leave their dead mother's side. It was horrific, dirty work, but ECI did it with unparalleled dedication and professionalism.

Our success with Lieutenant General Moonoo was not to last.

With his departure from the service, the pendulum swung yet again. With rhino losses – and arrests – on the rise, senior SAPS officers once more eyed the Kruger as a place that deserved their attention. It seemed to me that as many police as possible wanted to earn what I called their 'Kruger Medal'.

A new system, under the name of 'Operation Rhino', was introduced, in which teams of detectives drawn from around South Africa were rotated through Kruger on six-week deployments.

One very professional SAPS unit that served in the park for a few months, and that I requested for redeployment there at the height of the poaching epidemic, was the Special Task Force, the elite police tactical unit. The contingent was keen to join my force again. In fact, a detachment was already driving on the national road on its way to Kruger when they were ordered from Operation Rhino headquarters to turn their vehicles around and go home. It seemed the task force and I had fallen foul of internal police politics.

Whereas Moonoo had resourced and enabled a core team of detectives in Kruger who had become experts in the field of antipoaching, we now had teams of outsiders who had neither the experience nor the tenure to see cases through from arrest to conviction.

There was infighting over space and roles in the ops room and each new rotation had to be briefed at length on the situation. I tried to work with these contingents and their commanders, and brief them on the work we were doing in the field, as well as our engagements with Mozambique, but it was not easy.

Tempers sometimes boiled over. 'We are not here to babysit the police,' my head of Ranger Support, Mbongeni Tukela, said during one of the endless SAPS meetings. Mbongeni's sentiments were spot on, but they resonated upwards to Pretoria. I had to do some damage control, but did so on Mbongeni's behalf with no regret.

I once spent two hours in one of these meetings and raised the prospect of the SAPS doing more to engage with their counterparts across the border.

'This can't be done,' the senior police commander told me. 'Our current bilateral agreements don't allow us to do any more and this would require high-level intervention.'

Just then, there was a soft knock on the door. As the host of the meeting, I got up and answered. When I opened the door, I walked out and saw Kobus de Wet, head of ECI, with four Mozambican police officers who had come to question some recently detained poacher suspects. Kobus had excellent relations with his counterparts in Mozambique and had been instrumental in mounting many successful joint operations with them.

All of the visitors from across the border were wearing the 'Operation Lebombo' branded shirts we'd had specially embroidered. They were now regular visitors, but Kobus explained that they just wanted a minute to greet me. We shook hands and there were warm smiles and back-slapping. The irony was not lost on me that here we were, doing exactly what the police said could not be done.

It can be done, I told myself as I walked back into the interminable, unproductive meeting with our police service.

IN ADDITION to running a joint operation with partners who were either obstructionist or simply not interested, I lost a key supporter in early 2014 when David Mabunda's contract was not renewed.

The writing had probably been on the wall. There had been months of tension building, not only between the board and Exco, but between both of those groups and David. During this period, I had found myself in a unique position – I had access to top management, but very little management attention or supervision. That allowed me to carry on with my programme and make some decisions almost unilaterally.

The fallout from Pathfinder's sacking continued. Nigel Morgan, a Pathfinder board member, went on Tamara LePine-Williams's popular radio programme on Classic FM and lambasted the SANParks leadership for depriving the fight against poaching of the critical element of intelligence.

Nigel was understandably angry, but took it a bit too far with some claims of incompetence and corruption. In almost the same breath, he said: 'Huge credit needs to be paid to General Johan Jooste, who directs special operations at Kruger National Park, and his team of just under 400 rangers. Those rangers are risking their lives every day to try to keep the casualty rates of the rhinos down and they should be the ones getting the money, and not the fat cats sitting in the Pretoria head office of SANParks.'

Nigel's comments were well meant, but his allegations spread like wildfire through Groenkloof and the rest of the organisation. Abe Sibaya, who had been the head of Kruger, had been bumped up to acting CEO of SANParks after David's departure; he sent an email after the interview, which he saw as vindication of the decision to terminate Pathfinder's contract.

This is what happens if you let the enemy into your ranks, Abe wrote.

I was out in the field, visiting ranger posts and waiting for the helicopter to be refuelled at Punda Maria in the far north of Kruger when my phone rang. It was Danie Pienaar, who had been elevated to acting Managing Executive of Kruger.

Danie asked if I had heard about the radio interview and I told him I had.

'This is not good for you, Johan,' Danie told me, candidly.

'Shit, I know, Danie!'

Nigel had unwittingly played into the hands of my detractors.

Both Danie and Abe understood my quest and my situation, but they were intimidated by a board on the warpath. As well as losing support, there were some senior people in SANParks who were gunning for me. It seemed that the best I could hope for, when I tried to garner support for whatever urgent or controversial project I was pursuing, was a neutral response from the board or Exco. Often, I went solo and took bold decisions by myself; I was prepared to face the consequences and a few times this approach did backfire on me.

Danie would often offload to me after returning to Kruger from Exco meetings in Pretoria.

'Abe says I must manage you carefully,' he told me. 'Exco feels you have appointed too many whites on contract.'

I was never one to buy into conspiracy theories, but something else Danie relayed to me was particularly disheartening.

'Members of Exco feel you're acting outside your mandate in your pursuit of corruption after integrity testing,' he said. Although I had been legally unable to prosecute anyone for failing a polygraph – integrity testing, as we had euphemistically dubbed it – Danie was aware that I was using the results as a prompt for future investigations or to keep an eye on people. This, it seemed, was not popular.

At the height of the war, I had to frequently tear myself away from the park to chair meetings and intervene at head office. This meant getting up at 4 am and travelling two hours to Nelspruit for the early flight to Pretoria. I would have to leave Pretoria late afternoon, then transfer back to OR Tambo Airport in Johannesburg for the late flight back to Nelspruit. By the time I arrived home at my house in Skukuza it would be 10 pm and I would be up and back at action stations at five the next morning. So when my leaders at Groenkloof had the audacity to then question my travel expenses, that not only made me lose even further respect for them, but also more determined to carry on the path I had set myself.

Bliksem, I thought to myself, give a chap a chance.

12

'You must withdraw these two female rangers, General,' Rethea Myburgh-Fincham said to me.

Tannie Rethea, as the rangers fondly called her, was their psychologist. She had first been contacted at her practice in the picturesque town of Sabie by the former chief ranger in Kruger, Mbongeni Tukela, back in early 2011, when the rhino war had begun to heat up. Even in those early days, the impact of combat was being felt and observed in the ranger corps.

Rethea was now our on-call psychologist, a key person in ensuring the protection of our ranger base. She, more than most out of uniform, knew the horrors our people were confronted with, and the potential harm it could do to them.

Counselling was offered to rangers who had been in armed contacts with poachers, and to those who were feeling the accumulated stresses of the job. We were now experiencing an operational tempo in which it was quite conceivable for a newly trained ranger to be involved in a gunfight with poachers on his or her first patrol, or within the first month in the field. Sometimes, rangers were involved in multiple contacts in a single day.

Rethea had been in sessions with two of our female rangers from the Houtboschrand sector, who had been in several firefights, in which there had been fatalities. Added to the trauma of seeing bodies and being involved in shootouts, rangers had to deal with the constant, grisly spectre of dead or dying rhinos, or orphaned calves squealing for their lost mothers. At the time, it was common practice for us not to rescue orphans. They were left to be killed by hyenas or lions, as would have been the case if their mother had died of natural causes – not that there was anything other than old age that could have killed a full-grown rhino. It was not natural that their mothers had been killed by humans, but there was no recognised facility at the time that could care for orphaned rhinos. Rethea told me that I needed to speak to the two female rangers and tell them they had done enough. I made appointments to see them.

Tannie Rethea was diagnosing rangers with burnout and early symptoms of post-traumatic stress disorder, or PTSD, a condition first formally diagnosed among Vietnam veterans, but one with that soldiers from any conflict in history could probably identify – in the First World War the term 'shell shock' was coined. Initially thought to affect those people who were prone to anxiety, more recent research had shown that anyone who was exposed to a major traumatic incident, or a number of lesser incidents that posed a threat to their well-being could develop PTSD.

In an article she wrote for the Game Rangers' Association magazine she recalled the case of a young ranger who experienced psychotic-like symptoms, having lost touch with reality for periods of time. Triggers that reminded rangers of situations they had been in could cause them to act in an inappropriate or even dangerous manner.

Wives and the families of rangers were feeling the effects as well, with rangers returning home from duty unable to function as normal in social situations, often becoming moody or withdrawn.

Like other veterans with PTSD, some would turn to alcohol or cannabis to cope with their stress or to block the memories.

In late 2013, Rethea organised two 'indabas' for the wives of our special rangers and those working along the Mozambican border in the south of the park – these were the true frontline forces of our efforts at the time. She was able to listen to the concerns of the wives and partners, and help them with strategies that would assist them in dealing with ranger spouses who were physically and emotionally drained from weeks of battle and patrolling.

She talked to rangers who had been caught in the crossfire between poachers and a team of special rangers who had been called into assist them – how none of the rangers was wounded or killed was a miracle – and help these men and women deal with the mixed emotions of relief, anger and pity they experienced when taking the life of a poacher. Rethea herself talked of feeling sick when hearing the accounts of wounded rhinos that had been crippled by an axe blow, and the image of the blood trail an injured rhino had left when crawling, using only its rear legs to propel itself forward before it died.

Our rangers were strong, mostly drawn from cultures with their own deep beliefs and hierarchical systems, so it was something of a surprise to me when I gave a brief knock on the door of Rethea's office, walked in to ask her a question, and saw a tall ranger lying on his back on the floor, eyes closed and arms raised in the air.

I had no idea she was seeing a client. Rethea talked softly to him, helping him recount and express what was worrying him.

Seeing the disapproving look in her eye, I quickly and softly closed the door, retreating. I was left incredibly moved by the image of this tough guy from another culture lying at Tannie Rethea's feet, having placed his total trust, perhaps even his soul, in her soft but capable hands.

I followed up on my appointment with the two female rangers at their post.

'You've done your best and you must be proud of yourselves,' I said to both of them, 'but now let's not deploy you. I must take you out of the field.'

'No, General,' each of them said to me, respectfully, but firmly.

They refused to leave the fight.

. . .

FROM THE AIR-CONDITIONED comfort of the family car, or the elevated perch of a breezy, open game viewer, Kruger is paradise. On foot, tracking a man who is prepared to kill to defend his ill-gotten prize, it is hell.

Baking hot, with temperatures exceeding 40 degrees in the day in summer, and freezing cold on a moonlit night in the middle of winter, rangers also had to contend not only with snakes – one survived a potentially fatal bite from a deadly black mamba, thanks to immediate medical care and evacuation – but also big game, torrential rain, thorn bushes, crocodile-infested rivers, malaria and the constant threat of being shot at by a poacher.

Our rangers worked from remote outposts and patrol bases, often away from their families for protracted periods. When they went home on leave to local towns, such as Mkhulu, instead of being lauded as heroes, they and their families would sometimes be snubbed and shunned at the Shoprite supermarket, or even abused. One of our rangers ended up in a coma for a month after being beaten unconscious by members of a poacher's family.

The conditions bred tough, resilient people and the job required guts, courage and initiative. A ranger's strongest and weakest quality was obstinance. They needed to be rock solid, completely committed and unwavering when it came to chasing after a poacher for kilometres in a heatwave, or standing up to a charging elephant. However, rangers can be equally stubborn and fixed in their ways when it came to embracing renewal and change.

I had banished the notion that night patrols were little more than 'camping' expeditions, complete with tents, and had convinced them that entering and sharing intelligence would benefit them as well as others. I also needed to take more time to assist them on the journey needed to embrace and use our new resources.

They had moved on – the tents were gone and night patrols now went out with whatever they needed on their backs, and lay in wait, watching for the enemy. If a shot was fired or they heard the chop-chop of a horn being hacked off, the two-person patrols would advance to contact through the dark – which in itself took enormous courage.

What I had observed on my first World Ranger Day was that these individuals were hungry for a sense of purpose and pride that only good leadership could instil. All, if not most, had smart phones and could not avoid the daily barrage of negativity on social media. While the rangers were out in the bush, putting their lives on the line, arresting poachers – sometimes shooting them in self-defence – people around the world and in South Africa were telling them that the war was lost, that rhinos were doomed to extinction.

Building a sense of pride and esprit de corps was high on my list of priorities for protecting my ranger base. One of the things I thought the rangers were missing was a focal point, a place where they and the public could recognise the good work they were doing. In 2013, I enlisted the help of Honorary Ranger Ian Alexander, an architect, to design a ranger monument for me. I had a basic concept in mind. On each of my several trips to Washington, DC, I had taken time to visit the Vietnam Veterans' Memorial. This understated, curving wall of polished black stone, inscribed with names of every veteran killed or missing in action, is incredibly powerful. I wanted our own space where people could pay tribute to South Africa's rangers and reflect on their sacrifice.

In his design, Ian drew his own inspiration for his interpretation of that concept from the lines on one's palms. He came up with two curving rock walls, one higher than the other. The dominant was the 'life line', representing the lives of rangers dedicated to conservation; the second wall illustrated stewardship, the responsibility of the ranger in defending nature.

Anchoring the walls was the large trunk of a stout leadwood tree, whose qualities of strength, toughness and endurance we had highlighted in the rangers' creed at the last World Ranger Day, on 31 July 2013. A cairn provided the formal recognition of lives well lived, and the rangers who had sacrificed their lives in the protection of wildlife.

Minister Molewa could not make it, but on 1 August 2014, Barbara Thomson, the Deputy Minister for Environmental Affairs, came to the park to unveil the memorial. Some of the SANParks senior management had been worried that the memorial, located next to the gate, might overshadow the nearby statue of the bust of Oom Paul Kruger, founder of the park. It was ironic that African bureaucrats found a reason to be concerned about a memorial honouring the overwhelmingly black ranger corps overshadowing that of an old white president of the South African republic. Sometimes it seemed like I could please no one.

Minister Thomson at least spoke to the purpose of the memorial, as she addressed a crowd of dignitaries, rangers in their best uniforms and families.

'As a government we need to boost the morale of rangers by showing them their battle against poachers and other environmental crimes is not in vain,' she said in her speech.

'We want to tell you we understand and fully appreciate rhino poaching goes much deeper than mere physical security,' she told the rangers. 'Social and economic problems such as unemployment and poverty are part of the problem. In other words, it is a multidimensional problem that extends beyond provincial borders, countries and government departments and we are committed to develop a multi-dimensional combat strategy in support of your efforts.'

The Honorary Rangers had done an excellent job designing and overseeing the construction of the memorial. Their national chairman, Louis Lemmer, reminded us that a single day, World Ranger Day, was never enough to celebrate the commitment and dedication of people who put their lives on the line to protect our national heritage.

'This day is observed across the world on 31 July, and it is an opportunity to celebrate the work done by rangers everywhere and also to remember those who have lost their lives protecting South Africa's national parks.'

I could see, once again, the pride on the faces of the rangers present and it was truly inspirational. In the media, however, the talk was of the rhino death toll – 618 killed in South Africa already by that

August, and it was looking like the final tally for 2014 would be an increase on the previous year.

I remembered the chairman of the SANParks Board's words over and over again: When will the numbers come down, General?

WHENEVER I HEARD LAUGHTER, I knew there was a group of rangers getting together.

Whether it was at a prize giving, with all of them dressed to the nines, or standing around a braai or taking a break during training or at a conference, they laughed at each other's jokes and, in the way that men and women who come face to face with danger and blood do, sought refuge in camaraderie.

They played tricks on each other, revelling in the shock on the face of one of their number when he pulled on his boot and his socks squelched in boot polish; or the shriek in the night because someone had dropped the bones of their chops outside the tent of a fellow ranger who had then been woken by hyenas sniffing about on the other side of the canvas wall.

When we selected new rangers for training, we asked them what they did, not just for a job, if they were employed, but in their spare time. We looked for men and women who had an affinity for the bush, who had maybe learned to track small game or reptiles as kids; we sought out those who played team sports, because, at the end of the day, surviving a contact with an armed poacher or being able to put yourself and your friend out of harm's way when an elephant charged came down to teamwork. And, of course, we looked for the ones with a sense of humour; all of us who had served in the army knew the importance of that.

Camaraderie is forged through seasons, challenges, experiences and a shared purpose and ideals. Despite what the media and the Facebook warriors said, these men and women knew that they were stopping more poachers than those that got through, and because of their efforts, the species was hanging on – just.

When one of their number was caught out as an insider, poaching, it led to deep anger and profound disappointment. They saw the alleged poachers and their bosses in town, in their new clothes, driving a new bakkie, flaunting their wealth, yet the vast majority of them stayed strong, stayed honest and stayed side by side with each other.

They protected each other in gunfights, and against wild animals through their knowledge of wildlife and sheer guts, in order to carry out the mission. They were the celebrated 'thin green line' that people talked about on World Ranger Day, and I could not have been prouder of them.

In late 2013, Arina asked to meet all of the section and regional rangers, and so I introduced her to the senior leadership team. Naturally, she won them over, assuring them that they and their families had our support.

At the end of the meeting, Section Ranger Steven Whitfield moved that Arina should be known as 'Mama Ranger'. The name stuck, and for good reason.

Arina was no stranger to helping the families of men and women at war. At Christmas she travelled with me, visiting all of the ranger posts in Kruger, while I was frantically putting together our technology wish list for Howard Buffett. We were fortunate to have Ilze with us as well, and were able to show her parts of Kruger that few visitors to the park get to see. A part-time artist, Ilze made us a lovely album of pictures from the trip, covering all the ranger posts. Arina was touched by the effort the rangers and their spouses went to at many of the posts – having baked a cake for us in some instances – but at the same time she was concerned by much of what she saw.

'We have to help them, Love,' she said, and listed the problems she had observed. In many posts the rangers' families lived with them, but in these remote locations there were no play areas or equipment for the children; the womenfolk had nothing to occupy them after their domestic chores were done; no one was explaining the complexities and horrors of the rhino war to the spouses; cell-phone reception was weak or non-existent; and there were no leisure facilities for the rangers themselves.

We talked about her concerns and I realised that the rangers' morale, so often shaped by their home life and downtime, could be improved. From our discussions Arina came up with the idea for Project Relax, to support the rangers and their families.

'What can we do, though, if we have no money?' I asked her. I was still seeking funding for items such as helicopters and electronic monitoring systems, but I knew this was just as important, if not more so.

So it was that Arina arranged to meet with the Honorary Rangers' chairman, Louis Lemmer, and his wife, Erica. Project Relax, she told them, would involve sourcing equipment for leisure activities and ranger posts. Louis and Erica were excited to get involved and were assisted by Reverend Carl Lourens and the local congregation from the Skukuza NG Kerk. Reverend Lourens was the organiser of the popular annual Skukuza Half Marathon and he and the Marathon Club arranged for the proceeds from the August 2014 race to be donated to Project Relax.

With the funding from the half marathon, Arina was able to buy the first pieces of equipment we needed, from Makro in Nelspruit, to start improving life in remote outposts in Kruger. She bought soccer balls and netballs, kids' tables and chairs, and dartboards, as a start. As word of the project spread, colouring books and children's storybooks flooded in, and rhino ambassadors – school children who wanted to do something to help the cause – began raising funds.

Everyone involved knew the value of this project, but funds remained a problem. Arina and the Honorary Rangers came up with a solution: each of the HR regions would be invited to adopt a ranger post and raise funds to support the men and women working there, as well as their families.

This new twist on the programme turned out to be a huge success, with the most remote posts receiving jungle gyms, bicycles and toys for rangers' children; sewing machines, material and beads so that the wives could keep busy making clothes and other items in their spare time; and television sets so that each post could have a communal TV room.

The Adopt a Ranger Post concept led to two other spin-offs: Project Veggie, in which seeds, tools and skills were passed on to allow each post to develop its own vegetable garden, further helping with rations and fresh food; and Project Bafana, where posts that had the capacity established their own soccer teams, complete with sporting kit, for an inter-post competition.

These early support initiatives evolved into Project Embrace, which saw Honorary Rangers visiting posts to give talks to rangers and their families about how to proactively prevent the negative effects of trauma and manage stress. A survey of rangers found that more than 30% of them were suffering from high or moderate stress levels. Project Embrace provided advice on how to develop life skills, in order to build resilience, and how to recognise the signs, symptoms and effects of stress. It provided information on wellness tools and services available to manage and counter stress. All of these great initiatives were woven into a Ranger Wellness Plan, a key plank of our strategy to fight the war and transform the ranger corps by addressing their physical, spiritual, social and psychological needs.

Under the plan, we were building and improving accommodation and encouraging the rangers to take pride in their posts, and working hard to recruit the right people and establishing learning and career paths. I negotiated attractive allowances for rangers involved in specialised operations, such as extended clandestine patrols, in recognition of the extra hardship and deprivation associated with these responsibilities.

Having already instituted the new training regime, I knew that it had to be kept fresh and relevant. It was important to conduct refresher training so that rangers did not slip back into bad habits. I also identified the need for ongoing leadership training for section and regional rangers.

I made sure that time was taken to nominate outstanding individuals for the SANParks Kudu Awards and the Game Rangers' Association of Africa Rhino Conservation Awards each year, and that there were regular social occasions in the park where we could come together and celebrate our successes. At these events I encouraged older, more experienced members to share their stories and the lessons learned with the up-and-coming rangers.

For Christmas 2014, Imperial Logistics joined forces with the Honorary Rangers to put together and transport large cartons of groceries to every ranger household. Arina and I played Santa Claus, visiting the posts, and she delighted in the joy in the faces of the rangers' children.

It had been a long, hard year, and while the numbers of rhino killed were up on 2013, we were flattening the curve – more poachers than ever before were entering the park, but the runaway train had been slowed. The rate of increase was not as steep as it had once been and the growing number of incursions was not reflected in a comparable increase in rhino deaths; we were better trained, better equipped at catching, disrupting or, if it came to it, using our weapons in self-defence.

13

South Africa had faced down the threat of the extinction of our rhino once before in our history, and it was time for me to talk to the one man who had probably done more than any other to reverse the decline of the species – Ian Player.

Rhinos were slaughtered by white colonial hunters and farmers throughout the nineteenth century, the animals sacrificed for sport, their hides, meat and, of course, horns. As early as 1895, conservationists fearing for the future of the species established the Umfolozi Junction Reserve – today's Hluhluwe-iMfolozi Park. By then, and into the early twentieth century, numbers were estimated at somewhere between 20 and 100 individuals. At that time, there were no rhino in Kruger.

By the time South African-born Ian Player joined the Umfolozi (as it was then known and spelled) Game Reserve in 1950, after service with the 6th Armoured Division in Italy during the Second World War, there were about 400 rhinos in the reserve.

Rising through the ranks of the Natal Parks Board, to senior ranger then warden of the reserve, Player embarked on 'Operation Rhino' in the 1960s. In the course of this far-sighted and ambitious campaign, he oversaw the capture and relocation of Umfolozi's excess white rhino to other parks, most notably Kruger. Spreading the gene pool around allowed the species to flourish and white rhino numbers increased every year up until our recent poaching epidemic took hold. Player later went on to found the Wilderness Leadership School, Wild Foundation and the Wilderness Network.

In March 2014, I received a call from Player's office, inviting me to meet with him if I could spare the time. I, of course, said yes. I flew to Durban's King Shaka Airport, rented a car and travelled to the Natal Midlands. The countryside was rich and green, the air cooler away from the humid coastline.

Ian welcomed me into his office, set in an older, colonial-style farmhouse. We then went through to his lounge room, slowly – he was 86 at the time – where a lady served us afternoon tea, and scones with jam and cream.

With us were a couple of guys from Ian's advocacy foundation and Jack Greeff, a former recce major, who now headed up Ntomeni Ranger Services. Jack had trained rangers in the Kruger and his company had consulted to other parks as far afield as the Democratic Republic of Congo, Angola, Tanzania, Central African Republic and Malawi.

Ian Player was the master, the man who had made it happen, ensuring we were in the position still, although just hanging on, of having the most rhino in the world in one place – Kruger. I was there to learn from him. Although he was becoming frail, his eyes burned bright.

'You must make sure your rangers are well cared for,' he told me, 'and that you are consistent with your protection. The local communities must be involved.'

He made no attempt to hide his sadness at the current situation. 'I know these animals,' he said, his voice wavering. 'I know that the white rhino is such a docile animal. Why would they kill it? Why be so barbaric?'

He was complimentary about some of what we had been doing in Kruger. Far from his mind wandering, he zeroed in on me with some questions and I began to feel uncomfortable, knowing that other eyes were on me and that anything I had to say might be reported outside of our meeting.

'What about trade?' he said, his eyes, like that of the others, fixed on me.

I hesitated. This was a very emotive and politically loaded issue that came up often. Private rhino owners, such as John Hume, who had the largest single population of rhinos outside of a national park, were advocating legalisation of the trade in rhino horn. They had many conservationists, veterinarians and anti-poaching operators on their side. The argument was that South Africa's stocks of private rhinos could be farmed, their horns humanely cut off and used to flood the market in Asia, thereby satisfying demand and driving the price down to a level where poaching would not be worth it.

Like so many other solutions, it sounded like a silver bullet. 'I'm not sure what the long-term effect would be,' I said, dancing around his question, giving the same 'non-answer' I usually gave journalists when they asked the same question. 'Can it solve the problem? It's very hard to tell, so I'm not sure. This problem does not have a single, lasting solution.'

I held his gaze and could tell how disappointed he was by my response.

'General,' he replied, 'what the hell else will you do to win the war?'

I had an almost identical conversation, just as probing, with another respected veteran conservationist, Ted Riley, around a camp-fire in the bush in Eswatini. Back when his country was still known as Swaziland, Ted had joined forces with the small country's king to take a tough stance on poaching and introduce stiff penalties. Allied with that approach was an ongoing advocacy for legalisation.

There was a strong view in such circles that 'if it pays, it stays', meaning that wildlife had to be profitable, and not just as photographic subjects for tourists' cameras. I could see the rationale, but my concern was that this train had got away from us, and that the poaching gangs and middlemen had too much invested to simply hand the market over to 'legal' brokers and farmers.

The South African government had not taken a definitive stance on the legal trade in rhino horn, so I was extremely limited in what I could say.

I STOOD in front of the flip chart in my office. The members of our informal Rhino Steering Committee, which met at least quarterly, turned off their cell phones. The purpose of these meetings was to give us time to talk and think without the disturbances of our day-to-day roles.

Included in those present were our large mammal expert, Dr Sam Ferreira, head of research Danie Pienaar, and Kruger's senior veterinarian, Dr Markus Hofmeyr. I tasked Markus, as the youngest member, with taking the minutes of our meeting; they were never to be more than a page, and were to contain action points, one or two issues for each of us to research or pursue before the next meeting. 'What more can we do?' was the question we most often asked ourselves.

Here we discussed things other than anti-poaching, different ideas and strategies we could investigate or implement to help protect Kruger's rhinos and give the species a fighting chance. The group came up with four pillars to protect the rhino: effective law enforcement; good biological management; demand management; and community projects.

Work had already been done by SANParks and the private lodges bordering Kruger to the west to try to uplift local communities and give them a greater share in the benefits wildlife and tourism could provide, but to my mind that needed to extend beyond the lady selling beads and curios at the gate.

The fact was that the wildlife economy itself was relatively small. The few thousand local people employed in Kruger and the luxury safari lodges benefited, as did their families, but we needed to spread the wealth by thinking bigger.

'Why can we not have local people servicing all the safari vehicles close to the reserves; they could be making and repairing furniture for the lodges, and growing fruit and vegetables for the kitchens, not just cutting down firewood,' was a line I often pushed. There were schemes like these mooted, including setting up a precinct of support services on the old Lisbon citrus farm, on the southern border of the Sabi Sand Game Reserve. Lisbon had been the subject of an early land claim, but due to a number of disputes over ownership and previous failed plans for the property, most of its trees had gone for firewood.

What seemed clear to me was that it was not good enough to simply hand over land or set up a community-based business; ventures such as these needed to be supported with funding and mentorship. We needed to enable enterprise at all levels to encourage ownership so that more people saw and directly benefited from tourism. All of that would take time, and money.

At our leadership group meetings, I continually reminded the senior rangers that we must be responsive to the needs of the communities bordering Kruger. We needed to be ready to help them when problem animals escaped from the park, and to be sympathetic to their needs, such as drawing water from the Sabie River.

Other measures we discussed included the consideration that rhinos be relocated to other protected areas, including national, provincial and municipal parks, and private reserves where owners could meet certain criteria and requirements. We also came up with a protocol for relocations. Some of the smaller parks had been hard hit by poaching, but, like us in Kruger, had improved their security efforts. As we were finding in the IPZ, the concentration of effort in a smaller area was bringing results.

Ray Dearlove, a South African businessman who had moved to Australia, had set up a charity called the Australian Rhino Project, with the aim of relocating 80 rhinos to the Western Plains Zoo in Dubbo, New South Wales. Ray was, and still is, passionate about saving rhinos.

The idea was that in a worst-case scenario we would have a rump population of South African rhino safe outside of the continent. Already, there was another NGO relocating some animals, such as roan antelope and the last surviving northern white rhino from overseas zoos back to Africa. There was a precedent for moving rhinos to Australia – the media tycoon Kerry Packer had bankrolled the translocation of endangered black rhinos from Zimbabwe to the Western Plains Zoo in the early 1990s. Some had died of disease and other complications related to their diet, but valuable lessons had been learned and 10 calves had been born in captivity.

Ray's project was meticulously planned and well-resourced and he devoted a good deal of his own time and effort to it. Unfortunately, politics and personalities prevented the relocation of rhinos to Australia. This was a great pity and I often wished I could do more to help him. The whole story is related in Ray's book, The Crash of Rhinos.

One issue we had to look at, and give serious thought to, was orphans.

TOURISTS, at first delighted, stopped their cars during a game drive near Pretoriuskop Camp, amazed at the sight of a rhino calf making its way on the road, weaving between their cars.

This had long been one of the best areas in the park to see rhino, although as the visitors snapped away with their cameras and cooed with delight, it soon became clear something was wrong. No mother rhino appeared from the curtain of sourveld grass, long and golden in the middle of Kruger's mild, dry winter.

The calf began acting strangely, nuzzling up to a silver-grey sedan, perhaps mistaking its bulk for its mother as it tried to imprint itself on the strange object. As more cars appeared on the scene, the little rhino stumbled about, confused, but not afraid of the humans.

Word reached regional ranger, Don English, who, with a Kruger vet, drove to the scene in his bakkie. The calf was unsteady, dehydrated without its mother's milk, and Don was able to get out of his vehicle and approach it on foot. More pictures were taken and the tourists' initial wonderment was turning to concern. Some visitors were crying as the rhino was darted and loaded into the back of the vehicle.

A helicopter was called and Don and the veterinarian loaded the little rhino – small enough to be carried – on board.

Some rangers found it difficult to make the transition from conservationist to paramilitary anti-poaching operator; many had been unable to deal with the horror of countless rhino carcasses, or the stresses of armed combat, and had moved on. Don had found his own way to cope with the new role and had been recognised with awards for his courage and dedication in the field.

'I have taught myself to deal with the ugly stuff,' Don told me, 'but one thing I can't deal with is these little orphan rhinos. When you get these calves standing with the mother for days before you find them, and see what they've been through, it really cuts me up.'

For some time, the rangers in the park had been concerned about the plight of orphans. Until mid-2014, even if we had wanted to start rescuing orphans rather than letting nature take its course and for the poor little things to die of dehydration or be eaten by hyenas, there was simply nowhere to take them. There were also the naysayers who maintained that a rhino, once habituated to humans and dependent on them, could never be re-wilded.

I had heard the screams of orphan babies, and seen them, dead from a lack of their mother's milk, or a tiny carcass, devoured by predators. A solution, it now seemed, might be close at hand, thanks to Petronel Nieuwoudt.

Raised on a farm in Limpopo Province, Petronel had joined the South African Police Service's former Endangered Species Protection Unit in 1991, after finishing her university studies. After eight years, she had risen to the rank of captain in the ESPU and then left the service to set up a game capture school. From there, she moved on to set up and work in wildlife conservation centres, finally establishing her own Care for Wild rescue and rehabilitation centre near the gold-mining town of Barberton, in Mpumalanga, south of the Kruger Park.

In 2012, Petronel received her first rhino calf, from a private game reserve that did not know what to do with the little orphan. Unlike

SANParks at the time, the owner could not face the thought of just letting the precious animal die in the bush. Word soon spread and Petronel found herself the custodian and foster mother to four more orphans. Care for Wild subsequently moved to a larger property, with room for its new role, and it was at that point, in 2014, that we contacted her. By this time, the rangers were all of the same view – that the orphans must be saved.

The first rhino to be taken from Kruger to Care for Wild was Satara, a little calf found near the rest camp of the same name. As Petronel put it, in a quote on her website: 'I remember when they (SANParks) asked me to take the orphans from the Kruger. I was so deeply humbled. The enormity of the responsibility was certainly not lost on me. I took a moment just to breathe and acknowledge the responsibility I was about to undertake, not just to save the lives of the rescued orphans, but to safeguard the future of the species. Everything in my life had led to this moment. Not for one second did I hesitate or look back. It was my calling and I had faith.'

Now, with the latest little rhino on board, the SANParks chopper raced south from Pretoriuskop towards Care for Wild, hidden away in the Makhonjwa Mountains near Barberton.

En route, the little rhino, a male, stopped breathing. The veterinarian did her best to revive the tiny fellow, starting CPR, pushing down on his chest as a doctor would do to a human patient. It was no good. Realising the calf had died, they landed in the veld to remove the carcass from the chopper.

Feeling a mixture of rage, frustration and deep sadness, Don hauled the lifeless animal from the back of the helicopter, set it down on the ground and started thumping its little chest.

The rhino started breathing.

The little survivor was flown the rest of the way to Care for Wild and was named 'Don' after his saviour.

Sometimes one had to wonder whether there was someone or something more at work in the face of the evil we encountered on a day-to-day basis. Mostly, it was just dedication, determination and damned hard work. Don saved another orphan, Storm, a tiny black rhino calf no more than six months old, by pummelling its chest and resuscitating it eight times on the flight between Orpen, in central Kruger, and the Care for Wild facility.

I TOOK time out to visit Care for Wild, taking a solo drive from Skukuza to Nelspruit and then across the N4 to Barberton. With the windows of the Amarok wound up and the air conditioning on, I could also take a rare couple of hours to destress; I pressed play on an Elvis Presley CD and turned the volume up loud.

Done with The King, I arrived at the orphanage, keen to ascertain for myself the value of the work Petronel was doing, and if it was worth the time, air hours and resources it took to relocate rhino calves from Kruger. There was the emotional aspect of what was going on – no one wanted to think of baby rhinos dying of thirst or being killed by hyenas, and rescues were good PR, but I wanted to take the emotion out of the argument and determine whether it still stacked up.

When I arrived, Petronel greeted me, gave me a briefing and showed me around. I saw the bomas and accommodation for rhinos, where volunteers literally slept with the rhino calves to comfort them – many of the animals were traumatised by what had happened to them.

I watched calves being bottle fed by volunteers, while others mucked out the stables and cleaned faeces off the little ones. It was hard, dirty work behind the scenes, but I began to feel that it was paying off.

I could see the evolution and the value of what Petronel was doing. As the rhinos in her care grew, they were progressively moved from the bomas out into the open, still under the watchful eyes of volunteers and the resident anti-poaching unit, but beginning the process of returning to a more natural, wild state of life.

I had been told by scientists that rhinos could not be re-wilded, but Petronel was looking at expanding her orphanage so that the animals could live out in the bush, away from humans and enclosures, the next step towards one day being returned to a national park to live a natural existence.

'Are you funded?' I asked Petronel, as we walked, rhinos grazing in the background. Already I could see that the cost of her work – in food for the rhinos, administration, facilities, anti-poaching and veterinary care – must be huge.

She put on a brave face. 'We make it work.'

'You cannot say, "We make it work,"' I said. 'Do you know where the next quarter's funding is coming from?'

She shook her head. 'No, but we make it work.'

'You are doing an indispensable service here, you know. This is not just Petronel now – you've become an extension of the Kruger Park.'

I knew from her website that Petronel raised money based on the emotions that the plight of these orphaned calves stirred in people, but I believed that Care for Wild was bigger than that; it should also be recognised as an extension of the effort to conserve the rhino.

We now had the option of rescuing orphans and it was clear that facilities such as Care for Wild and others that were springing up around the country were going to ensure a significant offset to poaching losses.

Why must she live hand to mouth, I asked myself? I offered myself as an ambassador to the orphanage and determined that whenever and wherever I travelled to talk of the work we were doing, I would also promote Petronel and her staff and volunteers. Arina later visited the facility on a trip she organised for the wives of the ranger leadership group.

I had come to Barberton determined not to let emotion cloud my thinking, but it was impossible not to feel anything. I had seen and knew well the terrible things these animals had been through, but what moved me on this day was not the rhinos, but the people I saw.

This orphanage was not a temporary band-aid or PR exercise; it was bigger and more complex than I had imagined and there are now several more such facilities in South Africa also doing good work.

It was heart-wrenching for me to watch a wild creature having to rely on a human for its survival, yet at the same time I thought: thank heavens we have people prepared to do this work. In Kruger, I had seen the very worst, most heartless behaviour humans were capable of showing towards an animal, yet here I was seeing the best of human kind.

That is what moved me.

THE WAR CONSUMED all of our time. Full moons were an onslaught, with poacher bosses sending several gangs across the border, knowing full well that while most of them might fail, or be caught, some would not be caught.

The staff worked long hours, days and nights in the ops room, which by now was referred to as the MAJOC, the Mission Area Joint Operations Centre. Daytime was filled with the noise of drills and hammers as the dedicated centre we had marked on the ground with a bag of flour took shape.

The Honorary Rangers stepped up yet again, bringing their fundraising and other skills to kit out the new MAJOC. They fitted shelves, bought chairs and other furniture, and even had a lovely big central table specially constructed out of more than 20 pieces of wood from different indigenous trees.

At the house in the staff village I could be woken at any hour by a call from the ops room reporting a contact, but I also had another source of sleep deprivation. I'd told Arina we did not need a 'town garden', and she had gone ahead and created a nonetheless lovely paradise using native plants.

Whenever I heard the metallic clunk of the gate opening, I sat bolt upright in bed. The night before I'd been up at two, three and four in the morning, standing barefoot on the stoep banging a spoon against a saucepan to scare the elephants away. They loved Arina's new garden and some mornings we would wake to see a whole plant or tree missing, devoured in one sitting. I drew back the bedroom curtain and saw nothing, just a wall of grey blocking the view – a big cow and her calf were grazing right outside our window and it was only when I klapped the glass that the old girl sauntered slowly away.

IN THE BUSH, we were hitting the human intruders hard, but it was a constant grind.

'General, we had a contact and shots fired,' the operations staff would inform me on a typical day or night. 'We've got one poacher wounded and dispatched one helicopter to the scene 15 minutes ago.' There were always wild rumours circulating, such as one that we had unofficially instituted a shoot-to-kill policy – that was a lie. Another was that we never sent a helicopter to pick up a seriously wounded poacher, but rather let them wait until an ambulance arrived – that was also not true, as Arina and I had seen during our Christmas visits to the ranger posts.

Things were working with military precision and we had our support people, such as Coert, our legal adviser, and our psychologist, Tannie Rethea, on standby and ready to help. There were so many rangers involved in shootings that sometimes Coert would come to the park on a weekend, making several stops to give groups of rangers advice on their rights and procedures after the police had opened murder dockets on the rangers.

The ops room hummed like a well-oiled machine.

'Shot fired,' one of the Shangaan-speaking women would say to the Mission Area Manager (MAM), passing him a slip with the details noted; this was just one of many dozens of contacts they went through every month. The MAM would take up the radio handset and call the section ranger in question.

'We're on the tracks, bring forward a chopper, whisper mode,' the ranger would typically reply.

The MAM would then alert the pilot, who raced out to his aircraft. We had developed and refined our helicopter tactics. 'Whisper mode' meant the chopper would move to a location near where the rangers were working, but not overhead. If the helicopter headed straight to where the poachers were known to be, they would go to ground and hide, or bomb-shell, meaning we would have to split our forces. It was better if the rangers tracked the poachers in silence and then called the helicopter to their position once the gang was in sight and close enough to be engaged.

'Thunder mode', on the other hand, called for the helicopter to fly straight to the contact. The pilot would then take part in the chase, flying ahead of the poachers and then turning and hovering, deliberately forcing them to stop. There was a huge risk in situations like this that a desperate poacher would take a shot at the helicopter. In order to protect our pilots and their passengers, we fitted Kevlar armour plating to the aircraft.

Overseeing any contact required skill, experience and analysis. It was not just a matter of dispatching a helicopter and rangers to a particular grid reference. The MAJOC staff had to think two or three steps ahead. They might have to arrange that aviation fuel be moved onwards to a landing site where the chopper could refuel if the contact was a long way off; a dog team might need to be alerted and a pick-up arranged, or a second dog could be required if it was a hot day and the first animal exhausted itself in the chase. Another group of rangers might have to be flown ahead of the poacher's line of movement to act as a stop group. There were many working parts to one contact.

The rangers and the MAJOC staff were working together as a team. We were getting there.

GOOD AIR SUPPORT was crucial to our efforts in Kruger.

Grant Knight, the chief pilot of our Air Wing, had been flying helicopters in Kruger since 2004. For a young man interested in wildlife and the bush, this was a dream come true. Back then most of Kruger's pilots' work was taken up with aerial game counts and game capture; he had weekends off and Wednesday afternoons were, traditionally, used to work on one's golf handicap.

Like many others in the park, Grant was shocked when, in 2008, he first saw a rhino killed for its horn. This had been virtually unheard of in Kruger up until then. By 2014 his life had changed; he was in charge of an Air Wing that would grow to four helicopters and two Cessna fixed-wing aircraft. Our pilots now carried sidearms, and shrugged on body armour as they raced to board their aircraft. With night-vision goggles at the ready, the Air Wing's pilots were on call 24/7.

Grant and fellow pilot Charles Thomson had travelled to the United States to learn night flying and had been trained in advanced first aid – how to treat himself in the air if he was shot. In the day pack he carried with him on every mission was a first-aid kit with an emergency tourniquet. When not responding at a moment's notice to firefights and hot pursuits of poachers, Grant and the other pilots had their days filled flying ECI crime-scene technicians to bloody carcass after bloody carcass, or Advocate Coert Jordaan to deal with another ranger facing a murder docket.

Frequently, the pilots could be called to pick up the Kruger doctor from Skukuza on a mercy dash to treat a wounded poacher, who might then have to be flown to hospital in Nelspruit. Sometimes a bound poacher would be on board, under guard. If an orphan rhino was too big to be manhandled into the helicopter, that was not a problem – Grant and his comrades had become skilled at slinging larger rhinos under the chopper, dangling upside down by their legs as the animals were flown to a road where they could be loaded onto a vehicle.

I was also grateful to have Raymond Steyn on board as an aviation adviser. In his mid-fifties and a consummate professional, Raymond headed up the Pilatus aviation company in South Africa and was still also working as an intercontinental jet pilot. He had flown the game census in Kruger for many years and offered his services, pro bono, to help with the Air Wing expansion. He oversaw the complete refurbishment of our ageing Cessnas and other key projects. As part of the expansion, we also mapped and improved landing strips throughout Kruger.

Kruger already had one Bat Hawk light sports aircraft and I had a vision for one of these to be based in every region. The Honorary

Rangers had come on board to help support the acquisition of more of these aircraft by raising money for equipment and hangars. These lightweight, slow-moving aircraft could be piloted by section rangers, who could fly low and slow, looking for poachers. When the intruders were found, the Bat Hawk could be used in a similar manner to a helicopter, flying ahead of fleeing poachers in order to force them to slow down or take cover.

In addition to flying on poaching missions, the Air Wing had to make aircraft available for game counts and other conservation-related tasks. They also had to comply with and prepare for annual audits by the Civil Aviation Authority. The Air Wing passed these stringent checks without flaw.

With a concerted effort by all, we built up what arguably became the best small Air Wing on the continent.

LIFE HAD CHANGED for everyone in the ranger corps, not just the pilots. One 'typical' day remains seared in the memory of many. Sitting behind the pilot in the right-hand back seat of the helicopter was a mission leader, who, like some of the other regional and section rangers, had now been cross-trained as TFO, or Technical Flight Officer. Their job on board the aircraft was to advise the pilot of clearances, making sure it was safe to land or take off, but their main role was now airborne command and control of their rangers on the ground.

Three years earlier, section rangers had mostly been on foot or in a 4x4 vehicle, tracking poachers through the bush, and use of the park's one helicopter had been a luxury rarely afforded. Now, regional and section rangers would find themselves in a helicopter, directing operations from above, or even flying their own Bat Hawk.

On this specific day, the mission leader was on board with the pilot and a dog team after a report came through of a visual sighting of poachers. The poachers were close, so, staying low and flying fast, they would soon be overhead. On some missions they were able to get to the scene of a contact just eight minutes after the initial call was received.

'Contact!' a ranger said over the radio and the adrenalin levels ratcheted up – that meant shots had been fired.

When they arrived on-station, the pilot climbed to get an overall picture of the fight below, as the mission leader and the other ranger slid open the chopper's rear doors, for better all-round visibility.

'We've got visual.' Both the pilot and the rangers on the ground could see two poachers hurtling into the thick bush; a third member of the gang had already been arrested.

The chopper landed and the dog team was deployed to follow up on the fresh sighting. Back in the air, the pilot flew ahead, to suppress the fleeing poachers, forcing them to go to ground to give the dog and its handler a chance to catch them.

The tactic, which we had developed and used so often, worked yet again, and the remaining two poachers were caught and detained. The chopper set down, but as the rangers and pilot were discussing their next actions, the radio hissed to life again with news of another contact. The team was airborne in a couple of minutes, racing back the way they had just come.

By the time they arrived, the incident was over. Poachers and rangers had encountered each other at short range, in thick bush, and in the way of this man-against-man conflict, superior training and reactions had won out.

The helicopter touched down, and the mission leader made contact with the local section ranger. 'Is everything secure?' the leader asked

'Yes,' the section ranger replied. Another poaching gang had been prevented from killing a rhino.

Then a third call came over the radio. The pilot and mission leader boarded again, took off, and flew to an adjacent section of the park. As they helped the local rangers search for the poachers they were tracking, a new message came in, this time from yet another section.

'Shots fired, I need air support,' the section ranger said abruptly over the radio. The section ranger had been on foot, he and his rangers and their dog following a gang of three poachers in thick bush not far from the Mozambican border.

The poachers had been moving carefully, trying to cover their tracks, but they had then moved into a more open area where their tracks were suddenly plain as day. The well-trained rangers were immediately suspicious. The section ranger stopped to assess the situation.

He had noticed that two of the poachers had split off, one to the left and one to the right. The rangers slowly started following one of the sets of tracks, crossing a game path leading into thick bush again.

'Listen,' the section ranger had whispered to his team, as he realised what they were seeing, 'they are waiting for us.' The tracks were in a dog leg, heading in the direction from which they had just come – the poachers were setting up an ambush.

The section ranger was second in line and, as they took a few more slow, silent steps, he peered through the bush and spotted a man with a rifle, taking aim at the man in front of him.

A contact ensued and the poacher with the rifle dropped his weapon. Another man, hidden nearby, grabbed the precious firearm and ran off into the bush. That was when the section ranger had called for air support.

'Listen here ... we've just had a contact ... one person is running with the gun,' he told the mission leader and the pilot, who were in the air.

The section ranger heard a gunshot and his corporal came onto the radio net. 'The guy is firing at us.'

The chopper was called in, and, as it landed, the section ranger climbed aboard and sat next to the leader in the back. The dog picked up the scent of the fleeing men, and using that team's direction as a guide, the pilot flew ahead, all on board scouring the bush from the air. They spotted the two men, moving fast, but deliberately making use of the thick bush in that part of the park for cover. At least one of the men was armed and fired on the rangers on the ground.

The team on the ground, with the dog and its handler leading, managed to catch one of the men, but the one with the rifle carried on. The chopper forged on, the rangers on board leaning out of the open doorways in order to see better through the trees below.

The pilot noticed that they were getting close to one of the main tarred tourist roads in the park; in the distance, a game-viewing vehicle full of tourists had stopped to watch the low-flying helicopter with its doors open. Pilot and rangers scanned the bush below and then caught sight of the lone runner.

The suspect stopped, turned, raised his heavy-calibre hunting rifle and took aim at the helicopter. Time seemed to slow for the pilot behind the controls. The poacher fired. One of the rangers on board was close enough to see a long silencer on the end of the poacher's rifle, and the recoil of the rifle kicking back into the man's shoulder.

'We're taking fire,' the pilot said over the radio as he banked hard to the left, pitched the nose of the chopper down and raced for the cover of a stout, dead tree he'd just seen. This was not the first time a poacher had fired at one of our helicopters, and it would not be the last.

As he flew, the pilot was conscious that they needed to suppress this poacher as soon as possible, and that the contact was now moving closer to the tourists in the game-viewer. With the mission area manager monitoring the action in the ops room, those on the ground and in the air heard from another pilot, inbound in a fixed-wing Cessna aircraft to provide additional air support.

Everyone on board kept their eyes peeled as the poacher forged on. The pilot was trying to slow him down, while staying between him and the tourists on the tar road. In his peripheral vision, the pilot could see camera flashes going off.

The poacher stopped and fired at the helicopter again.

As the pilot circled around again, the leader saw a man lying on the ground. The man got up and ran on, this time taking cover in a dense thicket of bush. The rangers on the ground were closing in, but the pilot stayed on-station above him, thinking the man would stay put and give up, realising that the game was over.

The bushes below them parted, however, and the poacher showed himself again, took aim at the chopper and pulled the trigger.

The men on board the helicopter all saw the same thing. Coming towards them was not a bullet, but rather a spinning black cylinder, with sparks and smoke trailing from its tail.

The rangers ducked in their seats, instinctively crouching to avoid the oncoming missile and watched the cylinder shoot past. It was so close that one ranger thought it must have passed through the chopper's rotor blades. He wondered, briefly and incredulously, whether the poachers had managed to get hold of some kind of surface-to-air missile, or a rocket-propelled grenade launcher.

The pilot went into a turn so tight that a ranger's head was pressed against the door pillar. As the chopper circled around once more the rangers on the ground were closing in on the gunman.

'Stay above us ... this guy is just here ... don't leave us,' a ranger on the ground said over the radio.

Undeterred, the poacher broke from cover again, furiously worked the bolt on his hunting rifle, and fired more shots at the helicopter. Below them, the rangers caught up to the brazen poacher, and a firefight ensued.

The pilot of the Cessna had now arrived overhead and offered his support. 'You guys OK?'

'We're OK,' the chopper pilot said, almost in disbelief, 'but we need to land immediately, in case we've taken some rounds and sustained damage.'

When they landed, they discovered that, miraculously, the helicopter had not been hit and that the mystery projectile that had been coming their way had been recovered. It seemed that at some point the poacher tripped and fallen and in the process he had bent the home-made silencer on the end of his rifle. When he took his next shot at the chopper, the bullet sheared off the suppressor and sent it spinning towards the rangers in the air.

This was the operational tempo of the war our men and women were fighting. On that day, the mission leader had simultaneously coordinated and supported five follow-ups, of which four led to armed contacts and arrests.

Yet, still the poachers kept coming, and while the number of incursions and contacts rose, so too did the number of rhinos being slaughtered.

14

'I cannot stand here and tell you everything is OK now,' I told the audience at the Wildlife in Crisis conference organised by the University of Cape Town's Centre of Criminology in early 2015, 'but there is good progress in Mozambique.'

'If this sounds airy-fairy, it is not. We are pooling resources and we are getting results.'

It was true. The balance of incursions had indeed shifted. As a result of the success of our engagement with authorities and reserves across the border, through improved communications and joint planning and operations, the percentage of incursions from Mozambique into Kruger had dropped from 75% to just over 30%. The flow of poachers had not slowed, but they had changed their tactics.

There are strong cultural and even family ties between the people who live to the east of Kruger, in Mozambique, and to the west. Even before the poaching crisis intensified, the border was fluid, with thousands of illegal immigrants regularly crossing the border, risking their lives by walking through lion, buffalo and elephant territory in search of a better life in South Africa. There were even reports of people rustling cattle from South Africa to Mozambique, although those lower-level criminals were now not game or stupid enough to move through a park patrolled by what was becoming the best anti-poaching unit on the African continent. Some poachers had relocated to South Africa, easily melting into the communities of towns such as Bushbuckridge and Giyani on Kruger's western border.

My next challenge, which I had been working on, was to replicate the successes we had achieved with the likes of Lionel Dyck and Ellery Worth in Mozambique on the South African side of Kruger. There, a host of privately-owned reserves, from the Sabi Sand Game Reserve in the south to Timbavati, Klaserie and Balule to the north, was each doing its own thing when it came to anti-poaching and community engagement.

'We are the people who know you cannot win with law enforcement alone,' I said to the delegates at the conference. 'Intelligence is our greatest weakness – without it we are blind.'

I needed to make the point and was not afraid to speak candidly. The loss of Pathfinder had hurt me. While we were busy expanding ECI, we needed the police to do more outside of the park, finding and stopping the poaching middlemen and kingpins, who were now dispatching gangs from within our own national borders. There should have been nothing stopping us from going after these targets.

After my address there were other speakers. Moshakge Molokwane, national secretary of People and Parks, made the point echoed by many others that people living on the edge of national parks needed to have a stake in the management of wildlife reserves in order to see real benefit, and that their socio-economic needs should be met. I agreed with all of this, but from my perspective there was not enough coordination of the many community upliftment projects being sponsored by the likes of private game reserves. Greater coordination and focus, I felt, might lead to better results, rather than the patchwork of projects – all of them worthy – that existed. For instance, I was in favour of open days that would allow people from disadvantaged communities to visit Kruger for free, and, if anyone asked me, I always supported the amicable settlement of land claims on reserves, via appropriate compensation. The British High Commissioner to South Africa, Judith Macgregor, spoke about the work her government was doing at an international level to bring people together to talk about the broader strategy to combat wildlife crime. A delegation would soon travel to Vietnam, she said, to hold talks with the government there.

When the floor was opened to questions, one young man clearly had me in his sights, in a query that was also something of a statement. He said: 'With increased militarisation, there is an unintended consequence. People who get into [work as a] game ranger, or conservation, don't get into it because they want to become a guerrilla fighter. We have an issue here, and nor do we have good evidence that militarisation is a sufficient deterrent when the risk-reward ratio for poachers is relatively attractive. Do we not need to be a little more creative about our anti-poaching efforts?'

Another participant asked why we weren't doing more to combat corruption, concluding with a sweeping statement suggesting that 50% of rangers and police were corrupt. This was the sort of stance rangers were used to reading on social media regularly.

The term 'green militarisation' – the increasing use of armed rangers, paramilitary forces, soldiers and military veterans to fight poaching around the world – was a term often used by US academic, Dr Libby Lunstrum. She had visited Mozambique and in papers and lectures had highlighted her concerns about what she saw as an arms race between poachers and anti-poaching. She focused on Kruger and me, the retired general, as evidence of this new trend.

She talked of us following values 'that interpret rhinos as part of the nation's rich natural heritage and poachers as border-violating decimators of this heritage. The result is a heavily militarised and increasingly dangerous landscape.'

A source of irritation for me was that many academics argued an 'either-or' approach when it came to law enforcement and community care, as if the two were mutually exclusive. One had to pay attention to both areas, but to say, for instance, 'think what all this money being spent on anti-poaching could have done for the community' was both dishonest and misleading.

I had been guilty of whipping up anti-Mozambican sentiment at my first speech to the Game Rangers' Association of Africa Rhino Conservation Awards back in 2013, but since then I had been at pains to talk about cooperation between our two countries and the success of our joint operations. This had been manifested in a reduction in incursions from Mozambique.

Still, Dr Lunstrum's paper had set the tone for a more academic study that tried to paint the anti-poaching effort as racially based, or as a throwback to South Africa's apartheid-era strategy of interfering in neighbouring countries' affairs. I was concerned about the negative impact it might have on rangers, many of whom lived in the communities that academics claimed were suffering at the hands of this increased 'militarisation'.

Jasper Humphreys, from the Marjan Centre for the Study of Conflict & Conservation at the Department of War Studies at King's College, also zeroed in on my apartheid-era military service in his paper on the 'Rhinofication' of South Africa's national security. He theorised that I was playing to South Africa's historical predisposition to adopt a 'backs-to-the-wall' approach to external threats. He even gave a name to the 'war', saying in his paper, co-authored with MLR Smith: 'The "Jooste war" has thereby come to combine rhino counter-poaching with broader geo-strategic interests.' As flattering as that was, it was rubbish.

A number of subsequent articles carried the same narrative, with no alternative view. The tone suggested that the authors were projecting all of the wrongdoings of the past on to the current rhino war. It was as if they expected me, as leader of the campaign, to confess that I had invented colonialism and apartheid and that I was not prepared to serve the communities around the park.

In addition to the militarisation of the ranger corps and the use of the army, there was also discussion among academics of the perceived issues with the employment of foreign military veterans in the fight against poaching. I was contacted by numerous veterans from several different countries who had served in Iraq and/ or Afghanistan, offering me their services. Most were under the impres-

sion that we were in an armed struggle, in which our aim was to eradicate the enemy – we were not.

For a start, as I had to explain, it was illegal for a foreigner to own
a firearm in South Africa or to use their own for anything other than
hunting – hunting game, not people. There was nothing in our
charter or rules of engagement that would allow for anyone other
than rangers to take part in anti-poaching operations.

Many veterans offered to train our rangers, but this was already
being done very effectively by the Southern African Wildlife College.
I did not need a foreign veteran to teach my rangers how to be a
sniper, or how to blast their way into a building and rescue a hostage.
Time and again I stressed the importance of tracking, as this was the
way to find and catch poachers before they knew we were on to them.
I also needed people who could operate and survive in Big Five
country and this was something the rangers were adept at.

At the conference, I addressed the questions that had been put to
me about militarisation and corruption. I dealt with the latter first.

'Corruption is a factor,' I said, spreading my hands in front of the
microphone on the table in front of me. 'However, it is overempha-
sised. I'm telling you that. Forgive me the "I" message but I instigated
integrity testing in the Kruger National Park in the year 2013 and I
was the first one to go forward and be tested. Then all rangers did it
voluntarily, despite the labour regulations saying that you cannot do
lie-detector tests as part of their conditions of service.'

I added that the board and Exco and senior management had all
agreed to take lie-detector tests as well.

'There are corrupt rangers, unfortunately, and they cause
damage, but if you have evidence that 50% of rangers are corrupt,
then bring it,' I said, quietly but firmly.

I felt it was time to very clearly state my views on 'green militarisation' in order to cut through some of the assumptions and implied
criticisms that the term brought with it. My concern, which I
expressed to more than one academic via email, was that their
comments painted my rangers as 'war mongers', eager to kill.

I did not raise my voice. This audience was made up of students, academics and conservationists, and they needed to know the truth about what was happening in the bush, and the differences between a paramilitary force able to protect rhinos and rangers and an army.

'I'm not saying this as a general, but it is not the fact that we have militarised too fast – we had no option – that has caused the problem, it is the fact that the other actions have not kept up with the militarisation.' I was also using this speech to subtly but clearly point out what had not been done – that is, a concerted effort by the police and the army to match the efforts of the ranger corps.

It was also time to dispel some militarisation myths that I was somehow recreating the old South African Defence Force to stop the onslaught from some foreign peril, or that there was a better solution.

'If any person tonight can give me a responsible way to protect the rangers, I will do it,' I said, and I meant it. 'The anti-poaching doctrine you need in this fight is to operate in teams of two; we operate in extended clandestine patrols of five days or more. The military is not even trained for that – they train conventionally.

'It's nobody's fault here that the ranger's .375 hunting rifle had to be replaced with an automatic weapon, or that he's now wearing body armour. But it's by the grace of God and through good training and discipline that, in III firefights in one year, our people are unscathed.'

I watched the audience, hoping my words were sinking in. 'Will it remain this way – militarised? There is no guarantee, but it is up to me and the leadership to say that if we have this force, what do we do with it?

'If we want to demilitarise, which I support by the way, we mustn't take it too far and we have to step up the other actions of the other agencies, because we are at the receiving end. We have to equip the rangers, train them and care for them as people, because it is not pleasant out there.'

I shook my head. 'Nobody can just make this go away, but somebody has to address this. I can assure you, we would love, tomorrow, to go back to counting the roan antelope in Kruger, and looking at a new butterfly – all the wonderful things rangers used to do but now don't have the time for. It is sad. The money that goes into counter-poaching ... Can you think, if those millions went into conservation proper, what we could achieve?'

I took a breath. 'But let's not stop. Let's work towards that. Some-times, I wonder, why would the rangers do this? Why would they not tell me, "This is not my job, get the army to do it"? No, they do it because this war is happening on their beat.'

A LAW-ENFORCEMENT COMPONENT, as well as a form of militarism, had always formed some part of the various ranger corps across the African continent. We were now living in an era in which, through necessity, this dimension became the core business, bringing with it new complexities related to internal and external conflict. As much as the leadership – and, indeed, much of the community – wanted a military approach, the dirty work of fighting the fight carried reputa-tional and legal risk for all of us involved in the war. I continually had to walk the tightrope between the academics and purists who wanted rangers to return to only environmental tasks in the field. There were human-rights groups that – using inflated fatality numbers – bemoaned hard action against poachers, and the police and army felt threatened by my position of command and our rangers' successes. The 'thin green line', the ranger corps, was being left to do the dirty work, whether we wanted it or not.

Research was conducted in the communities adjoining Kruger on the South African side to see whether, as some claimed, the people living next to the park were being alienated by the tougher stand on poaching. Sam Ferreira and I then tried to operationalise the findings to establish much-needed context on this issue.

First, we tried to calculate how many of the approximately two million people living in neighbouring municipalities might actually benefit from poaching. From our own statistics, we knew that we had experienced 2 500 poaching incidents that year. Considering the size of what would be a typical gang, that meant about 7 500 individuals directly involved in poaching teams. If each of these poachers supported 10 people in their community, then that added up to about 75 000 community members, or about 3% to 4% of the local population.

Over the course of 30 public meetings and 24 focus groups conducted by SANParks in these communities, the communications section reported that there was no negative feedback on law-enforcement or ranger-related matters. Yes, we were aware of individual rangers and their families who were occasionally shunned by other community members – perhaps those who directly or indirectly benefited from poaching – but it was clearly not widespread.

By contrast, our calculations showed that, based on the number of people employed in Kruger and its adjoining private game reserves, and using the same multipliers, between 7% and 7.4% of the people living near the park directly or indirectly benefited from Kruger.

ONE OF THE best ways for me to counter this talk of green militarisation, and defend the rangers and promote the good work they were doing, was via the media.

I stood under a jackalberry tree near the new MAJOC, which was now nearly ready for its official opening. The cameraman had set up and Alex Crawford, a journalist from Sky News in the UK, waited for the video to start rolling.

Alex asked me, like those before her, why we had gone for the militarisation option.

'All the other options take time,' I said. By this time, after nearly two years and hundreds of interviews with reporters from South Africa, and visitors from as far afield as the US, China and Western Europe, I had my key messages down pat. As a military planner, I knew how to consider the most likely and most serious courses of action your enemy would take, and to be ready to counter them.

I most certainly did not consider the media to be my enemy. Rather, they were a means to get my messages across to the people of South Africa, the world and, most importantly, the rangers.

'Force on force alone will not work,' I said, not waiting for a question. 'You cannot shoot your way out of this and have victory in the bush – that is just treating the symptoms. The other solutions, like community programmes, technology, demand reduction, all of that takes time. You've got to think big, start small and act now. The "act now" is the ranger part in the anti-poaching role and hopefully one day it can change – hopefully they can become conservationists again.' I repeated a message I often emphasised: 'Victory over poaching will be determined in boardrooms, where the right decisions must be made, and in the courts where the right convictions and sentences must be meted out.'

Alex asked whether there were many ex-military people among the ranks of the poachers. In this war, like any, rumours spread and it was being claimed that ex-RENAMO guerrillas or FRELIMO soldiers were working as poachers; some wild theories had ex-Chinese military people training and equipping them.

'In terms of their bushcraft, their navigation, their utilisation of weaponry, the formations they use in the bush – those are typically insurgent military techniques,' I said.

'Are they heavily armed?' she asked.

'It depends. Sometimes they come with a second poacher, armed with a pistol, to protect the shooter, who is armed with a heavy-calibre hunting rifle.' This was an evolution – we were seeing this more often now, with gangs having an extra armed man, or the bearer or tracker now carrying a weapon. Occasionally, alarmists claimed that our 'aggressive action' in Kruger had started an 'arms race', with poachers becoming more sophisticated and better armed. However, there was no truth to this. While sometimes a gang might have two weapons, there was no suggestion of them coming with grenades or other military armaments, as some suggested.

'In that lies the danger for the rangers, as well,' I continued. 'You shoot at someone with that heavy-calibre rifle and you'll cut the person in two. So, in that split second when you arrest a poacher, you must decide what the danger is to you, because the rules of engagement dictate that you have to arrest, you have to try to catch the person. If you engage and shoot the poacher, the onus is on you to prove you fired in self-defence.'

'Is the war winnable?' It was another all-too-common question. 'If I can say to you that the war is winnable; you would say, "But look at the numbers," and that is the only measure. I'm not denying it; let me not try to spin anything here. The only measure is to stabilise and get the numbers down. That has not happened yet, but let us see what happens at the end of this year.'

A French journalist asked me the same question, but in a skilfully loaded and open manner: 'Why did you take on this un-winnable war?'

'Because it can be done,' I said, then filled the void with another of my key messages.

I had taken a decision early on to not to shy away from the media. I communicate well, but more importantly I knew my stuff and it made no sense to let well-meaning but relatively uninformed media liaisons handle the media for the sake of internal politics and preferences.

However, my discussions excluded statistics and numbers of rhinos killed. Minister Molewa communicated these as part of a well-thought-out strategy not to have ongoing, almost daily, coverage of rhino losses and few perspectives on the positive side.

She took a lot of flak for moving to quarterly briefings, but I supported her decision. We could not afford sensational coverage that focused on, say, multiple poaching incidents in one day. The media could well single out an individual event, such as a bad day, as if it were the norm. In some cases, the media were feeding off inaccurate social media reports. What we needed was for the media to get a better picture, overall, of what was happening in the campaign.

Minister Molewa personally chaired the quarterly work session where we prepared for the media briefing the day prior. I recall the earliest I left one of those sessions was about 1 am. She worked very hard.

At one of these media briefings, held in the auditorium at the Government Communication and Information System building in

Schoeman Street, Hatfield, I took my seat at the left-hand end of a long table. Stretched out alongside me were the important ministers from the security cluster – police, defence and state security – and my minister. The SANParks chief was beside me. In front of us was a contingent of media, about 40 or 50 journalists, photographers and television camera operators.

Minister Molewa gave a briefing on the numbers of rhinos killed. Afterwards, a journalist directed a question at the Defence Minister. Was she concerned, the reporter asked, about reports of armed foreign volunteers, ex-military people and veterans of overseas wars being employed in anti-poaching roles in South Africa.

The Defence Minister expressed her concern about such reports, and Minister Molewa then said: 'Let's ask the General.'

I did not feel unprepared or 'put on the spot' by the minister redirecting the question to me. Rather, it was at times like this that I appreciated how my minister put her trust in me.

'I can personally confirm that in our national parks there are no foreign armed combatants,' I said, stating the absolute truth. While foreign veterans besieged me, offering me their services, the laws on such things were clear when it came to national parks.

As I had said to Alex, the Sky News reporter, I could not 'spin' the figures – they were what they were – and I am proud to say that I never observed any attempt by my minister to spin the numbers either, or omit any of the bad news that we had to convey at those briefings.

They numbers did not lie, but nor did they tell the whole truth. They did not reflect the transformation the ranger corps had undergone, our own improvements in internal communication, the flourishing alliances around the park, nor the massive increase in poaching incidents. It was a difficult message to sell, but I used every interview to give credit to the rangers on the ground.

Some colleagues accused me of being self-serving and vain, but I saw this as a necessary part of my job. It could be intimidating and demanding, particularly when dealing with reporters who had their mind already made up that, for instance, green militarisation was evil and that I was refighting the apartheid-era border wars.

However, I fully believed it was worth me taking the lead in the media and PR campaign. Having entrusted the care of their national heritage to us, the public deserved to be informed about what was happening. Overseas audiences, including international NGOs, philanthropists and conservationists, needed to learn the reality of what was happening on the ground in South Africa, and what they could do to help us.

I knew that we needed to take all of these stakeholders along on the journey with us. I had seen the value of travelling abroad and taking our messages to the likes of Howard Buffett and the UK and Netherlands lotteries. In the course of an average year I might host up to 40 groups of international visitors to Kruger so that they could take the message back home with them.

I knew that potential donors would only contribute if they knew the facts and had assurances that their money was being spent wisely. This was something I had had to keep an eye on with the HGBF funding. By 2015, I was getting the feeling that all was not well, with Buffett's people pushing for a high level of detail on our expenditure and timetables, and with some in SANParks failing to comply with their requests. I was thus fighting not only the communications war, but also the day-to-day battle on the ground.

Leaders, like subordinates, also needed to be taken along on the journey, because when a leader is uninformed, he or she is effectively disempowered. The communications environment in which I was operating was as complex as the battlefield on which we were fighting, if not more so. As I faced multiple media interviews, I always had to watch my back, in case colleagues thought I was doing this to feed my own ego. All this gave a new meaning to 'big-match temperament'.

In some respects, I had been set up, not so much to fail, but to be the Messiah, something I tried to refute from my very first media conference. SANParks, under David Mabunda, had banked on my military background as part of its winning recipe, yet some academics and journalists opposed to militarisation saw this as my greatest evil.

I learned very early on that journalists fixated on emotive language to colour their reports. It was not surprising, then, that my early comments and those I allowed to be inserted into the very first SANParks media release, about 'taking the fight to the enemy', were seized upon.

The term 'Rhino War' was also controversial. Journalists loved that, just as they did my early, perhaps cavalier, remarks about the threat from Mozambique. These statements were, however, received as positive by many in South Africa and even the minister herself would sometimes refer to the 'War'.

Using the media was a high-risk, high-reward part of the strategy and I knew that a single wrong word could undo the gains of hundreds of previous 'good-news' interviews. Fortunately, I could say that, after nearly three years in the job, I never had a serious fallout with a reporter, and nor was I misquoted. Overall, I thought, the media had been a force for good, helping me to spread our message locally and around the world, and grab the attention of donors and supporters.

In 2013, we realised that the flow of illegal firearms into Mozambique was a significant factor in the increased poaching onslaught from that country.

ECI initiated an investigation that revealed the most common firearms used for rhino poaching in Kruger were CZ rifles, the Czech-made Brno in .375 or .458 calibre.

While Mozambique might have been awash with AK-47 assault rifles following its long civil war, the best weapon to take down a huge, solidly built rhino was one of these heavy-calibre hunting rifles. Our rangers had been issued with these to deal with big game, prior to us converting to assault rifles as part of the para-militarisation.

In mid-2014, while we were already investigating the source of firearms, SANParks was contacted by Kathi Lynn Austin, an American filmmaker and director of the Conflict Awareness Project who specialised in investigating the international arms trade. She was also interested in investigating the source of rifles used in rhino poaching, so I facilitated some meetings between her and the relevant authorities. At this time, there were several organisations involved, including ECI, the NPA, the SAPS Hawks, the police's Stock Theft Unit based at Skukuza, the Mozambican conservation authority ANAC, and the Mozambican police. The matter of CZ firearms being used by poachers was formally raised by us with the Mozambican police at this time.

In April 2015, Austin again offered to help with the CZ investigation and, again, I was supportive of this. We organised a meeting for her with members of ECI and Advocate Ansie Venter. During the meeting, Ansie asked Austin for a statement confirming her investigation and any information she had so far uncovered. Austin never complied.

The Kruger Park armourer, our resident firearms expert, compiled a list of all of the confiscated CZ rifles in our possession, together with their serial numbers, and provided it to the investigating team and Austin. Later that year, the matter was raised with Carlos Lopes Pereira, who later informed us that the issue had been raised to ministerial level.

In February, Austin attended another meeting with Ansie, the Skukuza Stock Theft Unit, ECI and the Hawks. It was decided that because this was now truly a cross-boundary matter, the Hawks would take the lead on it. Later, Austin told us that as she had received mixed reactions from the Hawks, she would continue with her own investigation, concentrating on Mozambique and Portugal. I was advised to let the police handle the investigation from then on in, but I did raise it again with ANAC and even the Czech Embassy, to see if there was anything they could do.

I had done everything I could to assist, stretching my mandate as far as possible. However, much later, Austin teamed up with the television current-affairs programme Carte Blanche to film a story about her investigation into the Czech-made rifles. We had handed over the investigation to the Hawks, and I had passed on all relevant information to the authorities in Mozambique.

Arina and our friends were quite excited to learn I was going to feature on Carte Blanche. When we sat down to watch it, I was left speechless to find that the story inferred that, because I did not intervene personally and internationally to stop a shipment of rifles from Portugal to Mozambique, I was somehow complicit in the trade. It was outrageous, and although I lodged a complaint with the broadcasting standards authority, I had neither the time, inclination nor the money for lawyers to see it through. To their credit, SANParks issued a media statement within 24 hours of the programme going on air, expressing their support for me.

'GENERAL JOOSTE, we want to honour the work your wife, Arina, has done for Kruger's rangers by giving her a special award,' the woman from the Kruger Lowveld Business Chamber said to me on the phone. I was at the house at Skukuza and Arina was with me, although she was out of earshot.

'Of course,' I said.

'The function is next Friday, General, but your wife mustn't know she's going to receive the award.'

'We will be there,' I said and hung up.

As part of maintaining a public profile and being accessible, I was also regularly called on to attend functions and speak. It was impossible for me to agree to everything. Ordinarily if someone had called me and invited me to an event with less than a week's notice, they would have received a prompt 'no', but this was different.

'Babe,' I said, finding her in the kitchen, 'we've been invited to this thing in Nelspruit next Friday and before you say anything, I said yes. I want to go, so let's make a plan.'

She raised her eyebrows – that Friday was going to be my sixty-third birthday so she seemed surprised I'd agreed to go to a dinner. On the afternoon of the event we packed our evening clothes and drove to the Riverside Mall complex just outside Nelspruit and checked into the Tsogo Sun hotel at the Emnotweni Casino. In the evening, we walked across the car park and into the convention venue. I was pleasantly surprised to see our good friends Leslie and Grant Coleman from the Lowveld branch of the Honorary Rangers. As I sipped my wine, I opened the programme for the evening's events. I felt mildly annoyed as on the list of awards I couldn't see any that seemed to correlate with what I'd been told about Arina's honour.

We ate our dinner and as the speeches were made and the list of awards and recipients were being read out, I didn't know whether to be irritated or anxious. The master of ceremonies was down to one last award and Arina's name had still not been read out.

'And the final award, for a special leader in the community for 2014, is presented to Major General Johan Jooste for his work in the Kruger National Park.'

My mouth dropped open. I wasn't sure I had heard correctly, but considering the applause and seeing Arina and our friends smiling,

I got to my feet and made my way to the podium. I was speechless, which was just as well as I was not expected to say or do anything beyond posing for photographs.

After learning that the award was indeed a special one, not presented every year, I returned to our table and smiles all around. I locked eyes with Arina. She and the organisers had cooked up the whole cover story because she knew I would probably have said no to an invitation at such short notice.

I was so fortunate to have Arina by my side and this was not the only spoiling or surprise for which she'd been responsible. Before she left to return to Pretoria, our fridge was always stocked with my favourites. Her support for me was loving and unwavering and Elvis's song 'The Wonder of You' could have been written about her. Heaven knows, I needed this backup from my 'roommate', as I often called her in jest.

I went to Arina, hugged her, kissed her, then put my lips close to her ear.

'Queen of my heart.'

15

'W e'll have to see about that,' one of the SANParks board members said when first I told him, still quite excited, that Howard G Buffett had agreed to finance us a second helicopter.

That one statement encapsulated and set the tone for the way SANParks handled this man's incredibly generous donation of some $25 million to the fight against poaching over the next two years.

Two other responses to the news further highlighted the problems I would have to overcome on all levels.

'Gee, Johan,' Ken Maggs said to me on the night I broke the news, 'are you not worried what this will do to your popularity?'

The morning after the function at the Golf Club I told the park head, Danie Pienaar, the good news.

'You realise the board will have to approve this,' he said.

The size of Buffett's donation was unprecedented in the world of conservation. It offered a one-off opportunity to change the anti-poaching landscape in the Kruger Park, with a simple, clear agreement that allowed maximum initiative and only limited governance prescripts. I cannot imagine there are too many deals in the business world of that magnitude that are finalised with a six-page contract.

Even setting aside the internal and international politics, there were difficulties when a dynamic businessman, supported by a justifiably demanding foundation, came up against the processes and procedures of a national parks bureaucracy bound by the rules of state procurement policies and, quite frankly, not used to doing anything with any great sense of urgency.

Buffett's foundation demanded – rightly so – regular, detailed updates on how the money was being spent and there were milestones and deadlines to be met. To be fair to SANParks, they may not have had the capacity to deal with this in the manner the HGBF expected. There were certain procurement procedures to follow, and there was little I could do to speed things along. I was chairman of a steering committee established to oversee the spending of the grant money, but to avoid any potential conflict of interest I could not be personally involved in procurement.

It was easy for Buffett to say, 'Buy a helicopter and send me an invoice,' but quite a mission to meet that intent. The scope and scale of this donation was also new ground for the HGBF; it was the plight of Kruger's rhino, in particular, that had attracted Buffett's attention and prompted him to commit so much money.

By October 2014, however, the first of the new Squirrel helicopters was in the air. Edna Molewa came out to Kruger with the media and, with Danie Pienaar and chief vet Markus Hofmeyr, flew on a mission to dart and tag five rhinos. The minister announced to the local community that these rhinos, now identifiable via their ear tags, had been nominally donated to them, and encouraged the community to help protect the animals.

Things were happening, but Howard Buffett and his team were growing impatient with progress. While he had told me that he fully expected that not all of the technological solutions we were proposing for the Intensive Protection Zone (IPZ) would succeed, he and his team remained frustrated at the slow pace of progress and lack of record-keeping, accounting and reporting.

Buffett had also earmarked money for aerostat balloons, and invited me to America for a week-long working visit to see them in action. He sent me a business class plane ticket, but I had to declare this to the SANParks management, and ask nicely whether they would let me accept it. With raised eyebrows, they agreed.

Buffett and I met up in North Carolina and toured factories and suppliers involved with balloons and related systems. I saw how the balloons were assembled in segments, so that if someone shot at one section the whole thing would not deflate and crash. I was interested in the payloads and how many and what types of sensors an aerostat balloon could carry – it was far greater than the drones available to us.

From there, we travelled to Texas, and spent time on the Mexican border, where we observed the aerostats in service.

I was taken with the idea of balloons mounted with long-range cameras and other sensors. I was still keen on the idea of radar and envisaged a system, perhaps smaller than the larger aerostat, that could be transported by vehicle and quickly relocated and deployed around Kruger.

With its long-range, early-warning capability, the aerostat was impressive. We agreed that a balloon fitted with cell-phone tracking technology would be useful, although I would have to work on getting the legislation changed to allow us to deploy it. Buffett was so keen that he offered to have a balloon sent to South Africa for a trial, saying that we could return it if it didn't work.

He was also mindful of the pressures I was under back home with SANParks, so together we drafted a letter from him to my organisa-tion, stating the conditions under which the balloon trial should go ahead. He agreed to have South Africans trained to operate the balloon and sensors, and specified that no more than one American at a time would be attached to the project; hopefully, this would placate those in government who were worried about American soldiers or spies infiltrating South Africa.

The technology in use on the US–Mexican border is impressive, with real-time information and video being streamed from sensors and cameras on the balloons to operators' laptops. As I sat there watching, however, I was struck by the fact that as with our struggle in South Africa there was a sense of futility in this type of border control. The Americans could see people getting to the border fence and crossing, then rush to arrest them, just as we hoped to be able to do with our systems, but I knew that what we really needed was depth and layers. We needed to be able to disrupt or stop poachers and their bosses before they came anywhere near our border.

After the border visit we flew to Decatur, Illinois, where Buffett lived. Waiting for us at the airport was his wife, Anne, and his dog, Bolek, a police dog that had dropped out of training, but wore a harness with sergeant's stripes. The billionaire had agreed to fund tracker dogs for the Kruger Park, but only on the condition that we drew up a retirement plan to ensure all the working dogs were cared for later in life.

From Buffett's place in Illinois I flew in the eight-seater Learjet back to the Teterboro Airport just outside New York; I had an early flight from JFK to South Africa the next morning.

During our week in the US, I had been mindful and respectful of Buffett's abstinence from alcohol. But now I found myself alone in a luxury private aircraft, so when the flight attendant asked if she could get me anything, I gave her a smile.

'I think I deserve a beer from that untouched stock.'

BACK IN SOUTH AFRICA, I started harassing the engineers and scientists at the CSIR.

'Radar,' I said over and over again until they became sick of me. Most of the time, I had to be careful to not use my former rank or platinum status to throw my weight around, but this was not one of those times. I was convinced, in my own mind, that what we needed was a combination of long-range, high-quality cameras, linked to a radar system, to provide surveillance of the IPZ. Time was of the essence – we were losing rhino, and Buffett's funding had a use-by date.

'General, it is unreasonable to expect us to do this in the time frame you are allowing,' said André le Roux, the CSIR's radar expert.

A consummate professional and a very reasonable man, he was becoming quite hot under the collar with me. 'Where must we find the resources? What about our professional reputation if we field a system that is not tested and does not work?'

But I pushed them and finally they got to work – mostly, I think, because they were sick of me bothering them and wanted me to shut up. At the same time, I was fast coming to the conclusion that I would not be able to convince the government to change the legislation to allow me to track cell phones, as per the original plan Buffett had requested. As the deadline to spend the money drew closer, and Buffett and his foundation made their impatience increasingly clear, I took a command decision to allocate the money he had earmarked for phone trackers to the radar project. It was a gamble.

I had brought the CSIR into Kruger to oversee the technology projects covered by the Buffett grant. Even that was a problem, with SANParks initially baulking at having another quasi-government organisation operating on its turf. It was maddening – the system was doing everything it could to thwart or slow me at every turn.

At the CSIR, André le Roux was cooperating with his optronics colleagues across the hallway, working together on the prototype of an array of sensors that would use radar to plot the movement of people and animals in the park. A laser target designator would be used to hone in on a particular radar intercept, and then direct a long-range camera on to the target, which could be several kilometres away from the base station. An infrared light could be used to illuminate the subject at night. They had even come up with a name for the system – the 'Meerkat'. Like the watchful little animals, our system would provide early warning of the predators hunting our rhinos.

Werner Myburgh, from Peace Parks Foundation, had also been sceptical about radar – the technology just sounded too abstract and fanciful: that radar, something used to track aircraft in the sky and ships at sea, could find people moving through the bush. However, one day Werner called me on the phone; he was escorting a party of potential foreign donors on a trip around Africa.

'How sure are you about this Meerkat?' he asked me.

The system the CSIR was working on was very much in its infancy. I had faith in the project, but there were problems with camera resolution and integration with the rest of the system. As persistent as I had been, I was by no means 100% certain it would work.

I took a deep breath. 'I'm sure, Werner.'

'I have a donor here with me who's interested. We might get two systems.'

'I'll make it work,' I said.

As WELL AS researching and developing new technology, Charl Petzer and the CSIR team were also proactive in promoting an existing system that the CSIR had developed for the 2010 FIFA World Cup in South Africa, and was busy refining and upgrading it.

Dubbed Cmore, the system had been designed to allow information sharing between different government and private agencies involved in management and security for the soccer matches held around the country. It seemed as though this could be a force multiplier for our rangers and our headquarters as we worked to become more proactive and more efficient at responding to incidents and following up on intelligence from the field.

Using the Cmore cell-phone app, a ranger who detected the spoor of a poacher could snap a picture of the footprint and share the image and its GPS coordinates immediately with the ops room and others on the system. As the ranger set off, we at headquarters could use this real-time information and to try to work out, say, if the poacher might be headed for a particular waterhole where rhinos were known to drink. Other rangers, or early-warning systems linked to Cmore, might also have made intercepts of poacher activity in the area. With all the information visible in real time, and shared, we could start to put together a picture of the gang's movements, past and future.

From the ops room, we could then alert stakeholders outside the park, such as anti-poaching units in the private reserves on Kruger's borders if the poachers were headed their way, and task our own assets, such as the Air Wing or a dog team. If a ranger heard a shot fired, then, using a function on the app, he or she could point their phone towards the direction of the gunfire and enter the estimated distance; with its built-in compass, Cmore would then record the bearing and estimate the location of the shooter. All the incidents recorded by the field ranger – a contact, the discovery of tracks, a gunshot or incursion – would be instantly recorded on the in-built map for all to see; the ranger with their cell phone and Cmore might instantly do the work of four or people in a more traditional military headquarters, gathering and recording intelligence. Stakeholders could communicate with each other by voice, video or text during an incident via Cmore's integrated chat group function, instead of, say, switching to WhatsApp.

When an arrest was made, the ranger could then take pictures of the suspects, their weapons and their shoes, as our people were taught to do, and then share that with everyone. Cmore was about bringing different people, systems and sensors together on one plat-form so that they could gain insights into what our enemy was doing. Armed with this information, we in the ops room could respond quicker, and make tactical decisions based on real-time intelligence and even some predictive modelling. Having all this data recorded and archived meant that after a contact with poachers, we could step back, analyse what had happened and use this as well as past inci-dents to help drive our tactical and strategic decision-making.

As with the introduction of any new technology, we had to take the rangers along with us when trialling a system such as Cmore – they had to be convinced of the value of recording everything they saw and heard.

'But I told you about the contact on the radio, why must I enter it on Cmore?' a ranger asked me more than once.

'Because everyone must know, not just me.' This was the essence of a force multiplier – a system that could save time and allow informed decisions to be made immediately by the sharing of timely intelligence.

. . .

'DOGS, DOGS, DOGS, DOGS, DOGS,' I would often say to the regional and section rangers, reminding them of my intent. There had been mixed reactions in the park to the use of dogs in anti-poaching so far.

The special rangers already had five dogs in the park. Dog handler Amos Mzimba and his legendary dog, Killer, had notched up many arrests and would go on to catch dozens of poachers, earning Killer a medal in the process.

Killer was a Belgian Malinois. Lessons were being learned already about the best types of dogs for working in the African bush. The Malinois, a hardy dog bred for herding sheep, was a good all-rounder and the breed had been used extensively in Afghanistan for sniffing out improvised explosive devices. Experience was showing, however, that in the heat of the African bush, dogs such as Killer were limited to missions of about two-and-half-hours' duration.

This meant that Killer and Amos were of most use in following up a fresh incident. If poachers had been spotted, shots fired, or very fresh tracks were found, the dog and his handler, part of the reaction force at Skukuza, would be flown to the scene. Once there, Amos and Killer would pick up the scent, and Killer would, more often than not, catch the poacher. Given that there were so few dogs at the time, and the fact that Killer was very good at these relatively short pursuits, it was no wonder he racked up such an impressive arrest rate.

Sometimes, however, the dogs would become confused by the scent of rangers who had already started following up on the poachers' tracks, or it would take the dog time to pick up the right scent. As far as some rangers were concerned, this was time that could have been better spent with humans tracking the poachers.

Howard Buffett had funded dogs for the park's entry gates, as well as for reaction force bases in the IPZ, and I organised some more donor funding to support Richard Sowry's initial trials to introduce free-running pack hounds. Our existing tracker dogs were 'line dogs', which meant they were attached to their handler by a leash for most of the pursuit and therefore limited to the speed a man or woman could run. They could be let loose at the end of the chase, but mostly had to move at the same pace as the handler. Free-running hounds were used in the US for manhunts, tracking escaped convicts or criminals. Richard took the lead, working in cooperation with the Southern African Wildlife College and an American 'houndsman' to determine whether the concept could be applied to Kruger. Full credit had to be given to Sowry for his pioneering work in this area. Richard was convinced that dogs could and would play a big part in our efforts.

EARLY ON, a new dog appeared in Kruger, and despite his unfortunate name, he proved to be a force for good. He turned out to be an unexpected, informal case study for the use of patrol and tracking dogs.

Hitler was a Doberman–bloodhound cross, who had been named and donated to Crocodile Bridge Section Ranger Neels van Wyk by a local breeder, Gavin Smith. SANParks would not have given a dog such a name.

Very soon, Neels learned that Hitler was, literally, a different breed to those that had been used in Kruger in the past. Not only was Hitler good at following fresh tracks, he could pick up a scent that was four, five or six hours old.

Hitler would lead his handler right up to a hidden poacher, then turn, looking back at his human as if to ask, 'Why can't you see him?' After Hitler's first contact with a poacher who opened fire, however, Neels was worried that he might lose this amazing dog. Hitler turned and ran, apparently alarmed at the change in behaviour of the handler and rangers around him, who were not only shooting, but yelling, as men do in the heat of battle.

Realising that dogs were as susceptible to trauma as humans, Neels started working on acclimatising Hitler to the sound of gunfire, taking him to the rifle range and progressively bringing him closer to guns firing. Unlike the Malinois and German Shepherd breeds being used elsewhere in the park, which had one dedicated handler, Neels learned that Hitler could work with up to three different human partners. They modified their own tactics, so that during a contact, when weapons were being fired, the handlers made an extra effort to reassure the dog and soothe him with some calm words – not always easy.

Hitler grew into the job and Neels eventually discovered that the dog was able to pick up tracks that were 24 hours old, and then stay on the scent until the poachers were captured. Big and strong, Hitler could cover more than 30 kilometres in a day. Once the poachers' direction of movement was established, Neels would move rangers ahead to try to cut the spoor. If they could find it, they could bring in another dog, to leapfrog Hitler and give him a rest.

After half a dozen successes in a row, news of Hitler and this particular breed spread and became a model for expansion of the use of dogs in the park. As well has having the nose of a bloodhound and the stamina and drive of a Doberman, Hitler had brains. One day Neels was trying to get Hitler to take a scent, using clear footprints on the ground. Hitler turned 180 degrees in the opposite direction and started heading in the direction from which the poacher had been coming. Neels tried to turn Hitler around and get him to move forward, but the dog was having none of it. Eventually, Neels stepped back and let Hitler do his thing. After a short while, still heading 'backwards', the tracks suddenly changed direction – the poacher, Neels now realised, had been 'back tracking', walking backwards to confuse the rangers. Hitler had simply followed the freshest scent.

The funds to construct new kennels and accommodation for dog handlers at key locations in the park and a Canine Training Centre near Phabeni Gate came mainly from the HGBF, but the Honorary Rangers took over the running of the facility and, in time, turned it into a centre of excellence. More Doberman-cross-bloodhounds were purchased and the free-running hounds programme was expanded.

We learned many valuable lessons over the next couple of years. It was one thing to raise money to buy a dog, but there was a whole logistics chain that was also needed to maintain a dog. They needed veterinary care, GPS collars in case they got lost in the bush, food and suitable, safe accommodation. Leopards love dogs and can rip the wire mesh off a kennel if it's not fixed properly. Dogs love their job – it gives them a source of enjoyment and reward – so even if they are not deployed, they need to be continually exercised and trained.

Just as the Good Lord has made only so many people who fly aircraft and carry out surgery, not just anyone can be trained to be a dog handler. We had to invest time and money in getting people with the right skills and temperament, who were also fit and motivated enough to keep up with a hard-working dog.

By mid-2016, the number of dogs deployed to the park had increased from 5 to 52. They were based at the gates – where electronic monitoring of entry and exit was being established – and ranger posts, as well as at quick-reaction bases.

The free-running hounds were proving extremely successful and also brought a new dimension of safety to both rangers and poachers. In the past, a typical face-to-face contact created a high level of anxiety and would often lead to a firefight. Now, with the dogs taking the lead, a shoot-out could be avoided. When the hounds reached and surrounded a poacher, the rangers could approach with caution and few surprises. By that time, the poacher was usually ready to give up the fight.

As well as being wonderful creatures, dogs – especially free-running hounds – were shaping up to be the game changer we had hoped for. Within three short years, they had been involved in about 90% of all arrests in Kruger.

WITH THE POACHERS shifting their main effort from Mozambique to Kruger's western borders, in South Africa, we needed to bolster our security and alliances with the private game reserves that lined that side of Kruger.

What we needed, I thought, was a GRU on steroids. The GRU (Game Reserves United), an affiliation of private game reserves to our west, was the brainchild of Andrew Parker, the hard-working and forward-thinking chief executive officer of the Sabi Sand Game Reserve.

Sabi Sand had been particularly hard hit by poachers, losing 50 rhino in one year, which meant that, proportionally, the reserve was being hit harder than Kruger. Andrew had made great headway in bringing together the owners of the various properties within the reserve and, where possible, getting agreement between them to share resources and intelligence. The luxury lodges in Sabi Sand are owned by some of the richest, most powerful families in South Africa and getting them to see eye to eye was often difficult; they guarded their internal borders jealously, with strict rules about which lodges could traverse on each other's properties for game viewing. Some needed convincing that it was worth spending the money to protect rhino.

I met with stakeholders in the private reserves on many occasions. Over time, we built on Andrew's work and created the 'GRU on steroids', the Greater Kruger Environmental Protection Foundation. The GKEPF would bring the reserves from Sabi Sand in the south into communication and cooperation with those in areas such as the Klaserie, Timbavati, Balule and Olifants River reserves to the north. Jacques Brits, general manager of the Timbavati Game Reserve, and the then chairman of the GRU, ably led the push from this side.

As it progressed, the GKEPF process was expanded to include the private reserves to the east, in Mozambique, and the Great Limpopo Transfrontier Park. In effect, it covered the whole of the Joint Protection Zone to the north of the Intensive Protection Zone, a vast swathe of land.

GKEPF's roles were: to develop human resources, such as ranger training and wellness; to share high-value resources, such as aircraft; to secure funding through reserve contributions, fundraising and donors; to build external and internal relationships through direct communication, workshops, training and regular meetings; to secure the JPZ through external community engagement, working with the national authorities and using Cmore to share information; and to come up with innovative solutions and interventions and to share data and research.

Basically, I wanted to apply all the lessons we had learned in

Kruger to the reserves on either side of us. At the heart of the GKEPF would be an operations room, similar to our MAJOC. It would need an experienced individual to run the mini JOC, and someone strong enough to stand up to and work with the many powerful egos involved. I recommended Otch for the job and this was accepted, bringing in another new era of firm alliances.

I'd faced down similar egos and objections to cooperating and sharing resources in the early days of forging alliances with landowners and concession holders in Mozambique. I remember saying to one businessman, who was throwing up objection after objection: 'When we next meet, I'll have an envelope for you with a piece of barbed wire in it.'

This was my none-too-subtle reminder to him that I was under pressure from the government and sections of the public at large to re-erect and strengthen the fence between Kruger and Mozambique. The Public Works Department had earmarked a few hundred million rand for fence improvements and Minister Molewa was keen to see that spent. In the end, I used the money to reinforce a problematic section near N'wanetsi, which had become a funnel for poachers and an area that we needed to keep under observation.

Sandy McDonald, the CEO of Sabie Game Reserve, called and asked if I could come to a meeting at the shady tree on the border, where we held our informal get-togethers. I flew out to see him.

'Do you know what I've done here?' he asked, concerned about renewed talk of strengthening the fence between our countries. 'I have an anti-poaching force under Lionel Dyck and we are doing good community work here, and now you are going to fence me out?'

I heard Sandy out and assured him that that was not my aim at all. Despite the threat I had made to the other concession holder, I was not in favour of reinforcing the fence between Kruger and the concessions across the border in Mozambique. While some people still clamoured for the fence to be strengthened, I started using another hashtag in my communications: #movethefence.

'The border of Kruger need not be the international border,' I told a joint meeting of government ministers from South African and

Mozambique in Massingir. 'I believe we should move the fence – that is, strengthen the fence on the eastern side of the concessions inside Mozambique.'

I glanced at Minister Molewa, who was present, and she gave me a terse look. Here was I, Chief Ranger of Kruger Park, now almost dictating international policy. Later, however, the minister took the concept to a higher-level meeting where bilateral talks were held between the two governments, and it was endorsed: #movethefence had worked.

Now, however, we began to see the early stages of 'threat displacement'. As our cooperation with Mozambique improved and we, in Kruger, became better at responding to poaching incidents, with the help of a four-helicopter Air Wing and dogs, poachers were voting with their feet and hitting the private reserves.

16

'Prince Harry is coming to visit,' I said to my staff, 'but it's a secret.'

The Prince had left the British Army early in 2015 and was undertaking a three-month working tour of Africa in order to be able to report back to the royal family on the real status of wildlife crime. His office had sounded us out about a visit to Kruger, and had made it clear that this trip, mid-year, would be very much under the radar. No one was to say a word about it to the media.

Initially, some of the usual bureaucracy played out between the various state departments here in South Africa, especially since the diplomatic status of a member of the British royal family was unclear. We were told to stand by and not to engage any party on the possible visit. A few weeks later, the visit was officially confirmed with detailed guidelines about maintaining a low profile and the safety of the Prince during the Kruger leg of his visit.

He had visited southern Africa many times and, from what I knew of him, he was passionate about conservation. His itinerary would take him to Namibia, Tanzania, Botswana and South Africa. In our country, he would spend time at the Care for Wild rhino orphanage, and then come to us. I hoped he would leave with a sound knowledge of what we were up against and what we were doing to fight poaching. The plan was, we were told, that he would return later in the year for a shorter and more public tour.

From our side, the South African government was still hypersensitive about the visit. Everything, Minister Molewa insisted, must be done properly and according to protocol. Importantly, the Prince was not to be involved in any contacts or arrests or chases of poachers.

Despite the veil of secrecy over the visit, a week before Prince Harry arrived I received a call from a newspaper in London asking me to confirm that he was on his way. The call lasted less than a minute, during which I courteously explained that I could not share any information about any visit. I probably should have cut my reply down by 50 seconds, because the story was too juicy for the media to ignore. The following Saturday they ran an article about the visit, with the journalist claiming to have inside knowledge of the visit following an exclusive interview with General Johan Jooste.

When he flew into Skukuza, we gave the Prince and his two staff members a briefing and tour of the MAJOC. Our new purpose-built headquarters was now fully operational. At its heart was a large 13-metre x 6-metre conference room with a bank of plasma screens on the end wall, covering 16 square metres. The displays showed feeds from cameras at Kruger's gates and our monitor at the Sabie River gap, a critical entry point for poachers from Mozambique, as well as maps, statistics of poaching incidents, other poacher infiltration routes and flash points.

There were a dozen cubicle workstations down one wall, each with computer connectivity, and I now had a dedicated office and mini meeting room adjoining the main area. I could at last break free from the administrative building at Skukuza Camp. There was also logistic support for the 24/7 staff, including a kitchen, storerooms, and ablutions with showers.

Early on, I had put up a framed quote, a favourite passage from the book *The Mind of a Fox: Scenario Planning in Action*, by Chantell Ilbury and Clem Sunter. It read:

Foxes are always paying attention to their surroundings; they're looking ahead, but also what's taking place around them. While it's impossible to forecast exactly what the future holds, by paying attention to what's happening around you, you can determine a few likely scenarios, and begin preparing accordingly – and then have the speed and agility to react to what you see.

The quote on the wall had given the whole building its nickname, the 'Fox Hole', which was now emblazoned on one exterior wall in a laser-cut metal sign.

'I tell all the staff when they come here,' I said to Prince Harry, 'that when they enter they must be situationally aware, focused and ready to act.'

From the beginning, I realised that Prince Harry was 'real'. It was clear that his intent to learn was serious and that with his military background he could grasp the impact of the threat and the effort it would require to counter that threat. He appreciated how complex the situation was and what we were able to do with the resources we had. He came across as unassuming and easy-going and could immediately relate to us. At the same time, however, he had an air of self-confidence and purpose about him. He was engaging and communicative.

I had arranged a two-week itinerary for him that would show him part of the park, and introduce him to regional, section and field rangers, and the other members of our Ranger Services team. He settled in well, in one of the guest houses in the staff village, and was very low maintenance. He was curious throughout his time with us and he and I had some frank discussions about strategy, tactics and the whole rhino issue. He called me 'General' and I addressed him as 'Sir', although most of our interactions were casual and relaxed. Prince Harry and I were able to connect, initially, because of our shared military background and that led us into some frank and to-the-point discussions.

Very early on in his visit we had a serious contact one evening in the south of the park; three poachers were arrested and one was wounded. When news of the contact broke, the media put two and two together and came up with five, reasoning that since Harry was in the Kruger Park, he must have been part of the operation. The next morning Jacaranda FM news carried an item claiming that Prince Harry had been personally involved in the contact.

He initially told me that he had chosen to ignore the media reports, but speculation ran riot, with UK and local journalists firing a barrage of questions at us. SANParks was forced to issue a media statement stating quite clearly that while Prince Harry had been exposed to the inner workings of Kruger, 'that exposure does not include operational activities involving engagements with poachers'. The statement further said that SANParks only allowed rangers and other law-enforcement officials to participate in actions against suspected poachers.

At all times I had one of my other staff or senior rangers with the Prince. When news of a contact came through, as happened during his time with us, Prince Harry immediately wanted to know where it was, how long it would take to get there, and what was happening.

I could see that, as an ex-military man, he wanted in on the action. A graduate of the Royal Military College, Sandhurst, Prince Harry had served in Afghanistan as an army combat air controller and, later, as a co-pilot/gunner and aircraft commander, or senior pilot, on Apache attack helicopters in action against the Taliban.

One Saturday morning, we were in the ops room when the helicopter and reaction force was scrambled. I could see how badly he wanted to be on board, or even behind the controls, and I felt for him as we watched the deployment unfold. While we'd been told he could not take part in a contact or follow-up, that did not stop him trying.

We had worked hard to improve our response times, but the Prince was, quite frankly, unimpressed at the just-under 15 minutes it had taken the pilot and rangers to get airborne and told me as much.

He was very critical; although he did not allude to it, the world had seen video footage of him in Afghanistan ripping a television microphone from the lapel of his uniform and sprinting away midway during a media interview when the siren had sounded, calling his Apache flight to action.

'Sir,' I said to him, hiding my personal irritation, 'this is the civil service of South Africa. Every time I call out a helicopter pilot after hours I start paying them overtime, whether they fly or not.'

He looked at me, incredulously. 'You have to pay them overtime?' He had come from a war where men and women on standby sat in their cockpits for hours.

'Yes, Sir, but I'm only allowed a certain amount by labour law. I have a budget for overtime and I can't exceed it.'

To his credit, he quietly attended an air support symposium sponsored by Stop Rhino Poaching outside Hoedspruit, the town servicing the private game reserves on the western border of Kruger's central section. Here was not only a member of the royal family, but a serious combat aviator bonding with all the rangers who operated from fixed-wing and ultralight aircraft and helicopters in an anti-poaching role. They were enthralled to have him there, showing his support, and to hear from him.

The Prince had a few beers with some of the other rangers and attendees after the conference. The word from the aviators attending was that the Prince was funny, down to earth and extremely committed and passionate about conservation. He really enjoyed being in the company of rangers and pilots, and had been reluctant to call it a night.

As his time in Kruger drew to an end, another visit was already being planned – he would return on an official tour, with the media in tow, in four months' time, in December. Initially, I thought it odd that he would make two visits in such quick succession, but the more I saw of him and the more we talked, it became clear to me that he genuinely wanted to learn and to formulate his own ideas and messages about conservation before he talked about such things in front of a camera.

During a wrap-up session with Kruger management and the ranger leadership just before he departed, Prince Harry expressed his gratitude to us and his concern about rhino poaching and the overall effort to curb it. He was appreciative of our effort in the park, but also smart enough to know that more could be done, if we were better supported.

Afterwards, he looked me in the eye. 'Did you apply for the job or were you approached?'

'I was headhunted, Sir,' I said.

'Then maybe you should be even more assertive.'

I nodded. I realised, then and there, that he had been watching closely during his two weeks with us, and taking in more than just the official briefings we had given him. I had been careful, or so I thought, to shield him from the internal and external political issues that complicated my life. He was perceptive and, of course, no stranger to the pressures of a high-profile position in the public eye, with all the baggage that brought.

It had been an honour and a pleasure getting to know this impressive young veteran.

HOWARD BUFFETT WAS NOT HAPPY.

The plan was that the CSIR would be contracted to do the project management and system design for the new technology initiatives that the HGBF grant would fund. That had been done because there was a memorandum of understanding between SANParks and the CSIR, which would become the main interface with HGBF. However, it took four months for SANParks to negotiate a service-level agreement with the CSIR.

Even once the CSIR was approved, there was distrust and suspicion of the organisation within parts of SANParks. Meanwhile, Buffett was losing patience – he had already given us one extension on the time in which the grant money had to be spent.

A steering committee was set up to oversee the grant programme. It was given neither support staff nor a dedicated project manager, which further hampered the execution of the plan. Ongoing negativity by some in SANParks and plain old-fashioned incompetence kept the donor's frustration levels high. This was all despite the sterling effort of Charl Petzer and his team, who were beavering away on implementation of the projects.

By mid-2015, three high-value projects were still outstanding – the eastern and western perimeter systems and radar – and several others were in progress. A final request for approval of a change on one of the perimeter systems was declined; in November, we were advised by the HGBF to speed up execution.

As well as the administrative delays and mistakes, there seemed to me – and Howard G Buffett – not much recognition by SANParks of the importance of the donation. There was very little thanks or public recognition given to the man or his foundation. Instead, the relationship became adversarial.

In some areas, though, the Buffett funding was indeed being put to good use. In the first quarter of 2015, we constructed five reaction-force bases, one in each section in the IPZ, adjacent to the existing ranger posts. Each base was enclosed and secure, allowing the rangers stationed there to maintain security in planning and executing their missions. There was a secured helipad at each base, set up for night operations, and accommodation for pilots, a canine team, and other specialists, such as CSIR staff, researchers or industry representatives working on new technology. In addition, each base had ablutions and basic shelters to accommodate detached forces, such as the groups of up to 20 police or military personnel who might be working in that section. The reaction-force bases gave us jumping-off points throughout the IPZ, allowing us more flexibility in responding to incidents and mounting proactive operations.

Some of the grant money had been used to fund the microwave communications system for the IPZ, six customised Land Cruiser 4x4s, half a dozen Polaris all-terrain vehicles, and an information system based on an informer network. The HGBF had also provided the funding for the MAJOC, which was nearly complete.

. . .

THE YEAR 2015 was also a turbulent time for me personally. A small but radical group in the Kruger Park issued me with a collective grievance for 'abuse of power'.

This was tied, generally, to the para-militarisation, but was, I believed, motivated by some in the park who were being shown up, or were unable to keep up with what we were trying to achieve. I had tried to have some rangers transferred within the park early on, and had been thwarted by senior management; this had caused some resentment.

I was subjected to an investigation and cleared, with no adverse findings against me. Fundisile Mketeni had by now taken over as the CEO of SANParks. I countered by telling Fundisile that I believed action should be taken against the individuals who had raised the false allegations against me, but the park leadership would not hear of it. They later paid the price for this through further labour unrest.

As vexatious as the complaints were, I could see where they were coming from. Although I still had just more than two years left of my contract in Kruger, I had already been talking about a succession plan. I knew that I could not stay forever and I also knew that my replacement could not be a white man – the radical element in Kruger kept on beating the drum about white leadership or ranger services. The senior management and board of SANParks did not seem to have the appetite to address these issues.

As a result, it was time for me to think big and to be a big boy, satisfied that I'd had the thousand days I had set myself to make the proverbial difference.

I spoke to Fundisile and he and I agreed on a plan to exit me to a position at head office, from where I could influence the anti-poaching campaign at a national level, as well as the unfinished projects in Kruger. We knew the problem of rhino poaching was not confined to Kruger. Gangs from Mpumalanga were targeting the rhino-rich reserves of KwaZulu-Natal and there were several other parks and clusters of reserves around the country that also held rhino. I believed that if we could replicate the initiatives we had implemented in the Joint Protection Zone in the central part of

Kruger and the private reserves to the east and the west elsewhere in the country, we could save even more rhinos.

Although our early relationship had been somewhat cool, I trusted Fundisile. When he was the deputy director-general of the Department of Environmental Affairs, he had only learned of my appointment via the media. After he was named as David Mabunda's eventual successor, Werner Myburgh from Peace Parks and Dr Mike Knight, one of Kruger's senior scientists, got together and planned a dinner at the Sheraton in Pretoria, to which Fundisile and I would be invited.

Werner and Mike's well-meant aim was to send a message to both Fundisile and me that we would do well to start working better together. Fundisile and I clicked that night and I then enjoyed his support; he had renewed my contract twice, and I found him to be a very good leader.

Fundisile asked me to help headhunt a successor and we settled on Xolani Nicholus Funda, a former ranger who had advanced himself through study and was lecturing in the Nature Conservation Department at the Tshwane University of Technology.

Nicholus's appointment as the new Chief Ranger of Kruger was announced on 3 November 2015. In a SANParks media release, he said: 'I have nothing but respect for General Jooste as he laid the foundation and formulated the strategies for a smooth coordination between rangers and other law-enforcement agencies when rhino poaching escalated in the KNP. He is my boss; and we will continue to work closely as a team, bringing in the different skills and experience when it comes to issues pertaining to wildlife crime.'

Before I left Kruger, however, I had another couple of VIP visits to deal with.

PRINCE HARRY RETURNED to South Africa, this time with the media in tow, in late 2015.

In the ops room we sometimes joked, morbidly, that we could never find the right carcass when we wanted to make a statement. On this occasion, we were able to show the Prince and the visiting media the full horror of the war, the remains of a mother rhino and her two-year-old calf. The carcasses were old and putrefying. Frikkie Rossouw and two of his technicians had been wading into the gore in search of evidence.

The Prince took time to talk to the ECI people working the crime scene; they showed him the spent cartridges from the poacher's rifle, and the butts of cigarettes the killers had smoked while going about their gory business.

Like the Prince, I was in the spotlight during the visits, with British journalists in the media 'pack' hounding me for comment and insights, particularly after the crime-scene visit.

'Did he wipe a tear away, General?' a reporter asked. 'Did he swallow a lump in his throat?' said another. 'Was he angry?' They were relentless.

Prince Harry had been to Petronel's Care for Wild sanctuary before visiting us, and had been pictured feeding Don the rhino. The orphaned calf Don English had picked up from the road near Pretoriuskop and brought back to life with rigorous CPR was growing fast and doing well. There were signs of hope amid the carnage. We took the Prince to the Southern African Wildlife College (SAWC) and he was keen to mix in with groups of students and rangers. Again, he seemed genuinely comfortable in the presence of rangers, including Cathy Dreyer and Lawrence Munro, whom he had met on his first visit and had requested for them to be invited to this event.

After the pair had done their bit for the media circus, Prince Harry said quietly to them, 'You nailed it.'

I was interviewed for the UK Daily Telegraph about the visit. 'His Royal Highness is not coming here with a bag of money,' I said to the reporter. 'If he can go away from here as an ambassador, understanding what we are up against, that is important to us. Somebody like him, as credible as he is, coming here from the royal family, coming from the northern hemisphere, that's extremely important to us. These are the world's rhinos, not just South Africa's.'

Prince Harry made a similar comment. 'If current poaching rates continue there will be no wild African elephants or rhinos left by the time children born this year, like my niece, Charlotte, turn 25,' he said. 'If we let this happen, the impact on the long-term prosperity of this country and on the natural heritage of the planet will be enormous and irreversible.'

We parted with a firm handshake in front of the SAWC. 'General, please keep me informed, as you may, through my staff,' he said to me.

As I told another journalist, Prince Harry was a friend of Africa, of South Africa, and of the rhino.

FUNDISILE CALLED ME FROM BRAZIL, where he was attending a conference. 'The President is coming.'

In the park, we kicked into overdrive, preparing for the visit. For a long time, Minister Molewa had been trying to get President Jacob Zuma to come to Kruger. She, as we all did, thought a visit would be a good thing, symbolically, to elevate the importance of the work that was being done.

The minister had written a cabinet memorandum, highlighting the rhino-poaching situation in Kruger and likening it to a war. She made a pitch for the president to come and see for himself and he had agreed. It was a short-notice visit and Fundisile would only return to South Africa two days before the president arrived in Kruger.

President Zuma arrived late on a Saturday afternoon in early November and was driven the short distance from Skukuza Airport to the luxurious Lion Sands Narina Lodge, one of the private concessions inside the Kruger Park. All of his official engagements in the park were to be the following day.

Having worked with quite a few senior politicians during my career, I would not have been surprised if the president wanted to do his own thing in the lodge, and perhaps unwind with a few whiskeys. Instead, I was invited to have dinner with President Zuma, two of his staff members and Kruger's new acting manager, Glenn Phillips.

All I can say about that evening was that the man I met, who drank only water while the rest of us had wine, was an extremely pleasant and engaging person. He asked intelligent questions, listened intently to the answers, and we enjoyed each other's company. We talked about matters ranging from the rhino war to national affairs.

At 6 am the next morning, right on time, President Zuma was ready at the airport, in the ranger's uniform we had sourced for him. We took him to a crime scene, and, with Minister Molewa, to watch a rhino capture and relocation. He flew in an Air Force Oryx helicopter to the bridge over the Sabie River and he laid a wreath at the ranger memorial at the Paul Kruger Gate.

After that, the president officially opened the new MAJOC building. This was a milestone and I had mixed emotions as he unveiled a plaque. We had achieved so much, yet there was still decidedly more to do across the country. A sound foundation, a tribute to what we had achieved, however, was there in equipment and facilities such as this.

As well as the MAJOC, we had constructed accommodation for 60 rangers and support personnel, five bases for reaction forces throughout the IPZ, the canine unit at Phabeni and five canine reaction centres. We had doubled our helicopter fleet and there were now more ultralight aircraft were in the air. Thanks to donors, there were more 4x4 vehicles and ATVs available for quick response, as well as dogs and new access-control systems at the park's gates. The rangers had more and better equipment, allowing them to operate in any conditions, with the added support of two new helicopters equipped to fly at night.

We had spent about R200 million and I was confident that I had come a long way to reaching one of my key goals – creating the finest anti-poaching unit on the African continent. And yet, still the death toll of rhinos was rising, albeit at a slower rate than before.

Nevertheless, I was proud of them all. On one occasion when the command group and I were discussing the army, I said to them, candidly: 'If I had to go to war today, I would be prepared to go with rangers.'

THERE WERE five of us in the helicopter. Pilot Brad Grafton and a new member of the SANParks Board, who we were taking on an orientation flight, were up front. Fundisile was in the rear on the left, I was in the middle, and Don English was on the right.

Brad tracked along Kruger's eastern border, with Mozambique on our right, giving the new member a view of the Lebombos and a feel for the vast wilderness area in which we and the poachers operated. As much as the job had consumed my life for the past three years, I knew I would miss the park. However, I would be back soon enough, I told myself.

No more than 10 minutes out from Skukuza Airport, Don received a call on his radio from a patrol on the western side of the Skukuza section, towards Pretoriuskop.

'We can see them,' a ranger whispered into his radio, and Don passed on the news that his rangers had made contact with poachers.

With no time to waste by dropping his passengers back at the airport, Brad turned and followed Don's directions. We were over the rangers eight minutes later and Don calculated that the poachers, if they were still running, would be about a kilometre and a half beyond where they were last spotted.

'That's far enough,' Don said to Brad over the internal radio, when he judged we were more or less in the right area. We all scanned the bush below as Brad circled. If we found them, our role would be to conduct suppressive flying, circling and hovering low, to force the poachers to slow or go to ground.

'There they are,' Brad said.

I leaned over Don and could see them, three men lying head to toe in a single line, trying to hide from the helicopter among some boulders in the lee of a big fallen tree.

As we waited, keeping an eye on the poachers, the rangers on the ground closed in. Just then the gang got to their feet and bomb-shelled, running in different directions.

Brad banked the chopper to begin the pursuit again, then noticed a poacher raise his rifle. There was a puff of smoke from the barrel.

'Hey, that bastard's shooting at us!' Brad yelled.

Brad immediately took evasive action, throwing the helicopter into a tight turn and heading away from the contact. The poacher fired again, but, fortunately, didn't seem to realise that he needed to 'lead' a moving target by aiming ahead of it. Brad swung the chopper around to continue the pursuit.

The poacher dropped his rifle and ran. Brad took the chopper right down, chasing him until he was almost on top of the suspect.

The man threw his hands up and Brad landed. Don clambered out of the chopper, rifle at the ready, and the poacher approached him, hands still in the air. Just as he reached the helicopter, however, the poacher ducked under the tail boom, just ahead of the spinning rear rotor, and dashed off into the bush again.

Don cursed, scrambled back on board, into his seat, and we took off again.

'Fly ahead of him,' Don said to Brad, 'then drop me off. I'll sit in the bush and wait for him, then you come back for us.'

Brad took off once more, followed the direction we'd seen the poacher running, then, once we were past the running man, touched down just long enough for Don to jump off. I slid across into Don's seat to better keep visual contact with the poacher. We flew after the fleeing shooter again.

Once we had located him, Brad flew a circuit around him. As we came down, I saw the unarmed poacher staring at me with a confused look that seemed to say, 'Who's this different oke sitting in the doorway?'

This brief pause gave Don the opportunity he needed to come up behind the startled man and grab him. I'll never forget the look on that man's face.

17

In 2015, 826 rhinos were killed in the Kruger Park, one less than the year before.

On the face of it, this was hardly cause for popping champagne corks, but when one considers that poaching had increased by 32% in the park between 2008 and 2014, it was proof that we had slowed the runaway train.

There were other important statistics behind the raw numbers that told the full story of what we had achieved so far. The stabilisation in numbers of rhinos killed had come despite a 7.7% increase in poaching incidents during 2015. We had prevented the customary and much-feared end-of-year holiday poaching spike by launching a concerted ranger and police task-force effort, resulting in us losing half as many rhinos as we had in the same period in 2014.

Another important milestone was the fact that at the end of the year every crime scene in Kruger had been attended to according to regulations and prescripts, despite the backlog earlier in the year. This was down to a super effort by ECI and police investigation teams.

During 2015, we had arrested 202 poachers inside Kruger and 115 in the adjoining reserves. The total, 317, was up 59 on the previous year. A total of 188 firearms were seized in the same greater Kruger area, 40 more than in 2014. To put the scale of the crime and anti-poaching effort into perspective: in the three years I had been in the park, 795 poachers had been arrested and 431 weapons seized in successes orchestrated from the MAJOC.

In addition to this encouraging news, I was hopeful that if even some of the ambitious projects and programmes we had initiated were carried on and seen through to completion we would see further falls during 2016.

The overall number of rhinos killed across South Africa had taken a dip, from a peak of 1 215 in 2014 to 1 175 in 2015. The early interventions initiated after the meeting of representatives of the national rhino parks at Mokala, in mid-2013, prevented a crisis like Kruger had experienced.

The other national rhino parks had finalised their plan for preventing and combatting poaching, and the document remains to this day one of the best of its type. Under the leadership of Property Mokoena, they had implemented in all six rhino parks everything we had discussed at the Mokala meeting. In some areas, they had done so faster and better than we had achieved in Kruger. To my mind, this was proof once again that if we'd had a similar drastic shake-up in SANParks prior to 2013, before things got so bad, we could have brought the numbers down in Kruger earlier.

When I handed over to Nicholus Funda, I made several human resources suggestions to him, specifically about succession planning in the ranger leader group. I suggested Tinyiko Golele be eventually promoted to regional ranger. Tinyiko was the ranger who had impressed me when I first met her, when her maiden name was Chauke. Rodney Landela, the other high-profile ranger who had flanked me on my first World Ranger Day in 2013, had recently been promoted to regional ranger.

Although many of our friends had been envious of us going to live in Kruger, it had been rare for both Arina and I to have time to truly enjoy the park. But, as I had been appointed by Fundisile to take charge of the overall anti-poaching effort in the parks division as well as Kruger, I would still be spending at least a third of my time in park. Now was our time.

One memorable Friday afternoon, when we did decide to treat ourselves to a game drive, we drove into a herd of aggressive elephant on the Afsaal road, close to Pretoriuskop. We kept our cool and later returned to Skukuza.

That evening we decided to dine at the Skukuza tourist camp and, lo and behold, just outside the staff village, we spotted an elephant on the road. I stopped and we decided to sit tight and wait for it to cross the road into the bush. As we looked around, however, we realised we were sitting pretty much in the middle of another big herd of elephants. We had to wait patiently for our safe passage. When Arina went for a walk the following Monday she also had to turn back because it seemed at least one of the herds had almost taken up residence in the village.

I wanted my departure from Kruger to be clinical and administrative rather than emotional, especially as I would continue to be directly involved in the park. Nicholus had stated publicly that he wanted to work with me and I was looking forward to taking on a more strategic role with a wider focus. For now, I was happy with the legacy I was leaving, and what the ranger corps had achieved. At the annual end-of-year function at Skukuza, my one concession to emotion was to pay tribute to what I called the 'Tungsten Club', those particular individuals who had helped me and the rhinos through the previous three years.

I thanked all the contracted staff who had worked tirelessly during the transition of the rangers into a fully fledged anti-poaching unit. Coert Jordaan, our on-call advocate, had provided legal advice to hundreds of rangers – not one of them had been prosecuted for murder, with all fatalities deemed to have been caused in self-defence. In the same breath was my thanks to Rethea, who meant so much to the rangers as she quietly listened to them and gave her counsel as their psychologist whenever needed.

Raymond Steyn had been my adviser on aviation matters, as well as one of our fearless and hard-working SANParks pilots; I also thanked Tokkie Botes, the volunteer pilot who gave generously of his time and aircraft for the cause. The Kruger scientists, doctors Sam Ferreira, Mike Knight and Markus Hofmeyr, as well as Danie Pienaar, had provided valuable input into the work in Kruger, and I was hoping to take some of their ideas and incorporate them in a national strategy.

I thanked Chris Serfontein, Charl Petzer and André le Roux at the CSIR – even though André was probably still cursing me over the ongoing development of the Meerkat system. In the courts, dealing every day with stonewalling defence tactics and threats of death and assault from poachers' criminal associates and families, prosecutors Ansie Venter, Isabet Erwee, Petra van Basten and Joanie Spies were doing the vital, often unsung, work of putting criminals behind bars. Of course, I also thanked all the branches of Ranger Services and their leadership, of whom I had become incredibly proud.

Arina and I were always conscious of not showing personal displays of affection when on official duties. 'Thank you,' I said to her, without fuss, at the year-end function, but I know she could read the deep appreciation and love in my eyes as I looked at her across the room. 'Mama Ranger' had her own special send-off at Skukuza, where she was recognised for her hard work in improving the lives of rangers and their families in trying times.

After our time in Kruger, we could also showcase a harvest of SANParks trophies, including an award to Ranger Services for Best Section in Kruger, and the coveted Kudu Award for Best Section in SANParks.

With our exit imminent, Fundisile suggested that I find offices for myself in Pretoria, somewhere other than SANParks HQ at Groenkloof.

'If I put you there, you'll end up just doing budgets and paper-work,' he said.

Someone would have to fund this alternative accommodation and the Peace Parks Foundation board chairman, Johan Rupert, came to the party. He generously contributed resources to fund the establish-ment and management of a new Wildlife Crime and Corruption

Combatting Coordination Centre, the WCCCCC. Chris Serfontein once again stepped up to oversee the fitting out of the new centre in Brooklyn, Pretoria. With Chris's help, we could link into the Cmore system and keep an eye on what was happening in Kruger and the adjoining reserves in real time.

My work in the park itself was, however, far from finished. While I now had a home and my wife and dogs to return to in the evenings, I was still on the move.

In early 2016, I travelled to Edinburgh and the Netherlands with Werner Myburgh to 'sell' the Meerkat concept to the UK and Dutch Postcode lotteries. The Postcode Lottery, pioneered in Holland, is a subscription lottery; when more than one player from a particular postcode area wins, then all players from that postcode also win money. Nearly a third of all players' contributions are distributed to various charities.

It was Werner who had introduced the Meerkat idea to the lottery organisers, and they were interested, which was a godsend, as Howard Buffett's funding ended in April 2016. He and his foundation had grown frustrated at the continued delays, errors and inefficiencies on the part of SANParks. I had managed to convince him to switch the cell-phone tracking funding to Meerkat, but SANParks still had to contribute some funding to the prototype, which was being commissioned for trials. If we could get that right, then the lottery money would allow us to develop production versions of the system.

A last-minute effort to save the grant funding was mounted by SANParks, and Buffett agreed to extend the deadline yet again, but only if certain conditions were met – SANParks failed. As a result, he pulled the plug and we lost just over half of the promised money. Some people tried to pin the blame for Buffett's withdrawal on me, but an external investigation and a forensic audit by the Treasury failed to find any evidence of wrongdoing by me. Subsequently, a third and final report, prepared by the SANParks CFO, found that systemic problems were to blame. My input on the report highlighted the absence of a reporting structure with clearly defined roles and responsibilities and a lack of internal capacity for enterprise and project management as the most devastating causes of the termination. This investigation came at a low point of mutual trust and respect within the whole organisation, with various individuals covering for themselves. Millions of rand were wasted through these inquiries, which were almost like management by tribunal.

Instead of leaders opting for open and fair resolution of conflict and controversy – saying what you mean and meaning what you say – it was easier to order another investigation. All of this stoked a fire inside me that burned more fiercely than the flames around me. Despite the end of the funding and all that happened, I am still in contact with Buffett, whom I regard as a friend and supporter of our cause.

In the UK, I contacted Kensington Palace and told Prince Harry's staff what I was up to. The Prince agreed to meet me. I reported in a dark suit, crisply ironed white shirt, perfectly knotted tie, and here he was looking suitably African and relaxed in jeans and vellies.

We talked about my new role and, as before, he left the door open for me to keep him informed via his staff – I subsequently visited him a second time.

I RETURNED to Kruger to have my day in court.

On the day I had to appear to give evidence about the poacher shooting at us in the helicopter back in late 2015, I was feeling good, relishing my chance to contribute in some small way to the execution of justice, even if it was in a case against a single poacher. Ansie Venter had tried to get the man to plead guilty to a number of charges, but when he changed his mind at the last minute, she klapped him with five counts of attempted murder. By this time, after Isabet had resigned, Ansie was carrying the bulk of poaching prosecutions. She was also directly involved in ensuring all poaching cases were heard at Skukuza, which had now happened.

The courthouse was a dusty, neglected little building, and I still had a plan on my to-do list to have it renovated. As I arrived, I saw the police leading a parade of young males into the court waiting area.

Seeing so many alleged poachers in one place at one time, I was suddenly struck by the impact that just this one day in court would have on many families, and the future lives of the accused men.

Inside the courthouse, while I waited for our matter to be heard, I watched and listened to a number of other cases being finalised. In one, the poacher was charged with the usual string of offences: unauthorised possession of a firearm, illegal entry into a protected area and conspiracy to poach wild animals, which were state assets. He was found guilty and sentenced to 17 years in jail.

When we mentioned such things in the media, it was always with a sense of triumphalism, but watching this young man standing in the dock I was struck by the futility of what he had done; he represented a family that had just lost a breadwinner, as well as a husband, son, brother or a good friend.

How, I wondered, could we get to a point where these young men had enough other options beyond risking their lives for what seemed to them a high payout from a poaching boss, but was, in reality, a con in itself? How, I asked myself again, could we collapse the networks behind the poaching?

Yes, these young men were often victims of poverty, operating out of desperation, but all too often those who achieved success went on to become middlemen themselves, dishing out cash to the relatives of the foot soldiers they sent to their deaths or painting themselves as philanthropists or role models in their communities. The victim then became the predator, perpetuating the line that poaching was a form of upliftment, a way out of circumstances that had been thrust on them by others.

In reality, it came down to two things, that toxic mix of poverty and greed. The man who shot at us was convicted and sentenced to a total of 37 years in prison.

AFTER KRUGER, the next highest concentration of rhinos was in the Hluhluwe-iMfolozi Park (HiP) in KZN. The two game reserves, now referred to as one by the acronym HiP, had been the breeding ground for Ian Player's return of rhinos to southern Africa. But, as we increased our effectiveness in Kruger, poachers were moving their sights to the rhinos under the care of Ezemvelo KZN Wildlife, known as the Natal Parks Board when Ian Player had instituted Operation Rhino.

Cedric Coetzee, the former South Coast park conservator for Ezemvelo, had been appointed to head up anti-poaching around the same time I had arrived in Kruger. We met several times over the years, and I remember one meeting in particular.

We were walking through the car park to our respective vehicles when Cedric stopped me, took me by the arm, and looked me in the eyes. 'We have to formalise a joint plan to ensure a more effective approach. We must work together.'

As part of my brief for my new role, Minister Molewa had told me to engage with the other provinces in which rhino were found. And so, once I was set up in the new offices in Brooklyn, I contacted Cedric and invited him to a meeting in the WCCCCC. It was time for us to start working better, together.

In the Joint Protection Zone we had found that that was all it took – working together and communicating. If it had been difficult to get the various owners of private game reserves bordering Kruger to talk and work together, then it was going to be a mission to replicate that same system at a national level.

SANParks and Ezemvelo KZN Wildlife were completely separate organisations.

HiP, at the time, was going through the sometimes-painful process of establishing a fully-fledged anti-poaching unit, emulating but also customising the Kruger solution. They had to achieve all of this within a complex external environment in which politics also played a part. Elsewhere in the country some rhinos were in provincial wildlife parks; Pilanesberg National Park, near Sun City, for example, was under the control of the North West Parks Board. There were also rhino on private game reserves and farms scattered across the country.

I turned to my flip chart and, with Cedric's input, started writing.

Under 'Aim' I wrote: 'To ensure an integrated approach to intra-province application of best practice in rhino protection.'

We knew that the approach needed to be a joint one, with people working together and 'inter-agency' – we had to get better at bringing government law-enforcement agencies together. Cedric had already flagged the need for better intelligence and one of my tasks at the WCCCCC was to identify high-value players in the rhino-horn trade.

As it had been with me at Kruger, Cedric was also responsible for parks that bordered or were close to Mozambique, just across the border, so we also needed to take a multinational approach. As we had shown, despite scepticism from some in the police, this could indeed be done.

At the tactical level, we needed to improve information sharing between the Ezemvelo parks and private reserves; I recommended they start using Cmore. Based on what I had learned in Kruger, we talked about using small teams of rangers, and having specialists and joint task teams on standby. We looked at technology and capacity-building, and I suggested that there should be cross-pollination, with rangers from KZN visiting Kruger to see what we had been doing.

And so our planning session gave birth to Project East Gate. It would form a model for rhino protection and conservation across South Africa. On my staff in Pretoria I had intelligence analysts and people seconded from ECI. We started analysing poaching and the rhino trade in the eastern part of South Africa, ignoring park, police, jurisdictional and provincial borders in the process. Our centre, with its over-arching view of the problem of poaching, had both the mandate and the powers to gather this information, and then pass it on.

With a joint and integrated approach, we identified 10 or so king-pins operating from the Lowveld of Mpumalanga to the northern part of KZN. We then effectively engaged in intelligence-driven operations with other law-enforcement agencies, which in time led to the arrest of a number of these individuals.

In doing so, we reconfirmed a valuable military lesson that borders and boundaries can easily become fault lines and these obstacles tend to benefit only the criminals. While we had to accept that policing operates within jurisdictional borders, we were now better able to monitor how and where the poaching threat was being displaced, and address the new hot spots more proactively.

From the WCCCCC office, we were able to assist with all of this by filling a critical void, namely, having a dedicated analyst function that allowed for some predictive modelling, while at the same time closely monitoring action, trends and tendencies on the ground.

In Kruger, the rangers had diligently arrested suspects and inevitably been the first responders at crime scenes, but they were not the police. It was the job of detectives to see investigations through to court appearances, and for the prosecutors to then take over. The prosecutors had been doing their job, but more effort was needed by the police to follow up outstanding cases and target kingpins and poachers outside the park before they made it to Kruger's boundary.

By taking a top-down approach and not being hampered by provincial and police borders and silos, we could pass on the information we gathered to the right people. So much of this came down to communication and cooperation. From Pretoria, I could organise meetings between people and agencies, fund work sessions and send people to learn from each other.

My guiding principle and motivation was that the second decade of the rhino war could not be as tragic as the first. I had known that one of our greatest weaknesses was our lack of crime intelligence, but now I was in a position where I could drive that, and bring people together in the process.

THE SCIENTISTS and engineers at the CSIR had mixed feelings about my return to Pretoria. I was now close enough to their offices to pay them regular visits.

With the Buffett money gone, I could not allow the Meerkat project to go on forever – SANParks would eventually call a halt to their top-up funding and all would be lost. I told André and his team to work harder and faster. They pushed back. In a turbulent meeting in the CSIR boardroom, I let fly.

'In my time as Director of Army Programmes we faced many more – and more daunting – challenges than this. If people were not up to it, I would get someone else to do the job!'

In my heart, I knew this was not possible, but André and his team, to their credit, endured my berating and carried on tirelessly. Eventually, in 2016, on a remote rocky outcrop somewhere in the Houtboschrand section of the Kruger Park, CSIR technicians set up the array of sensors and radar, collectively known as the Meerkat.

The system had been designed to be transportable and low profile. The installation itself, with a footprint of just a few square metres, was not more than three metres high, and the whole thing was shrouded in camouflage fabric. Its reach, however, was phenomenal, allowing us to watch over a very large chunk of Kruger.

André and his team worked day and night, in the heat of an oncoming Kruger summer, and in a location that was being hammered by rhino poaching. If the war had seemed a long way away in Pretoria, they were now on the front line.

I appointed Mark McGill to oversee Meerkat's commissioning. I had headhunted him from the Sabi Sand Game Reserve where he had been working for Ntomeni Rangers in an anti-poaching role. He had a degree in Zoology, could think tactically, and was a fixed-wing pilot. He was also tech-savvy and I thought he was the right man for the job.

Mark's early exposure to Meerkat left him feeling slightly underwhelmed, thinking the scientists and engineers working on it had been 'smoking their socks'. The Reutech radar system had been designed for maritime use, so it gave the engineers the reach they needed in the open expanses of Kruger, but rather than empty seas with the occasional ship, this screen was cluttered with terrain and animals. Looking at the screen, Mark could see a wavy, fuzzy line, which indicated the recent path of an animal on the move.

Initially, the system was difficult to use and apply tactically. While the radar and optronics engineers worked to perfect the collection of data, software experts tackled the display of the radar intercepts and Mark provided tactical and operational input. The whole system was still evolving, but it was ready, we thought, for launch.

The most exciting moment and a huge turning point in the whole project was when we first realised it could work. Mark contacted a forward tactical headquarters located at the Houtboschrand Ranger Post to let them know the system had detected a team of nine poachers entering the park en masse and then splitting into three groups. I was contacted and there was a continuous flow of information back and forth via phone as the Meerkat tracked the three gangs.

It was frantic inside the small tactical headquarters and, man, I have to say, we were clumsy. Here we had all this real-time information – even video footage of the poachers – and now we needed to push ourselves to see whether we could deal with so much intelligence at once. The poachers split up – a team of special rangers was sent to intercept one group, while a helicopter was circling a second group, but unlike the Meerkat operators, the pilot could not see the poachers in the dark below.

We realised, after that busy night, that it was one thing to be able to detect poachers like this in the dark, but we would now have to refine our tactics in order to retain these targets through the night and then intercept them at a time and a place to do so safely. This is not as easy as it appears in Hollywood, where generals and politicians watch live feeds from a drone on a big screen, and glowing figures rush across the landscape to neutralise a target. In reality, it was incredibly risky to send rangers out in the middle of the night, in pitch darkness, and vector them into the location of an armed gang; in such an instance the chance of one side or the other opening fire too soon, and casualties occurring, was just too high.

In December 2016, Meerkat was unveiled to the public, and a launch was held at a secret location on top of a hill in Kruger, attended by about 30 guests, representatives of SANParks, the CSIR, Reutech Radar Systems, PPF and the Peoples' Postcode Lottery from the UK.

Two large outdoor screens showed what operators would see

when they worked on the system, sitting in an air-conditioned shipping container at a ranger post. We took care to keep some details secret, including the location of the two systems we were about to deploy.

Soon enough, the operators picked up a couple of rhinos and zoomed in on them, much to the delight of the crowd watching the screens.

'Poachers!' someone in the audience piped up. On screen was a trio of intruders making their way through the bush.

'Are we safe?' a concerned onlooker asked.

'You should have known this can happen,' another guest countered.

A ranger spoke into his radio in front of the crowd, scrambling a helicopter and a reaction force. Just minutes later, the chopper was overhead, its powerful searchlight picking up poachers no more than a kilometre from where we all sat at a perfect vantage point. The reaction force went in and 'captured' the criminals.

At this point, everyone in the crowd realised it had all been an elaborate demonstration, with rangers playing the part of their adversaries. Cheers and applause broke out under the African sky.

Now it was time to see the Meerkat in action, for real, and to determine whether we had refined our tactics enough to make it useful.

FIFTEEN HOURS into the first deployment of the first shift, a group of three poachers from Mozambique was detected on the Meerkat's screens. A reaction force of rangers was immediately deployed and all three poachers were arrested before they could kill a rhino.

On the screen, overlaid with a map of the swathe of the park covered by the particular system, was a mass of blue (historical) and red (live) dots that represented radar intercepts; the software improvements now allowed the intercepts from the radar to be seen as clean, crisp symbols, rather than the confusing, wavy line Mark had seen. With minimal training and a few hours' experience, operators could quickly learn how to differentiate between animals and humans.

Once a camera zoomed in on an intercept, the operator could then record still or video images of it, which were saved on the system. A new operator coming on shift could then see what had already been identified, as well as intercepts of interest, such as a crash of rhinos moving together. The Meerkat operated day and night, and in all types of weather.

Tools on the system allowed an operator to record the speed of movement and distance travelled by animal or human. While its primary objective was to detect poachers, we were keen to announce in the initial burst of publicity that the Meerkat potentially had an important future role to play in research, by allowing people to monitor and observe animals from afar without disturbing them. This was particularly useful in letting us know exactly where the rhinos were located, but operators had to take care not to be distracted by leopards patrolling their territories at night or prides of lion making kills.

The launch of Meerkat gave me huge satisfaction, since I had been able to help conceptualise it, assist with raising the R30 million we needed to build three systems, and to push, pull and cooperate with the team from the CSIR and Reutech who put Meerkat together. Ultimately, I was also involved in the development of the concept of operations for Meerkat's utilisation.

Very quickly, we found that Meerkat would pick up every group of poachers that entered the area of coverage. The next thing we had to work out was what to do with the information; how to react in the quickest and most effective manner; what criteria we should use to evaluate the system's success; and how best to operate and deploy it.

Our concept of operations for the Meerkat, we decided, was to save rhinos. We now had a sophisticated surveillance system that could detect poachers but could not, on its own, arrest and convict them. We could use a gang's location to vector in a reaction group, which would hopefully catch the gang, but we would be equally happy if, say, we were unable to catch the poachers, but had caused them to fail in their mission.

In some cases, Meerkat could see a trio of poachers, but for reasons of time of day, weather, terrain, resources or other inhibiting factors, we could not physically get to them to catch them. Mark thus developed a number of tactics and techniques, which I will not specify here for security reasons, that could be used to 'disrupt' the poachers by letting them know they had been spotted. If they then escaped the park without killing a rhino, we considered that a win for Meerkat.

Mark found that just as rangers, trained to live and work in the African bush, made the best anti-poaching operators, so too did people with a knowledge of the veld and conservation make good Meerkat system operators.

'It's about understanding the natural patterns of life and the veld on the ground,' he explained. 'If you know how animals move, when they sleep and what their normal behaviour is, then you quickly start to recognise when things are unnatural.'

Operators soon became familiar with the area they were watching on screen; if they saw animals scattering or running, it could be an indicator of people moving through the area. If a herd of impala was not in the area where it usually spent the night, that could mean there were poachers hiding there.

The morning after the first Meerkat success, Mark sent me a black-and-white video of the poaching gang, recorded by the system. It was only once the video started circulating that all of the naysayers finally accepted that radar could work. That video enthused the team at the CSIR and impressed Peace Parks – they forwarded it on to the UK lotteries people as firm proof of the value of their funding.

Now that we had proved that Meerkat would work, my next challenge was to have it embedded, staffed and resourced. To some in Kruger's senior ranks, this was just one more piece of expensive technology, another legacy of my time as chief ranger. I was disappointed to see that there was already a reluctance to follow through with some of the initiatives I had introduced.

This unintended consequence of me taking the 'big-boy' decision to leave Kruger earlier than planned caused me one of the biggest disappointments, after ranger corruption, of my time working in conservation. Granted, some of the technology I had introduced was ambitious and not fully compliant by the time I left, but because of prejudice, or short-sightedness, or a lack of courage or resilience, or people simply not wanting to step out of their comfort zones, the follow-up work was not done and the IPZ plan was set back. This was the price I paid for being trusting, and nobly leaving two years before the end of my original tenure.

However, undeterred, I hit the road in search of donor funding for logistical support and staff for the Meerkat. PPF was already a major donor, but I did manage to find corporate sponsorship for three 4x4 vehicles for the Meerkat staff to use around the park.

On one of my fundraising trips to the UK, I was talking about Meerkat in a speech I gave at the Royal Geographic Society in London. I spoke of the difficulty in manning the system; the CSIR staff who had been with the project since its inception were getting burned out and there was basically only Mark McGill and another SANParks employee working on the system full-time.

After the talk, I was approached by a representative of a UK veterans' charity, which was looking for ways to support wildlife conservation. The idea was that military veterans might offer their skills in some way, and benefit themselves from giving something back. I was, of course, mindful of the implication of armed veterans of foreign wars coming to South Africa, so I was quick to point out from the start that what I needed was volunteers who could sit in front of a screen and monitor and interpret the data that came through. I did not want ex-military men and women in uniform or carrying guns – no firearms were required and none would be permitted. To further cover myself, I insisted that anyone working on the Meerkat would be subject to a polygraph test, no matter where they came from.

The charity agreed and its local manager, Andrew Crichton, a South African who had served in the British Army, coordinated the transport and movement of a number of ex-military volunteers, who, in short time, had been given training and were manning the Meerkat on a rotational basis. Author Tony Park, who divided his time between Australia and a house in the bush near Kruger, was doing PR for the charity. He had served with the Australian Army in the past, including service in Afghanistan, and he, too, did a couple of shifts on the Meerkat.

Meerkat was a tribute to the resilience, talents and skills of the people at the CSIR. I had cajoled, even bullied them, and made an empty threat to find another organisation to develop the system, but the fact was that no other group in the world had the same winning combination of knowledge, determination and good-old South African 'make-a-plan' attitude needed to make this a success. Many of them had served in the military, so they also had the grit and toughness required to live in the bush for days and weeks on end, seeing the project go from strength to strength. Night after night, month after month, Meerkat continued to prove its worth.

WITH THE HIGHS, however, came the lows. Not all of our technology projects worked as well.

The technology plan had its weak points and some of the systems unfortunately failed. The magnetic cable detection system to the west of the IPZ and the seismic system to the east both suffered from Africa's climatic conditions, and the seismic system, in particular, was susceptible to interference from animals. The root cause of the problems, however, could be traced back not to hardware or software, but 'wet ware' – people.

Sophisticated technology demands extraordinary effort and commitment. If a reserve does not have the capacity and personnel to embrace and maintain specialised technology throughout its life, then the purchase price may be money wasted. Such systems are force multipliers, but to make them work requires not just a one-off donation, but ongoing, dedicated funding for trained technical staff and equipment. Rather than trying to convince rangers that such systems were worth their time in training and maintenance, we might have been better off negotiating service-level agreements with the suppliers.

The biggest problem in Kruger was, however, the failure of the KNP and ranger leadership to carry through with these projects and find a way to make them work, or at least come up with workable alternatives. (This abdication of duty and lack of courage has left the IPZ with unanswered questions on the feasibility of some systems to this day).

There was even more disappointing news when, in July 2016, Rodney Landela, who had been promoted to regional ranger on my recommendation, was arrested and charged with offences related to poaching.

Rodney and and an employee from the KNP's veterinary science department, were found near the carcass of a freshly slaughtered rhino; both of the animal's horns had been removed.

Like many others in the park, I was shocked and devastated by the allegations. The case was still before the courts as this book went to print.

Also of concern was an increase in elephant poaching in the north of Kruger and across the border in the Limpopo National Park (LNP). In 2016, the numbers of elephants killed for their ivory had risen to more than 60 and there was a public outcry.

In a cab, in New York City of all places, I brainstormed how to tackle elephant poaching with Werner Myburgh from PPF. We had just delivered a presentation to the United Nations Environment Programme after a busy week of fundraising.

'We need good old-fashioned, consistent and disciplined anti-poaching operations in the Great Limpopo Transfrontier Park, and an IPZ,' I said.

We discussed the fact that this had been happening to the south, in the Sabie Game Reserve under Colonel Lionel Dyck. Dyck's contract was coming to an end there – he was getting pushback from some of his philanthropic donors in the US because big-game hunting was taking place in the reserve he and his men were guarding. 'We need to get Lionel into the Great Limpopo Transfrontier Park, and I'm prepared to do it,' Werner said in the back of the cab.

'You're right,' I said.

And so we came up with a concept for a new initiative, Project Ivory, which would apply the lessons of the JPZ to the issue of elephant poaching. Inside the LNP, Colonel Dyck's DAG would set up a forward operating base within the park's own IPZ, using his team to support the local anti-poaching rangers, and deploying a helicopter and dogs to respond to incidents. Within a year, elephant poaching dropped to single digits.

Added to this good news was that there were now small pockets of rhinos alive and thriving in the private concessions across the border in Mozambique. These seemingly small wins were proof that we had come a long way from the day I'd had to send a helicopter on a five-hour flight to shepherd the last living rhino out of the LNP.

18

The numbers came down.

In February 2017, Minister Molewa released a statement saying that the number of rhinos killed by poachers in the Kruger Park during 2016 had fallen from 826 the year before to 662, a drop of almost 20%.

Across the country, 1 054 rhinos had been poached, 121 fewer than in 2015. We had achieved what I termed a hard-fought, moderate win.

Increasingly, ECI were arresting people outside of Kruger and the other parks before they even had the chance to go about their unlawful business. For the first time, there were more poaching-related arrests outside of Kruger than within its borders. It is very hard to fight a thief when he is already inside your house, which was why I developed the strategy of clearing the park from the outside – and, finally, it was starting to happen.

Of course, many in the media and other commentators were quick to assume and point out that the reason fewer rhino were being killed in Kruger was because so many had been lost that it was getting harder for a poaching gang to find an animal to shoot. I cannot deny that that was a factor. However, the 'fewer rhino' angle was most definitely not the main or only cause of the drop in poaching. To suggest that was not only false, but also an insult to the rangers of the Kruger Park and everyone else who had worked so hard to bring about change.

Our strategy was working, as evidenced by the percentage of the rhino population being lost to poaching. When I moved to Pretoria from Kruger I could sit back and take a breath, and look at how we were measuring out success or otherwise. There had been so much focus on the raw numbers of rhinos lost that we were losing perspective. I called Sam Ferreira in to have a look at the losses as a percentage of the estimated rhino population – this, I thought, would give us a better indicator of the effectiveness of our strategy. It was interesting to note that from 2014 to 2015 poaching was responsible for the loss of 10% of Kruger's rhino population. By 2016 to 2017, 7.2% of the population was killed by poachers. Had we done nothing, or if our strategy had been unsuccessful, we would have lost about 170 more rhinos that year, based on the 2014 percentage.

Kruger's highest density of rhino had always been south of the Sabie River, in what was now the Intensive Protection Zone. Yes, we lost many rhino, but I believe that if nothing drastic had been done, if the IPZ and the JPZ had not been established, resourced and monitored as they were now, Kruger would have lost a hell of a lot more rhino and we would have been in a far worse situation. Of concern when it came to the 2016 figures, from a national perspective, was that poaching had increased by 38% in KZN. Our successes in Kruger had resulted in poachers heading south. We had been successful in Kruger and at bringing down the numbers across the country, but we had also displaced the threat to another part of South Africa. Fortunately, we were already working on Project East Gate to address the KZN problem. The lessons learned in the JPZ, put into practice with the help of Cedric Coetzee at Project East Gate, have been rolled out across the country since 2017.

From the WCCCCC we could finally establish the forerunner of a national analyst capability, from where we could feed the various role-players intelligence on poaching syndicates. To fight a war on crime one does not just need information – in fact, you could drown in it if you do not have analysts who are able to convert that information into intelligence, preferably actionable, that can ultimately be used as evidence in securing an arrest and conviction. The new capability resulted in three successful joint operations with other agencies, netting several alleged high-level criminals. This may not sound like a huge number, but it took a great deal of pressure off rhinos in protected areas.

The process of seeing an arrest through to a conviction, however, particularly for some high-profile individuals, is a long one. Some of these cases are still before the courts, years after arrests were made.

In 2018 I embarked on Project Southern Cross, managed from a new Environmental Enforcement Fusion Centre (EEFC) at the Department of Forestry, Fisheries and the Environment. This centre evolved from the lessons learned in the WCCCCC and ensured fusion of management information, crime intelligence and statistics, and coordination of anti-poaching projects.

The EEFC formed a basis for joint planning and execution, with the common goal to get poaching numbers down and to increase arrests of the high-level criminals driving the poaching networks. The centre ensured a dedicated focus and resources were applied to rhino poaching within a department that has other challenges, but at the same time provided a benefit to all wildlife.

The overarching approach to Project Southern Cross was to ensure all the key rhino populations in South Africa received the same level of standardised protection, no matter where the animals were or who owned them. Tied to this was a need for a stronger, better-coordinated and more focused campaign outside of protected areas; this was the only way to regain the initiative in the fight against poaching and to end the current war of attrition in the bush.

We have done this by establishing Integrated Wildlife Zones (IWZs). Building on the JPZ model, I was able to incorporate the four pillars we had come up with in Kruger's Rhino Steering Committee – effective law enforcement, good biological management, demand management, and community projects – into the planning of Project Southern Cross.

The IWZs brought together smaller national parks, which had previously operated as islands, together with private game reserves, game farms and provincial parks around them. The basis of this work was already being done in some areas because of successful rhino parks planning sessions, such as the one at Mokala in 2013 and many thereafter.

The IWZs were demarcated around key rhino populations, mindful of the fact that more than 50% of rhino in South Africa are in private hands. I have always maintained that a rhino has no number plate and that we should allocate resources to protect the national herd of rhino regardless of ownership. We also plan to include all communities in the zones in the protection effort, and are striving for the best practice in private–public partnerships, well aware that much of the future of conservation in South Africa will depend on the private sector. We are thus looking for the most integrated and cost-effective solutions possible.

Each of the current zones includes at least one national park, one provincial park and several private reserves, with the zones spread throughout the country. In the north, we have the Waterberg and Premier zones, the latter including the central part of Kruger and Karingani in Mozambique; to the east are the Zululand and Frontier zones; in the south is the Garden Route zone; while north of that is the largest IWZ, the Kalahari zone. Finally, we have the Platinum zone in the north-west, bordering Botswana.

As WELL AS this strategic work, I have continued to maintain a hands-on approach to the development and introduction of technology in environmental asset protection. I firmly believe that one day there will be a technology 'wow' that will give rangers a decisive advantage, although it will, of course, never replace them.

Currently, the ranger community is in the either/or paradigm when it comes to technology and this inhibits creativity. We owe the rangers their slice of the fourth industrial revolution; it may have begun with Meerkat but more is yet to come.

In the near future, technology will give rangers greater advantages at night and in all weather conditions. Surveillance systems need to be layered so that they can first give early warning of a breech, then detect an intruder or gang, and then track them. This intelligence needs to be actionable – that is, if a warning is received or criminals detected, rangers have to be able to do something about it, immediately. These types of systems exist, but to be truly effective they have to be supported, sustainable and able to be effectively deployed by leadership.

In Kruger, we looked at ground-based systems – seismic, magnetic and radar, with Meerkat being the standout – but in the future I believe more will be made of the vertical layer of surveillance. Technology will evolve to make this more effective and more affordable. I am still convinced that the aerostat balloon concept – in an easily transportable configuration – will enhance the value of radar, and other sensors.

Despite being accused of being anti-drone in the past, I do believe that future drones, within the budgets of African operators, can play a role in tracking, if not yet detecting, incursions. A whole array of sensors – radar, cameras, optronics, infra-red, magnetic and others – can be mounted on UAVs, manned aircraft, vehicles, and even on fixed towers or platforms in a well-designed configuration to provide greater reach. Sensors can also be placed on rangers and animals to allow visibility and real-time information on both. I believe there will be a role for satellites, eventually, for persistent surveillance and situational awareness, as well as early warning and reaction. Improvements in artificial intelligence will also allow satellite monitoring of valuable assets, such as individual rhinos, and be able to instantly tell the difference between an animal and a human. We need to think of putting a 'dome' over a protected area – the bigger the reserve, the bigger the dome needs to be, perhaps with longer-range drones, fixed-wing aircraft and aerostats.

Threat/risk assessment of the future concept of operations, availability of sustained technology and funding will all determine what and how many sensors are needed to protect wildlife in the years ahead. Also, we must never forget that environmental asset protection requires several layers. It is far better to be disrupting kingpins and middlemen, and arresting people outside of a national park or reserve, than detecting them once they breech the perimeter.

THE CHALLENGE of protecting a national park the size of a small country remains a concept difficult for many people to comprehend. Add to this the abundance of a species sought after by affluent consumers abroad and neighbouring populations that lack widespread employment and basic services, and you have a perfect, never-ending storm of crime.

A decade into the rhino campaign, my overwhelming realisation is that we cannot afford another 10 years like this, even with our successes. We must avoid another 'runaway train' situation at all costs. At the time of writing this book, we are losing about one rhino a day, and while this is a significant improvement on the loss of three animals per day – in Kruger alone at the height of the crisis – we need to be aiming for a loss of one rhino per week.

I do not think, in the short term, we will see the demand for rhino horn dry up completely and nor will any effort, no matter how great, in any one protected area alone bring the figures down to 50 rhino per year. To contribute to that elusive strong win, we need to continue to coordinate anti-poaching at national level to ensure proactive measures that will help collapse crime networks. We must heed the lessons learned in Kruger, particularly in relation to the way we employed composite solutions, bringing in all parties.

My exposure to wildlife crime over the past decade has left me with a lasting sense of alarm as I have come to realise that our planet is being degraded at an astonishing rate. With so much coverage in the media and online about climate change, overpopulation, pillaging of natural resources and pollution, people can become both overwhelmed and jaded. It can all seem so hopeless that one might throw one's hands up, convinced that there is nothing we can do.

When it came to coverage of rhino poaching, I observed that

people fell into three broad categories. There were those who thought the problem was overstated, that we were crying wolf, and that the serious money being raised and allocated to fighting poaching could have been better spent on something else; a second group, who declared all was lost in the fight to save the rhino and there was nothing the state could do to stop the scourge; and a third group, fortunately the largest, which remained broadly supportive of our efforts.

If I have a message for the people of South Africa and those around the world who share our passion for rhinos and the environment, it is this: Let's give meaning to a whole-of-society approach to conservation. Those who can contribute should; those who can give their time as profile ambassadors should do so; and let us ensure that we all work together, basing our approach and our arguments on facts – if we don't have the right information, we should seek it out. I believe it is incumbent on all of us to fight crime, in all its forms, by supporting law-enforcement agencies, despite what prejudices we might harbour against them. The city of New York was able to bring down its murder and serious crime rates by first starting with litter and petty crime – we can do the same thing. In the IWZs, we are using our new lines of communication to not only fight poaching, but also other crimes.

Our continent, our country and especially our parks are blessed with a unique biodiversity of species, subspecies, flora and fauna, which, in some cases, may be the last remaining specimens on earth. This is our heritage, but in more concrete terms it is one of the economic engines we can use to create wealth through tourism. The current poaching of environmental assets, particularly our rhinos, is happening on our watch – surely this deserves greater attention and action by all of us as Homo sapiens.

All the efforts of our people and many of our projects in Kruger have started to pay off. Yes, many rhinos were killed on my watch, but many were saved, and in recent years the numbers of rhinos killed in Kruger have continued to decline: 504 in 2017, 422 in 2018, 328 in 2019, and 247 in 2020. This continued fall in poaching deaths has given the species some breathing room and we are once more at the point where births per annum are exceeding deaths.

However, through the actions of poachers and Kruger's never-ending battle with drought, the park is now reportedly left with less than a third of the rhinos it held just over a decade ago. Despite all of that, this is still one of three meta-populations for the species in South Africa. Even after the hell we went through, we still hold 80% of the world's rhino, of which about 30% are to be found in national parks.

In response to our efforts in the bush, poachers switched their tactics from speculative night-time incursions into the park to a more sophisticated, perhaps even more evil, campaign of targeting, intimidating and bribing rangers. They had come to realise that the only way to get into – and, more importantly, out of – the IPZ was to do so with the aid of someone on the inside.

I had confidently said at the wildlife crime conference in Cape Town in 2015 that I believed the problem of corruption at that time was overstated, and I stood by those remarks then. Now, however, this planned and coordinated campaign of subverting rangers is one of the poacher's main weapons.

From the beginning of my time in Kruger, lie-detector testing and integrity management were in stark contrast to our liberal labour dispensations in South Africa. This made people in management nervous and the unions and their members suspicious. Adjacent to the Kruger, however, the Sabi Sand Game Reserve, under the leadership of Andrew Parker, worked closely with the CCMA, the Commission for Conciliation, Mediation and Arbitration, to draw up its own integrity testing policy and it has proved to be a great success. A polygraph could only ever be considered one small part of a possible criminal investigation, but the private reserves had the benefit of being able to refuse the right of admission to employees who failed their testing. As a highly unionised and state-owned national park, Kruger simply could not go down the path of locking people out. My issue was that so little management attention and resources were contributing to this facet of the rhino problem;

corruption was an uncomfortable truth that some chose not to tackle head on.

However, in late 2015, before I left the park, I was able to secure funding to formally institute integrity management. In 2016, SANParks announced that in Kruger and the other rhino parks regular polygraph testing would be carried out, with a policy in place to guide it. What is needed is a holistic management of staff integrity, including appropriate responses and real consequences for devious behaviour, or aiding and abetting poachers.

Poaching, whatever the tactics, and the international wildlife trade will remain part of the African conservation scene. It is not a question of 'if', but rather 'how' we deal with it. The allocation of resources will always be an issue simply because this noble work competes with many other law-enforcement challenges and more popular demands. The only way forward is to optimise the use of available resources to bring better results through sustainable action and, one day, gain the upper hand in combatting environmental crime and corruption.

Even though we are now better at protecting rhinos than we were in 2012, we still need to think big. When it comes to the future of Africa's iconic wildlife, there are long-term strategic matters to consider. In 2019, the South African government appointed a High Level Panel (HLP), made up of representatives from the tourism, hunting and game-farming industries, conservation bodies, academics, community leaders and other stakeholders in wildlife management and protection. Its role was to review policies, legislation and practices relating to elephant, lion, leopard and rhino management, breeding, trade and handling.

The HLP recommended that South Africa be promoted as a destination of choice for legal, regulated and responsible hunting of the species covered by its report, including a return to rhino hunting. It further recommended that our country take a global leadership position on rhino conservation. That would require gaining consensus from other African countries with rhinos in relation to the legalised international commercial trade in rhino horn, which could be taken to CITES as a proposal. However, before that could happen, the HLP said that a number of security concerns raised by its Rhino Committee of Inquiry would have to be addressed.

The committee of inquiry recommended that South Africa's ability to counter transnational crime be upgraded, including looking at extradition treaties and memoranda of understanding with countries where rhino horn is consumed, and those through which it transits. More work needed to be done to ensure we are able to track and trace individual horns and know exactly where they come from before a regulated legalised trade could be considered. It is high time that the findings of the panel receive the attention and allocation of resources needed to inform decision-making and allow policy formulation. This will enable firm decisions on strategic issues, specifically the legalisation of the trade in rhino horn.

Wearing my start small hat, I would argue that we need to ensure a much-needed whole-of-government approach, as we address the root causes of the problem of poaching, including unemployment and poverty, and ensure lasting solutions. A complex problem like this does not require a complex solution, but a composite one. The existing National Joint Operational Intelligence Structure in our country could make this happen now, and execute consistent joint and integrated operations that would lead to the collapse of organised crime networks.

When it comes to act now, we have to think beyond enforcement and put more thought into how we manage the asset – the animal and its horn – and tackle the elusive matter of community ownership.

A few initiatives proposed by the Rhino Steering Committee for managing rhinos can and are being put into place. Sensors are being placed inside horns so that both the animal and horn can be monitored and tracked; rhino guardianship schemes are being put in place where people are able to monitor and almost live among rhino in the field; and dehorning is being carried out.

Dehorning has been used as an asset-management tactic in South Africa and other countries in the past. It is most effective in smaller reserves or well-defined and protected areas, such as an IPZ. If poachers know that every animal in an area has been dehorned, then there is less incentive for them to risk entry. Dehorning deprives the poacher of an asset, but then the question for the authorities is how to manage the horn – which, in turn, leads back to the question of legalising the trade, with the attendant suggestion that the proceeds be used to improve conservation and protection. Dehorning has been carried out to good effect in the Greater Kruger Environmental Protection Foundation, a well-defined area, and in parts of Kruger.

When it comes to community ownership, many projects are being executed with too little coordination, focused mostly on education and awareness, which of course are much needed. However, there is a social economic dimension where the state and private sector must join hands to address real and urgent needs in communities bordering wildlife areas, including issues such as water, infrastructure and basic services. Local government does not have the resources and capacity to provide these.

The private–public partnerships approach, which includes NGOs, needs to be central to future conservation and environmental asset protection in South Africa. This will require mature relationships and customised structures to ensure good governance, while allowing flexibility in execution by a multitude of role-players. Good communication, connectivity and situational awareness, fusing into a well-developed management system, will be paramount. This should occur without the artificial constraints of borders and boundaries, but rather in inclusive demarcated zones. Then, of course, the ultimate spice to the recipe will be good leadership on all levels.

New models for fundraising, including internationally, will have to be pursued based on the implementation of credible projects by competent teams that ensure both compliance and fully verified transparency when it comes to expenditure and performance. This will have to include, if not focus on, carbon and biodiversity credits funnelled through natural capital economies and impact bonds.

Corporations around the world are increasingly expected to show that they do not allow or condone child labour, deforestation or harm animals, and there is an onus on them to invest in initiatives that prove their social and environmental responsibility. South Africa needs to capitalise on this. A pioneering example is Rhino Impact Bonds, an accredited scheme in which companies can invest in Addo Elephant National Park and the Great Fish River Reserve to support clearly defined projects to enhance rhino conservation and numbers.

While all of the above is pursued, the rangers and associated services will still have to hold the fort. In my current role, I have overseen the introduction of Project Braveheart, a ranger-leadership training programme at the Southern African Wildlife College. Much effort had gone into the training of many rangers, but almost no attention had been paid to leadership development, a factor pivotal in empowering those who must lead under difficult and complex circumstances. I believe that the role of the anti-poaching ranger needs to be standardised and classified as a distinct occupational group in South Africa. If anti-poaching unit rangers are trained and developed in the correct way, they can be deployed in the right way, anywhere in the country.

We need to continue to acknowledge and manage the potential unintended consequences of fighting the war against poaching, including the human cost, the real cost (in rands) and the neglect of the park rangers' core business of conservation. Although the war will not be won inside the park, we must never neglect our duty and responsibility towards our custodianship of wildlife.

It is my fervent wish, however, that future chief rangers will be allowed to focus on their core business – conservation, of which law enforcement will, unfortunately, continue to be a major part. A chief ranger should not have to continually liaise with politicians and the media, raise funds, manage a multitude of high-value projects, pioneer technology, forge international relations, and plan and set up alliances. Other specialists, organisations and project managers should fill these roles as part of a whole-of-government and whole-of-society approach to conservation and protection.

.   .   .

My time in Kruger was an amazing race during which I also experienced remarkable grace, comradeship and support from around the world.

Sadly, some of those who were with me on my journey have since passed. Minister Edna Molewa, Ian Player, Abe Sibaya, ranger Louis Olivier – who, unlike some, greeted me so warmly on my first day in Kruger – and Nigel Morgan, from Pathfinder, are no longer with us.

It was a daunting time – a real battle, not just for the protection of a key species, but for the soul of this iconic park. The impact of environmental crime is destructive and excruciating to witness. The onslaught we face is arguably the most intense and protracted on a species and a park in modern history. This is due in no small part to the fact that South Africa had the best record in the world when it came to rhino conservation and it is important to remember that we have been here before – at the turn of the twentieth century there were fewer than 200 rhino in our country and none in Kruger.

This chapter of my life played out in a very specific era in the history of my beloved country, which today is still in the throes of a protracted and painful transformation, with all the associated social and economic stressors and tensions change carries with it. Rhino poaching was one more embarrassment our political leaders did not need.

The line leadership in the responsible state departments faced many other challenges during the 'rhino war', with other pressing priorities and limited resources. I, too, had to navigate these tricky waters and my actions brought much unwanted pressure, thanks to the very prominent and exposed role I played. Although I have been critical of the contribution of various other players in the fight against poaching, it is not up to me to speculate on the reasons for their level of effort. However, the fact is that without their buy-in and future success in collapsing crime networks, and further addressing community ownership and demand management, we will simply not progress from the current moderate win to a strong win. This fight cannot be left to the rangers, no matter how good they are or become.

When it comes to the role of government and our leaders, yes, more could have been done earlier, but credit should be given to the late Minister Edna Molewa and Dr David Mabunda for taking that first, decisive and controversial step in 2012 to 'go paramilitary'. Even with the unintended negative consequences that came with the decision, that bold move set the tone for the creation of competent and professional anti-poaching units not only in Kruger, but also across the country. I will keep the men and women of this thin green line in my heart and prayers always, and I salute them for their service to our wildlife and our country. The image of the Kruger Park's soil, drenched with the blood of its rhinos and the sweat of its protectors, is engraved on my soul.

In looking back on my time as Chief Ranger of the Kruger National Park, my only regret is that at times I did not lead my team as well as I knew I could. The scope of the tasks I undertook, and the many and conflicting urgencies and priorities I experienced, meant that I could not always schedule enough time to really listen and interact with everyone around me. This could have helped take many more along with me on the journey I envisaged.

The stress of external and internal organisational politics served only to aggravate the situation. Sadly, these factors consumed and drained my emotional energy more than the poaching scourge itself. The resulting stress often caused me to be unnecessarily impatient.

I am thankful for the opportunity to have been allowed and trusted to formulate and execute a strategy. I had believed that this was a strong skill I learned and developed during my various careers, but, ironically, had never really put fully to the test. Although I had at one point been responsible for the army's overall strategy, my plan for the future at that time had been curtailed, perhaps understandably, by competing national demands and limited funding. In the private sector, working for the local branch of a multinational company, I was often disillusioned to learn how disconnected strategy, planning and execution were on the various levels.

As someone still involved in the fight against poaching, and as a citizen of South Africa, I am reminded daily that we are the custodians of a wonderful corner of our planet and continent. To me, as a

Christian, this comes with an obligation to use my talents and skills as best I can to help protect our natural paradises. I feel privileged to have been given the opportunity to do so.

I am firmly of the opinion that when we all truly rediscover the benefit and power of working together for a common cause, and when a critical mass of all role-players and resources are focused on a worthy cause, we can triumph. The threat to wildlife will, sadly, never vanish, but we can learn to keep it in check and to overcome it.

This is all happening on our beat, as a nation, and the rhino and other species depend on us. It can be done, as long as we remember that old African proverb: If you want to run fast, you run alone; if we want to run far, we run together.

#4therhino

ACKNOWLEDGMENTS

I would like to thank my wife, Arina, for her undiluted and undying love and support. In so many respects, she stood by my side throughout the challenges and joys of our special third career, selflessly serving our cause with love and dedication.

My household and family were always there to support and cheer me on. It meant a lot to me and I love them for it.

I thank all those friends, local and around the world, as well as colleagues and ex-colleagues, including leaders, who were part of this chapter of my life – I am because you are. A special word of thanks must all go to those who contributed to the content of the book.

To have worked with Tony Park as my co-author was a pleasant and constructive experience, as we share a real love for Africa and, yes, he is a professional, well proved by his track record. Our interaction with the Pan Macmillan South Africa staff, led by publisher Andrea Nattrass, was equally cordial and professional. Salute to the team.

Tony would like to thank his wife, Nicola, and mother, Kathy, for their initial proofreading of our book and providing feedback, and Ray Dearlove for introducing us to each other.